An Autecological Theory of the Firm and its Environment

NEW HORIZONS IN INSTITUTIONAL AND EVOLUTIONARY ECONOMICS

Series Editor: Geoffrey M. Hodgson, *Research Professor, University of Hertfordshire Business School, UK*

Economics today is at a crossroads. New ideas and approaches are challenging the largely static and equilibrium-oriented models that used to dominate mainstream economics. The study of economic institutions – long neglected in the economics textbooks – has returned to the forefront of theoretical and empirical investigation.

This challenging and interdisciplinary series publishes leading works at the forefront of institutional and evolutionary theory and focuses on cutting-edge analyses of modern socio-economic systems. The aim is to understand both the institutional structures of modern economies and the processes of economic evolution and development. Contributions will be from all forms of evolutionary and institutional economics, as well as from Post-Keynesian, Austrian and other schools. The overriding aim is to understand the processes of institutional transformation and economic change.

Titles in the series include:

Deep Complexity and the Social Sciences
Experience, Modelling and Operationality
Robert Delorme

Creative Industries and Economic Evolution
Jason Potts

Institutional Variety in East Asia
Formal and Informal Patterns of Coordination
Edited by Werner Pascha, Cornelia Storz and Markus Taube

Capitalism and Democracy
A Fragile Alliance
Theo van de Klundert

Foundations of Economic Evolution
A Treatise on the Natural Philosophy of Economics
Carsten Herrmann-Pillath

How Markets Work and Fail, and What to Make of Them
Bart Nooteboom

Law and Economics from an Evolutionary Perspective
Glen Atkinson and Stephen P. Paschall

An Autecological Theory of the Firm and its Environment
Colin Jones and Gimme Walter

An Autecological Theory of the Firm and its Environment

Colin Jones

Queensland University of Technology, Australia

Gimme Walter

University of Queensland, Australia

NEW HORIZONS IN INSTITUTIONAL AND EVOLUTIONARY ECONOMICS

Edward **Elgar**
PUBLISHING

Cheltenham, UK • Northampton, MA, USA

Published by
Edward Elgar Publishing Limited
The Lypiatts
15 Lansdown Road
Cheltenham
Glos GL50 2JA
UK

Edward Elgar Publishing, Inc.
William Pratt House
9 Dewey Court
Northampton
Massachusetts 01060
USA

A catalogue record for this book
is available from the British Library

Library of Congress Control Number: 2016962565

This book is available electronically in the **Elgar**online
Business subject collection
DOI 10.4337/9781784711016

ISBN 978 1 78471 100 9 (cased)
ISBN 978 1 78471 101 6 (eBook)

Printed and bound in Great Britain by TJ International Ltd, Padstow, Cornwall

To the diversity, richness and warmth of

Iman Lissone

17 February 1963 – 21 July 2016

Contents

Figures

Tables

Preface

Life persists in all corners of our social and natural environments, through a constant process of problem solving. Historically, our investigation of the breadth of this problem solving has seen a sharp demarcation between the natural and social scientists, despite the common elements to their discourse, mainly in their reference to environment and adaptation. This book is designed to unite aspects of those natural and social perspectives and thus consider the ecology of firms and the social processes through which their persistence is possible. This work is the product of our mutual curiosities to explore ideas and circumstances, doing our best to avoid dogma and idealism, and guided by our observations on the persistence of individuals through their adaptive mechanisms. Time after time, we find ourselves drawing upon past thinking as we attempt to synthesise the old with the new in developing a schema by which to investigate ecological phenomena from the natural and social perspectives.

One of us (Jones) is an ecological novice, an enthusiastic and ever curious social scientist. A lack of satisfaction with current explanations of why firms persist led Jones intuitively to decouple individual firms from the populations to which others would ascribe them membership. The result has been a growing fascination with *the* firm and *its* environment. The other of us (Walter) is an ecologist. His focus on individual organisms and their interactions with the environment, as mediated by their species-specific adaptations, casts doubts on the predominant ecological and evolutionary generalizations, those based on the view that the environment, and therefore natural selection, is primarily competitive.

We aim to lay a strong foundation for others to apply autecological ideas to the study of firms. We hope we have made the case that firms do persist through matching the requirements of their environments, and that understanding the ecological nature of this imprecise and difficult process is worthy of our time. We believe this book marks the necessary start of an on-going conversation from which many new and/or contradictory ideas may yet emerge. But in the spirit of Robert Hutchins's "Great Conversations", we choose to add to the progress of knowledge by sharing our present thinking. At this stage we do not have all the answers regarding the persistence of firms, but we believe our present thinking is worthy of your time.

Introduction

People are trapped in history and history is trapped in them. (Baldwin, 1964: 154)

In this book we develop an autecological theory of the firm and its environment. An approach we argue is necessary to fully understand the ecological interaction between individual firms, or specific types of firms, and the unique environments they both experience and modify. We outline the need for this new approach and also the theoretical and philosophical foundations of an autecological theory of the firm and its environment. We also present empirical evidence of the type of new knowledge gained from using this approach. Writing this book is a difficult challenge, for the ideas contained within will be swimming against a strong historical tide of intellectual currents. Given that we cannot rewrite this history, the best place to start is by explaining the historical literatures these *new* ideas interact with, intentionally or otherwise. Through this process, the underlying fundamental assumptions that govern differing ecological logics can be more fully appreciated. It is not the intention to merely demonstrate a sound understanding of the historical literature, but rather to illustrate an empirical *pathway* that has remained unexplored for the best part of 100 years. This book represents an intellectual endeavour to reopen that pathway, and to assist others to navigate it guided by a specific set of theoretical and philosophical insights.

It has previously been said that to 'understand the behaviour of an organization you must understand the context of that behaviour – that is, the ecology of the organization' (Pfeffer and Salancik, 1978: 1). This ambition represents the starting point of our intellectual journey, to fully explain the ecology of a firm (or identifiable types of firms) and the unique operational environment they experience/modify. To do so we must travel back in time to reconnect to a previously advocated method of ecological investigation. Through this process we discover a void that has waited a long time to be filled. A void that has narrowed due to dominance of sociological theories that have ignored the individual firm in order to give preference to the collective actions of populations of firms and higher-order community relations (see Hawley, 1950; 1968; Hannan and Freeman, 1977; 1989). The front cover of this book demonstrates our specific focus on the uniqueness of individual firms. We assume that, if we could observe the firms that others so neatly categorize using discreet industry codes through a set of autecological binoculars, the diversity of their features would be obvious to see. That said, we do not seek to elevate our autecological approach over the established organizational ecology approach (hereinafter OE), just simply to restore a balance to the use of ecologic reasoning in such investigations.

For a moment, we invite you to think about the streets where you live, where there are firms that quietly survive. Firms like restaurants, which refuse to accept credit card payments, whose décor is seriously dated and who close their operations earlier than we might like. Yet they survive just fine over long periods of time in environments apparently characterised by significant environment change. The nature of such survival is *untouched and unexplained* (to draw upon Darwin's phrase) by most theories of the firm. This book is focused on the survival of such firms. Small firms increasingly contribute significantly to local employment and production globally, yet they are virtually invisible in many studies. They are either deemed too simple to study or are stripped of their individuality in aggregated datasets. Nevertheless, they are numerically the most dominant form of business globally, and therefore are worthy of our attention alongside all other forms of business. The ideas contained here are not limited to small business; they apply to all business types. However, just as common fruitflies provided Dingley and Maynard Smith (1969) with access to a unique context to observe the process of evolution, so we believe that understanding the uniqueness of the firms we are surrounded by and the unique operational environments they experience/modify will aid the development of our approach.

It will be demonstrated that such firms are rarely selected for or against uniformly by the presence of a common environment, as assumed in population ecology models (Hannan and Freeman, 1977). Neither should we expect these firms to possess superior resources and/or routines in comparison to other firms that have already failed, as might be expected if studied from the perspectives of the dynamic capabilities approach (Teece, Pisano and Shuen, 1997), resource-based view of the firm (Wernerfelt, 1984) and/or evolutionary economics (Nelson and Winter, 1982). These firms may not even conform to their industry's assumed requirements, as expected in institutional theory (DiMaggio and Powell, 1983). Firms, that may indeed seem unrestrained in shaping the nature of their operational environments, unlike the central assumptions of the resource dependence approach (Pfeffer and Salancik, 1978). Finally, firms that may also appear to be less efficient than other firms that have already failed, in contrast to the central assumptions of transaction cost theory (Williamson, 1985). If we are right, that ordinary simple firms do defy the logic of so many well-developed theories of the firm, then perhaps our autecological theory of the firm and its environment has a place in investigating such common resilience.

We are suggesting that a great many firms are capable of matching the requirements of *their* operational environment, using their internal cognitive abilities to develop intuitive situational awareness (Endsley, 1995). Although we will spend a great deal of time in Chapter 3 explaining exactly what is an operational environment, for now we offer a simple definition. The operational environment of a firm is all environmental phenomena *observed* to have *operational relations* with any firm. The operational environment must always be first observed, rather than merely inferred. The operational environment is directed, timed, ordered and spaced by and across the lifeline of a given firm. This conceptualization of the environment is quite radical in comparison to existing definitions of environment in organizational studies, drawing heavily upon the original ideas of Mason and Langenheim (1957) and Spomer (1973). As the title of this book suggests, we argue that a firm cannot be defined in isolation to its operational environment, and vice versa.

We argue that previously too much attention has been directed to the big economic, social and technological events occurring in our economies, assuming uniform impact, whilst forgetting that such period effects (Aldrich, 1999) may not actually impact all firms equally. Herein lies the central story of this book, a fine-grained consideration of what actually happens on the corners of our streets for those firms that simply maintain their existence. There will be no grand theory produced that will lead to bankable predictive expectations. The aim of the book is to furnish the reader with an alternative ecological approach to explain the selective survival of all manner of firms we encounter daily as researchers, customers and resource providers.

THE UNFOTUNATE BIRTH OF HUMAN ECOLOGY

Imagine you were a stranger walking down a street of a small town in its infancy, a town nevertheless with much construction activity happening. Imagine that elsewhere you were already recognised as an experienced and innovative builder, and you offered your services to the people of this town, only to be rebutted for not complying with their specific and rather concrete building practices. Worse still, imagine that the specific building practices chosen by the people in this town ultimately became the standard for the next 100 years, immune to criticism and/or paradigm challenging improvements; despite you receiving endless acclaim elsewhere during your lifetime.

This unlikely scenario provides a neat analogy of the actual reality of how early thinking in sociology, specifically in the Chicago school of urban ecology, set the tone of ecological thought in the social sciences from 1915 to present day. Given the direction this book will take, and the clear distinction to be developed vis-à-vis the underlying philosophical and methodological foundations of OE, it's worth travelling back 100 years in time to consider this history. Through looking at the positions of various contributors to the literature around this time, it will become obvious why a vacuum for autecological thinking in the social sciences has persisted for so long.

In 1917 a Scottish sociologist named Robert MacIver published his first major work, *Community: A Sociological Study*, building on previous ideas published in the prominent journal, *Sociological Review*. This major work was instantly acclaimed to be the most important sociology book of the decade (Ellwood, 1917). Conversely, it was also claimed by Park (1918: 544) that MacIver had demonstrated 'no particular familiarity with the sociological tradition' and that the terms used in his book were 'more or less improvised, consequently lacking in precision, and on the whole ... [the] ... volume is vague, thin, [in]plausible, and innocuous'. While not uncommon for any published work to draw competing opinions, one of these opinions matters in the context of this chapter.

Robert Park would be central to the development of the Chicago school and its research in urban ecology. He would publish the seminal *Introduction to the Science of Sociology*, and in doing so would ultimately centre his approach to human ecology on the processes of competition and collective action. His outright rejection of MacIver's early ideas of community would seem to have prevented their use in ecological research. As a consequence, MacIver's explicit focus on the importance of the interests of individuals as driving community evolution and his unique conception of the relations between man and his environment were (it would seem) not further developed in the domain of human ecology and then its successor, OE.

As a result, social ecologists ignored the early ideas of MacIver regarding environment, community and the importance of the individual. It is difficult not to think what might have become of human ecology (and therefore OE) if MacIver's ideas had gained at least some approval by those developing the field of human ecology 100 years ago. Nevertheless, his ideas are very central to the work being developed in this book. Several of his key ideas can be considered briefly here, and they will be themes that will be continually developed throughout the book.

The Ideas of MacIver

MacIver (1917: 361–362) believed 'we all inhabit a single world, but the world is somehow different for every species, nay for every living thing within it'. He added that the 'environment is infinitely complex, never quite the same for any two living creatures; it is ever present, never to be entirely known or estimated; it is modified by the beings whom it modifies, in an endless and never wholly calculable reciprocity' (ibid: 364). Here the seeds of what would eventually be defined as the operational environment (Mason and Langenheim, 1957) were being cultivated. Explicit consideration being given to the individual nature of reciprocity between individual and the unique environment they both experience and shape. Such thinking was clearly very novel to many sociologists of the day.

With specific reference to the importance of the individual in shaping community evolution, MacIver (1917: 21) stated that 'to those that understand the true relation of "individual" and "social," it will appear no paradox that the fundamental social laws are thus individually determined'. Here the determination of individual humans is central to shaping community evolution at higher levels.

Part of the reason for the rejection of MacIver's ideas by early human ecologists was his strident rejection of sociology adopting scientific methods rather than social methods of inquiry. He famously stated that 'detail has therefore been ruthlessly abandoned for the sake of comprehensiveness' noting 'that the most essential features of the community are the most often misconstrued' (ibid: vii). For the autecologist, the concerns of MacIver remain as true today.

The Task at Hand

The most significant challenge we face writing this book will surely be providing clarity around our intended use of a range of novel concepts and theories. Likewise, our reinterpretation of a good many ecological concepts already in use in the organizational studies literature will also most likely challenge many readers. So we will commence this book with a challenge to you, the reader. We are attempting to provide you with an *alternative* ecological explanation of firm survival. This will require you, the reader, to suspend judgment as to what you may already assume constitutes an ecological explanation of firm survival. It is our intention to provide you with sufficient new information from which to accept the validity of the developed alternative explanation. Essentially, there is an unavoidable challenge of engaging with the extant organizational studies literature germane to this topic, so thoroughly reviewed by Aldrich (1999) and Baum (1996) and Baum and Shipilov (2006). They are the direct artefacts of a long running evolutionary play being played out on the stage of a scholarly ecological theatre. The new ideas developed in this book seek to enable you to add in new actors, previously ignored, and to reinterpret the meaning attributed to the events discussed previously in this play.

It is important that the contents of this book are not viewed as an attack on existing ecological and/or evolutionary approaches to the study of the firm. What is being offered is an *alternative* ecological approach to the study of the firm and its operational environment. There has always existed 'two internally homogeneous sets of ecological theories, or research approaches that stimulate the collection and interpretation of ecological data' (Hengeveld and Walter, 1999: 141). Given the minimal overlap in the two theories vis-à-vis their underlying premises and research priorities, 'they represent two separate and alternative paradigms' (sensu Kuhn, 1962). This book aims to introduce to the domain of organizational studies a pre-existing, alternative ecological approach that has not previously been applied to the study of firms. Our only hope is that you will persist in your consideration of the ideas contained here, as our attempt to describe this alternative approach should, in all fairness, only be judged after the entire book has been fully considered as a whole.

A HISTORY OF FIRMS AND ECOLOGICAL THOUGHT

Explanations of progression and organization in society have long been of importance to sociologists. They have enrolled many ecological and evolutionary ideas and concepts since Herbert Spencer (1864) coined the phrase 'survival of the fittest'. The longevity of this particular phrase has greatly influenced conceptions of evolution and ecological relations in the social domain; with the assumed presence of competitive relationships consistently thought to shape the organization of society (Park, 1936). However, as Carr (1965: 29) stated, 'the function of the historian is neither to love the past nor to emancipate himself from the past, but to master and understand it as the key to the understanding of the present'. That is our intention in recording this selective history of ecological thought, to enable you the reader to better appreciate the emergence, development and suppression of key ideas that have shaped the theoretical and empirical world we share today.

For example, we acknowledge the role afforded to competition in many ecological approaches, but seek to explain why this is so, not whether it should be so. Human ecology, the forerunner to OE, emerged from a veritable intellectual potpourri formed by philosophers, sociologists, naturalists, biologists, botanists, economists, zoologists, anthropologists and geographers, to name but a few. It is from such eclectic beginnings that the ecological investigation of man and his or her institutions was founded. Critically, this period of time was not free from translation errors and such errors, we claim, have disproportionately shaped the development of human ecology and subsequent OE theory and empirical practice. Therefore, we aim to draw attention to specific events and publications that have influenced the thoughts and opinions of scholars in this field of enquiry for nearly 100 years. Events and thoughts that left the possibility of an autecological theory of the firm and its environment in their wake.

So, with direct reference to developing an autecological theory of the firm and its environment, we will focus upon three issues. First, those significant events that have altered the trajectory of socioeconomic ecological thought away from autecology. Second, the trajectory of socioeconomic ecological thought from the early twentieth century to today. Finally, the implications of this path-dependent thinking upon our quest to develop an alternative autecological approach.

Getting Blown Off Course

Ecology is typically assumed to be 'the study of the relation of organisms or groups of organisms to their environment, or the science of the interrelations between living organisms and their environment' (Odum, 1959: 4). Such definitions are common and assume two things. First, the ecologist is on firm ground in seeking to understand the relationship between any given entity and the environment it interacts with. Second, the ecologist is also right to concern themselves with the nature of relations between entities of the same or different form. However, a commitment to the first issue should not be at the expense of factoring in consideration of the second, and vice versa. Herein lies a big problem, which can be philosophically described as committing an epistemic fallacy, or to conflate what we *think is*, with what actually *is*, or confusing epistemology for ontology (Carolan, 2005; Bhaskar, 1975).

We identify specific events within human ecology and also now OE, which suggests an epistemic fallacy is being committed. We argue that the knowledge developed in these domains has not been sufficiently tested, with preference given to seeing knowledge as progressively developed rather than something forever open to critique and challenge. As we noted at the beginning of the chapter, 'people are trapped in history and history is trapped in them' (Baldwin, 1964: 154). Despite the many disciplines related to early human ecology, it was primarily sociologists who produced the major works in human ecology (see, Park and Burgess, 1921; McKenzie, 1924; Park, Burgess and McKenzie, 1925). From this starting point a lasting imprint from the founders has survived to this day. An imprint largely based upon overriding concern for community relations and competition as the chief organizing agent (Park, 1936).

Much of our concern relates to the interpretation of important ecological concepts central to how an ecologist would typically be expected to investigate interactions between entities and their environments. Whilst there have always been differences in the usage of many ecological terms given that ecologists act at different levels of analysis and/or ecological scale (Reiners and Lockwood, 2010), the current usage of the term commensalism in organizational studies is totally at odds with *all* other ecological domains of enquiry. At present within the organizational studies literature, commensalism is a descriptor for a *range of competitive relations* (see Aldrich, 1999).

Alternatively, in every other domain of the ecological literature (since its original conception in 1869) it is clear that the term commensalism has been used to account for *one discrete type of relation* in which one entity benefits and the other remains unharmed (see van Beneden, 1869; 1876). That is, it is not used as a descriptor for any form of competitive relation. This difference in usage can be traced back to the original works of van Beneden being misunderstood by first Warming (1909), and then by Fuller and Conrad (1932) who mistranslated the seminal work of Braun-Blanquet (1928). Subsequently, this translated work was used exclusively by Hawley who concluded that 'the most elementary and yet salient expression of commensalism in nature is competition' (1950: 39). Since then, Hawley's work has remained highly influential to many organizational scholars with reference to the issue of competition (see Hannan and Freeman, 1977; Pfeffer and Salancik, 1978; Astley, 1985; Carroll, 1985; Barnett and Carroll, 1987; Barnett and Amburgey, 1990; Baum and Singh, 1994; Aldrich, 1999; Greve, 2002; Rao, 2002). Sadly, within the domain of organizational studies the assumption that commensalism is a form of competitive relation continues unchallenged.

At the heart of observing, understanding and explaining commensalistic relations in an organizational setting is the need to understand the nature of coactions present across time and space. Coaction theory proposed by Haskell (1949: 46) provides the means to reconnect organizational studies to the original meaning of commensalism and all other forms of coaction. Haskell asserted that the major properties of any society vary with coaction, noting that weak and strong 'classes can only have nine, and only nine, qualitatively different [coaction] relations toward each other' (that is, +/+, +/0, +/−, 0/+ (commensalism), 0/0, 0/−, −/+, −/0 and −/−), where + denotes a positive gain, − a negative loss, and 0 a neutral outcome. In the natural sciences, Haskell's classification scheme and its adaptation by Burkholder (1952) have stood the test of time as the accepted way of accounting for population coactions (see Odum, 1971).

Aldrich (1999) adopts Hawley's (1950) symbiotic and commensalistic axes to frame his eight possible relations between organizational populations, with commensalism accounting for the following coactions; 1) –/– full competition; 2) –/0 partial competition; 3) +/– predatory competition; 4) 0/0 neutrality; 5) +/0 partial mutualism; and 6) +/+ full mutualism. When commensalism is taken to account for all other coactions other than those that are symbiotic (see Rao, 2002), then the opportunity to understand and investigate how firms, populations and communities originate and grow is decreased due to an inability to correctly account for relations that are predatorial, parasitic, mutualistic, or based on commensalism.

Locking in a Fixed Course

Putting aside our obvious concern that OE is out of sync with every other form of non-sociological ecological inquiry, another concern looms large. The process of elevating competition over all other types of ecological interactions produces an over-reliance upon law-like generalizations that are founded upon poor ecological logic. For example, in developing *his* resource partitioning theory, Carroll (1984: 71) acknowledges OE as an intellectual descendant of Hawley's (1950; 1968) human ecology. Not surprisingly, Carroll (1985: 1278) relates his notion of resource portioning to Hawley's description of competitive social process claiming they both 'predict a shift from competitive to symbiotic relations between organizational forms'. Carroll's model is widely interpreted (Baum and Amburgey, 2002: 312) as predicting 'that increasing market concentration increases the failure rate of generalists and lowers the failure rate of specialists'. Evidence presented in Chapter 5 differs, with a combination of firm features and environmental factors rather than ecological laws used to explain the distribution of so called specialists and generalists.

A review of ecology literature related to the term resource partitioning again reveals an apparent disconnect between its usage in the natural and social sciences. The term resource partitioning was originally coined by Schoener (1968) and further articulated in his later works, most notably in his 1974 classic paper titled *Resource Partitioning in Ecological Communities*. Whilst the idea of resource partitioning 'is intuitively understood, it is not necessarily straightforward to decide what does and does not qualify as a case of resource partitioning ... at one extreme, ... [resource] ... partitioning may be defined as any difference in the resource utilization among species' (Tokeshi, 1999: 162). It is commonly defined as 'the differential use by organisms of resources' (Begon, Harper and Townsend, 1996: 967). Further, Pianka (1969) produced a major work that identified three specific areas of focus when considering the process of resource partitioning, they being habitat, food and time.

Despite prior reference to specific ecological literature (see Hutchinson, 1957) that is heralded as providing 'a precise language for the description of resource partitioning' (Schoener, 1974: 27), Carroll appears to claim resource partitioning as his concept. This despite the fact that the concept of resource partitioning (see Schoener, 1968, 1974; Pianka, 1969) had substantially been developed, and at least 58 papers directly related to the coexistence of specialists and generalists (see Wilson and Yoshimura, 1994) already published prior to 1985.

The assumption that competition must drive the resource partitioning process is inconsistent with its development in the natural sciences where other forms of coaction are taken into account. The above discussion suggests a different trajectory of thinking that has accompanied the development of the concept in the OE literature than in the broader ecological literature. Historically, there has clearly been a lack of on-going ties between both literature bases, with many of the many of the most seminal ideas in ecology (Watt, 1947; Schoener, 1974; Connell, 1980; Wiens, 1989; Levin, 1992) absent from OE research. Such a disconnection would appear to have resulted in an over-reliance upon very strict interpretations of what is, for example, competition. Hannan and Carroll (1992: 30) in acknowledging the difficulty of observing competition within populations, argue that increasing a focus on intra-specific competition simplifies the problem 'because one can safely assume that members of the same population have very nearly the same fundamental niche'. Similar approaches that focus upon vital rates, influenced it would seem by past works from Clements and Shelford (1939), Park (1954) and Odum (1959), reconcile the determination of competition with the outcome of interactions. This contrasts with Milne's (1961: 60) definition that 'competition is the endeavour of two (or more) ... [entities] ... to gain the same particular thing, or to gain the measure each wants from the supply of a thing when that supply is not sufficient for both (or all)'.

What we observe is a complete lack of focus on the type of coaction, on the type of resource usage, the time of consumption, the specific location, and the mechanism of interaction missing in the OE literature. In Chapter 5 we present compelling evidence that Hannan and Carroll's (1992) central assumption regarding homogeneous populations is most unlikely to ever be *directly* observed.

There are also many well-established ecological theories, like Brown and Wilson's (1956) theory of character displacement yet to be applied to the study of firms. This theory would seem to perfectly explain how firms adopt or reject particular forms of organization to avoid competition. Especially when it is recognized that this approach is used in the field of ecology to further develop the idea of resource partitioning. Further, another concept common within the broader ecological literature, but rarely considered in the organizational studies literature is facilitation (Rathcke, 1983). Enrolling this concept offers us the opportunity to rethink apparent competition as potentially something else required to support survival of many diverse types of firms.

In summary, the initial and current thinking in OE has followed a very similar trajectory to that proposed by Hawley and his predecessors. Homogeneous environments exert selection pressure upon populations of firms, with many unable to survive due to a lack of fitness. Worse still, the ability of individual firms to change so as to achieve better fitness is not viewed positively due to structural inertia and/or environmental change occurring too quickly. The assumed opaqueness of the environment is believed to prevent firms from being able to comprehend what aspects of the environment are indeed changing.

Such assumptions have been carried forward by generations of OE researchers, along with the accompanying philosophical, theoretical and methodological assumptions that underpin this thinking. These are choices made by others, and do not reflect the choices made here in our attempt to develop a theory of the firm and its environment. To do so we must develop an alternative ecological approach, an approach with diametrically opposing philosophical, theoretical and methodological assumptions.

To this end, we will leave the last word to Hawley (1988: xvi), who, with reference to Fombrun's (1988) suggestion to consider firms as ecologically capable of adaptation through shaping their environments, said that 'this calls for a rethinking of the strategy of organization ecology. The proposal is unquestionably constructive. Perhaps, however, it is looking further down the road than organizational ecology should travel at this time'. Given the accompanying philosophical, theoretical and methodological assumptions explicit in OE, we agree with Hawley. It would be a tortured journey for all. That is why an alternative ecological approach is required to free individual firms from limiting ecological assumptions made about them. More importantly though, we need an ecological approach to the firm based in the first instance on narrow observations rather than broad inferences. The remainder of this introductory chapter provides a brief overview to the structure and focus of the remaining chapters.

CHAPTER SUMMARIES

Chapter 1. An Alternative Ecological Theory of the Firm and its Environment

There are many theories of the firm, and all serve a purpose. Alvarez (2003: 260) argues that at present most theories of the firm are diverse in nature and 'developed to address a particular set of characteristics and behaviours of interest' to different fields of study. In addition, her concerns extend to the type of firm to which such theories typically relate, i.e. the traditional asset-intensive firm. This chapter seeks to sow the seeds of a new theory of the firm that is applicable to all firms, large or small, physical or virtual, private or public and/or knowledge or asset intensive. This chapter seeks to position the proposed autecological theory of the firm and its environment relative to existing theories of the firm. In doing so, this chapter highlights the potential unique contribution this new theory can make through the adoption of a new set of ecological assumptions regarding the interaction between individual firms and their direct environments.

Chapter 2. What is a Firm?

Firms that survive do so by continually adapting to their surroundings in unique ways. They operate in environs that most certainly differ from their neighbours in ways that are mostly confidential, even secret. Such differences may be small or large, but they are ever-present, and this inevitably leads to observable differences in the firms we see across the world, but one may have to look closely enough. This chapter is about firms and the unique relations they maintain with their operational environments to ensure their survival. It will be argued that neither routines nor firms can be seen as isolated from their own external environments; they constantly interpenetrate each other. In defining the firm as a *non-autonomous entity, located in an operational environment, that is socially constructed, goal-directed, boundary maintaining and maintained through sustenance activities*, we redraw the traditional relationship between firm and environment. We achieve this by considering the nature of organization in firms that is dependent upon a range of sustenance activities, these being organized regularly and enduring activities aimed at supporting firm survival (see Gibbs and Martin, 1959). Our aim is understand the adaptive mechanisms of the firm relative to the environmental factors it maintains operational relations with.

Chapter 3. What is an Environment?

A fundamental premise of the autecology approach is an assumption that individual firms operate in and are adapted to environments particular to their operations. We start this chapter by defining the firm's operational environment as *all observable environmental phenomena that are operationally related, directed, timed, ordered and spaced by and across the lifeline of a particular firm.* This definition draws upon the specific works of Mason and Langenheim (1957), Spomer (1973) and Rose (1997). We will draw upon many other ideas to explain our conception of an environment, remaining true to the assumptions that underpin an autecological approach. We do not start with the presumption that firms based in an industry experience a common environment. We therefore do not believe it is possible to consider the selection of individual firms from the perspective of an assumed homogenous selection mechanism that sorts firms based on individual differences. The actual structuring process within firms, a human driven response to perceptions of the environment, is entirely different in a socioeconomic context than it is in nature. Therefore, we see firms as related to environments operationally in unique and historical ways. As a result, we do not need to enrol the process of natural selection to explain evolutionary outcomes within industry contexts. Instead, we confine ourselves to ecological scales consistent with the firms we investigate and rely upon heuristic generalizations to guide our investigations of firm–environment interaction, as is the focus in ecology/autecology (Walter, 2013).

Chapter 4. Modification and Matching

This chapter offers the reader access to several existing theoretical frameworks that provide a new lens to view firm–environment interactions. It has long been recognized (McKenzie, 1924) that firms interact in ecologically distinct and important ways. Relative to plants and animals, firms have a greater array of mobility options and also possess greater capacity to deliberately seek to acquire, control and/or modify resources from within their local environment. However, such interaction is too often not visible once firm-level data has been aggregated to the level of assumed populations and communities. Building on the past work of Luksha (2008) and Jones (2009), this chapter explains the process of environmental modification, demonstrating the value that this ecological framework holds for understanding the feature–factor relationship between firms and their environments. This issue is at the very heart of an autecological approach to the firm and its environment. Therefore, this chapter places great emphasis upon ensuring the reader can comprehend from an ecological perspective how to account for the nature of environmental interaction occurring between any given firm and its local environment. It will be argued that firms both make and are made as a consequence of interaction with their environment. Importantly, the ideas contained in this chapter differ fundamentally from other ecological explanations of firm adaptation in that individual firms are not required to be assigned membership within a population prior to their adaptive abilities being explained. The focus remains upon the individual firm and its local environment, and a curiosity for contemplating the degree to which firms desire to *tinker* with factors in their local environment (Sahlins and Service, 1960).

Chapter 5. A Model of *Transferred Demand*

In the earlier chapters consideration has been given to explaining the nature of an autecological theory of the firm and its environment. This chapter demonstrates how such a theoretical approach can be used in the field to develop new knowledge on how firms achieve above-average survival. The empirical context is predominantly local restaurant industries in Australia and England, although data from other industry and country contexts will also be presented and discussed. The aim is to illustrate the primary importance of understanding the industry-specific properties of individual firms and the nature of their local environment interactions. It will be demonstrated that individual firms exhibit specific actions that have a profound influence ecologically. Even within an industry, observable specific evolution can be seen to have produced several different types of firms through independent adaptive change (Walter and Hengeveld, 2014). A key feature of this chapter is the presentation of research methods used to conduct research such research.

Chapter 6. Methodological Issues

If the preceding claims that an autecological approach is significantly different are true, then it stands to reason that there will be specific method requirements associated with this approach. It has been said that *nature loves to hide* (Morton, 2013) and Møller and Jennions (2002) highlight six factors that will prevent organizational ecologists from being able to envisage, capture and explain all the variation in their studies. First, the contexts we choose to study are not perfect; there are lags between events and selection and between selection pressures and responses that precede eventual selection (for or against). Second, there is inherent randomness in the contexts we study; no two towns, cities or regions are the same. Third, there are so many possible responses that firms can attempt in response to perceived environmental change, yet typically only a few are focused upon. This leaves space for confounding variables to create sufficient noise to blur the assumed relationship between other variables. Fourth, many firms' actions vary considerably across time and space and are therefore difficult to measure. Fifth, it is difficult to capture the evolutionary past of all firms being studied. Thus, the capacity of each firm to respond differently is difficult to explain. Last, the actions of one firm can alter (negatively or positively) the outcomes of other firms and their environments, a difficult dynamic to observe. Therefore, this chapter will consider the types of approaches and explanations best suited to conducting autecological research. Of primary consideration, reinforcing the specific philosophical and methodological assumptions upon which autecology has historically developed.

Chapter 7. Opportunities and Future Directions

Given the embryonic nature of autecology in organizational studies, and the fact that its future development depends upon broader intellectual curiosity about the approach, this chapter serves as an invitation to other scholars. In contrast to Aldrich (1999) whose invitation chapter sought to 'create a little distance between ... [his] ... efforts to be balanced in the preceding chapters and ... [his] ... desire to be more provocative' in his final chapter, we attempt to do the reverse. In seeking to claim a distinctive intellectual space for an alternative ecological theory of the firm and its environment, we have already been sufficiently provocative. Therefore, this chapter serves as a bridge to reach out to scholars sympathetic with ecological and evolutionary theories. We aim to highlight a range of issues that have remained problematic to organizational theory researchers and offer suggestions as to how an autecological approach may offer new avenues to solve such issues.

Glossary

One of the challenges of introducing an alternative ecological approach is that some concepts, ideas or processes used are either used differently, used in a different context, or new to organizational studies researchers. A comprehensive glossary of all concepts, ideas and processes used throughout the book will be provided. Emphasis will be placed on: 1) providing an accurate ecological definition; 2) references related to the original and current development of the concepts, ideas or processes; and 3) where necessary, an example of how the concept, idea or process is useful to the field of organizational studies.

PART I

An Alternative Theory of the Firm

1. An alternative ecological theory of the firm and its environment

> To understand the behaviour of an organization you must understand the context of that behaviour – that is, the ecology of the organization. (Pfeffer and Salancik, 1978: 1)

The central thesis of this book is that we need an alternative ecological approach to studying *the* firm to fully appreciate the relations between any *individual* firm and its *operational* environment. This approach must accurately account for all resource flows back and forward between firms and *their* operational environment, centre on the degree to which an individual firm's operations *scale* the environment, must generalize at a level that accommodates idiosyncratic *noise* often ignored from the spatiotemporal context of *individual* firms, and must focus on the unique feature–factor relationship of any given firm and its environment. In short, an approach is required that aims to explain the *adaptive responses* of individual firms from the perspective of *their* interactions with regards to the distinctive operational environment they experience. The development of the ideas here draws heavily upon the works of Walter and Hengeveld (2014), Walter (2008), Hengeveld and Walter (1999) and many other related works associated with the on-going renaissance of autecology in the mainstream ecology literature (Rohde, 2005; 2013), works that ultimately seek to bring to life the pioneering works of Daubenmire (1947) and Andrewartha and Birch (1954; 1984) within which the individual entity is the interactive unit. None of these works have been written with the study of firms in mind and, therefore, it is through our interpretation of how autecology is developed elsewhere that guides the development of this book. That said; we believe this work to be the first time a recognized ecologist has contributed directly to theory and method development in the domain of organizational studies.

There are many theories of the firm, and all serve a particular purpose. Alvarez (2003: 260) argues that at present most theories of the firm are diverse and have been 'developed to address a particular set of characteristics and behaviours of interest' to the different sub-domains of organizational research. Further, she expresses a concern as to the type of firm to which such theories typically relate, that is, the traditional asset-intensive firm. This chapter seeks to sow the seeds of a new theory of the firm that is applicable to all firms, large or small, physical or virtual, private or public, knowledge or asset intensive and/or deemed to be entrepreneurial or non-entrepreneurial. This chapter seeks to position the proposed autecological theory of the firm and its environment relative to existing theories of the firm. In doing so, this chapter explains the expected contribution this alternative approach can make through the adoption of a different set of ecological assumptions regarding the interaction between individual firms and their unique operational environments. It will not be the aim of the chapter to critique the merits of other theories of the firm, but rather, to explain the nature of their underlying assumptions vis-à-vis those being advanced here from an autecological perspective.

To establish a clear distinction initially between the alternative autecological approach and what is currently accepted as organizational ecology (Hannan and Freeman, 1977; 1989), we can initially consider the contrast illustrated in Table 1.1. Although, these differences will be explained in greater detail throughout the book, this preliminary discussion seeks to establish within the reader's mind the essential underlying differences of the autecological approach. Non-controversially both approaches accept the existence in society of firms as social entities identifiable as having goals, boundaries and activities systems as outlined by Aldrich (1999).

However, that is the only similarity the two approaches share. In OE, firms are assigned membership to specific populations and/or communities that are deemed to experience a common environment. These are the primary conditions upon which the process of competitive selection is expected to optimize the fitness of surviving firms. Alternatively, firm autecology (hereinafter referred to as FA) does not rely upon arbitrary human abstractions (Reiners and Lockwood, 2010; Martinez and Aldrich, 2012) to construct boundaries so that individual firms can be provided membership of assumed populations and/or communities. Rather, selection processes that affect individual firms are assumed in the first instance to be related to the local events between any given firm and the operational environment, as Spomer (1973) envisages for individual organisms across the different circumstances they experience/create. The operational environment must always be first observed, rather than merely inferred. Following the lead of Mason and Langenheim (1957), we see the operational environment as being directed, timed, ordered and spaced by and across the lifeline of a given firm.

Table 1.1 Alternative ecological assumptions

Organizational Ecology	Firm Autecology
1. Firms exist ...	1. Firms exist ...
2. Firms exist in populations sharing a common environment ...	2. Firms exist in proximity to other firms, frequently sharing a common external environment ...
3. Firms exist in populations sharing a common environment that has limited resources and therefore compete ...	3. Firms exist in proximity to other firms, frequently sharing a common external environment, but typically have their own distinct operational environment ...
4. Firms exist in populations sharing a common environment that has limited resources and therefore compete and this leads to the differential selection of organizational forms with a better fit to the environment.	4. Firms exist in proximity to other firms, frequently sharing a common external environment, but typically have their own distinct operational environment maintaining their existence through solving problems in their operational environment.

This conceptualization of the environment is quite radical in comparison to existing definitions of environment in organizational studies, and draws our explicit attention to specific environmental phenomena with which individual firms maintain *operational relations*. That is, those specific environmental factors, which any particular firm interacts with, and processes used in order to perform the resource exchanges necessary to maintain its existence.

While the existence of populations and/or communities is not denied, such aggregations should be viewed in the spirit of Hengeveld and Walter (1999), as ephemeral epiphenomena. That is, populations and/or communities are the transient by-product of individual-level behaviours and are in reality more conceptual than real. So while we may observe firms being situated in the same spatial or temporal zones, this does not mean that they experience a common environment through joint *assigned* membership. However, it is acknowledged that such structures may exist and indeed influence the process of selection experienced by any individual firm.

In OE, competition is the central mechanism through which one organizational population supposedly 'reduces the hypervolume of environmental space in which another population can sustain itself' (Hannan and Carroll, 1992: 28–29). Viewed as ever-present, the process of competition is the foundation upon which niche theory (Hannan and Freeman, 1989) and its related concepts of density-dependence, legitimacy and carrying capacity have been developed. However, within the OE approach, competition is assumed to be difficult to observe directly and therefore indirect estimates of competition are developed from 'analyzing the densities of interacting populations'. Thus, the process of competition is reduced to mathematical modelling, rather than direct observation. In contrast, the FA approach views competition as only one of many potentially influential ecological processes that may influence firm survival, and it is not around which all investigation and organization is structured.

The FA approach requires that analysis does not reduce all other environmental factors down to a density-dependence explanation (see Andrewartha, 1984) and/or seek to focus upon pairs of interacting populations to formulate models based on competition. As such, assumptions about relatively homogeneous populations in relatively homogeneous environments are replaced by a concern for specific types of individual firms and the spatial-temporal variations present in their local conditions. There is no default assumption that particular traits held by firms predispose such firms to being able to better compete for resources and therefore achieve higher fitness vis-à-vis other comparable types of firms. Indeed, once we view individual firms as situated in highly variable environments, we can also entertain the idea of local adaptation detached from comparable measures of performance and therefore fitness (Nei, 2013). That is, we can imagine firms decreasing the degree of complexity within their activities in order to better match the requirements of their local environment. While firms may be located in proximity to other similar or dissimilar firms, what matters from the FA approach is the matching process between any particular firm and the operational environment it experiences and creates.

Finally, from the OE perspective, the individual firm is 'characterized by relative inertia in structure and in the other characteristics that define membership in a population' (Hannan and Freeman, 1989: 66). When too many firms enter a population relative to those that leave the population, the carrying capacity of the environment for that population is assumed to be exceeded, resulting in a process of intensification of competitive selection removing those firms with less fitness vis-à-vis other firms competing for available/scarce resources.

In contrast, the FA approach has already taken a different pathway to accounting for firm survival. Located in their unique operational environments as Spomer (1973) portrays organisms in an environmental setting, each firm is challenged by different circumstances and resource configurations; 'adaptive improvement is relative to the adaptive problem' encountered (Sahlins and Service, 1973: 15). From this perspective the most upwardly evolving and complex firms can exist alongside the simplest and seemingly static firms, each prospering in a common industry, rather than a common environment.

Whereas OE seeks to understand the ecology of populations of firms (with the environment considered homogeneous), FA seeks to understand the local ecology of individual firms (within their local and operational environmental contexts). Such a difference in purpose extends beyond mere semantics. Whereas OE researchers see firms as being similar in principle and expected to conform to natural ecological laws, FA does not. From an FA perspective, the researcher is focused on understanding the nature of the interaction between individual firms and the environments they experience, create and/or modify. Consistent with the theoretical foundations of autecology, and to paraphrase Walter's (2013: 342) perspective on organisms, firms have industry-specific 'adaptations that mediate their interactions with the environment, and thus are the primary influences in what we call their ecology'. It would be expected that any industry could contain several *sub-types* of firms and therefore care must be exercised when generalizing even at the industry level. For example, previous research into the restaurant industry (Jones, 2009) has shown there are at least six distinct types of Pizza firms operating in unique ways. These different types of firms are observed to adapt to their operational environments in distinctly different ways.

Following the lead of Walter (2013: 351), the FA researcher should also rely upon 'heuristic generalizations that provide guidance on how to investigate the adaptations that underpin' firm–environment interaction. The focus is upon understanding the special ecological circumstances associated with firm adaptation. Further, such circumstances will be expected to align to the degree to which any individual firm scales its environment. To import ecological processes from beyond the scope of a particular individual firm's operating space increases the risk of developing pseudopredictions (Wiens, 1989). Essentially, an autecological approach seeks to avoid applying incorrect spatial and temporal scales to the study of local ecological processes.

In conclusion, this introductory section has sought to introduce the idea of FA, relative to the existing paradigm of OE (Hannan and Freeman, 1977; 1989). It is now appropriate to consider the development of ecological thought in the social sciences so that the current omission of autecology in the social sciences can be understood more clearly. The aim of this section is to illustrate how population/community level thinking has become so dominant in the study of firms. One other caveat worth noting is that the primary concern of FA is understanding ecological interactions *within* time and space, as they pertain to specific *types* of individual firms. Once such an understanding is achieved, further consideration can be also be given to accounting for evolutionary change *across* time and space. So FA is first and foremost an *ecological approach*, which can also potentially contribute to the eventual development of *evolutionary explanations*.

A SHORT INQUIRY INTO ECOLOGICAL THOUGHT

Many have contributed to the development of ecological thought in the social sciences. However, as will be demonstrated, a process of premature convergence has largely led such thinking fundamentally down a set of closely related, and convergent pathways. While much progress has been made in developing and improving ecological models, many important ideas remain unseen, misunderstood and/or unexplored. This section aims to revisit, reorient and reexplain several ecological ideas and concepts, that while present during such thinking, have so far contributed little to our ecological investigation of individual firms in society. The specific focus of this discussion will be upon: 1) how we account for the interactions between firms, 2) the ability of firms to change their mode of operations, and 3) the capacity of firms to modify aspects of their operational environment. From an FA perspective, the past development of these three issues in OE has clearly proved to be intensely problematic.

To understand OE we must understand its intellectual roots. Whilst this inquiry into ecological thought will intentionally be short, and narrow in its focus, it will also not align neatly to the conventional history as documented elsewhere (Gibbs and Martin, 1959; Wallace, 1969; Young, 1974; Berry and Kassarda, 1977; Mlinar and Teune, 1978; Hawley, 1988; Hawley, 1998). Rather, it will retrace many important intellectual positions that were adopted and retained, and other ecological ideas that have yet to influence the domain of OE. The aim being to reveal the latent ecological foundations of an alternative ecological approach to the study of firms that have always been present, just not recognized, and therefore remaining undeveloped.

The OE paradigm gained most traction with the seminal work of Hannan and Freeman (1977), and this is commonly recognized. This work was significantly influenced by the proceeding work of Hawley (1944; 1950; 1968) and his work on human ecology. Hawley's work in turn drew upon the pioneering works of Park and Burgess (1921), McKenzie (1924; 1934a) and Park (1936). These initial works imported many ideas from plant and animal ecology (Young, 1974; Hawley, 1998) for use in sociological domains. It is therefore important to understand the nature of how certain ideas were imported, ignored, or eventually forgotten. Clearly, Hannan and Freeman's (1977) work did not appear from within a vacuum. The argument being made here is that a great deal of ecological *consistency* has remained within the sociological domain from the 1920s until present. Further, this consistency in thought has, as a natural consequence, worked against the appreciation that firms operate and interact within a heterogeneous environment, and thus against the development of an autecological approach to the study of firms in society.

Accounting for Interactions

Of primary concern to any ecologist is accounting for the nature of interactions occurring between observed entities within a given environmental setting. If we accept that Park and Burgess (1921) represents one of the first major works in the field of sociological human ecology, then the initial ideas developed within this work are of great interest. They drew upon the ideas of many influential ecologists of the time, including Warming (1909), Wheeler (1910) and Clements (1916). Beyond drawing upon their natural sociological orientations to place the community at the centre of their research, Park and Burgess also adopted Warming's nonconforming definition of commensalism. As noted previously, an ecologically *inconsistent* interpretation of commensalism based on competitive relations was therefore introduced during the initiation of human ecology as a discipline. Commensalism was first defined by van Beneden (1869) and its ecological meaning as an *interaction between two entities in which one benefits from the other, but the other is unaffected*, and this has not altered across time and/or domains of enquiry as meaning anything other than that (see Dana, 1872; Clements, 1907; Alcock, 1911; Thomson, 1917; Borradaile, 1918; Flattely and Walton, 1922; Hegner, 1924; Pearse, 1926; Kudo, 1931; Allee, 1931; Odum, 1959; Reid, 1962; Pennak, 1964; Clarke, 1967; Rees, 1967; Martin, 1983; Blood and Studdert, 1988; Morris, 1992; Allaby, 2003; Rittner and McCabe, 2004).

The definition of Warming (1909), based on absolutely competitive relations, was offered without explanation, other than to say it is different from that which already existed. To further confuse matters, the Fuller and Conrad (1932) translation of Braun-Blanquet's (1928) classic work contains a translation error that reversed the ecologically consistent meaning attributed to commensalism by Braun-Blanquet. This incorrect translation of Braun-Blanquet's (1928) work is of great importance, given the significant influence of Hawley's (1950) work on so many subsequent researchers in the organizational studies domain (see Hannan and Freeman, 1977; Pfeffer and Salancik, 1978; Astley, 1985; Carroll, 1985; Barnett and Carroll, 1987; Barnett and Amburgey, 1990; Barnett, 1994; Baum and Singh, 1994; Baum and Mezias, 1992; Aldrich, 1999; Greve, 2002; Rao, 2002). It would seem that human ecology; the intellectual forefather of OE was built upon the initial adoption of an incorrect interpretation of an important descriptor of ecological relations. Worse still, this inconsistent meaning was reinforced when Hawley (1950) adopted Fuller and Conrad's (1932) incorrectly translated meaning of commensalism. As a result, OE and other related evolutionary approaches (see Aldrich, 1979; 1999) have continued to use this central ecological concept in ways that preference the assumption of competitive relations over a range of other relations, mostly almost invariably non-harmful.

What remains a mystery is why Hawley (1950) adopted this over-reliance upon competitive relations that has to this day remained so influential in the formulation of OE. He clearly was very mindful of Kropotkin's (1902) idea of mutual aid and was mentored by Roderick McKenzie, whose writing on such matters was crystal clear. McKenzie's (1934b) collection of readings in human ecology provides a standard definition of commensalism, attributable to the work of prominent ecologist, Arthur Thomson (1914). It is somewhat ironic that Hawley (1944: 399) observed that 'the difficulties which beset human ecology may be traced to the isolation of the subject from the mainstream of ecological thought'. Whatever the reason, the adoption of a position relegating commensalism to be a descriptor for all manner of competitive relations (see Aldrich, 1999) has deprived OE researchers from accounting for all nine forms of coactions (see Haskell, 1949) in a manner that is ecologically consistent. It has ensured a strong emphasis remains upon competition as the primary organizing process of population/community relations. To be clear, and consistent with mainstream ecology, within the FA approach a commensalistic relationship connotes an *interaction between two entities in which one benefits from the other, but the other is unaffected*. In Chapter 2, the full range of coactions that an individual firm may experience will be discussed in detail. The next issue relates to the structural inertia attributed to firms in the OE approach, as contrasted to the idea of firm plasticity proposed in the FA approach.

Firm Plasticity

Many theories of the firm consider the ability of firms to adapt to changing environmental conditions a fundamental issue (Teece, Pisano and Shuen, 1997). While new ideas related to dynamic capabilities (Winter, 2003) emerge from scholars with many decades of thinking in this space, OE remains condemned as being too pessimistic (Dew, Goldfarb and Sarasvathy, 2006) vis-à-vis the ability of firms to remain agile and capable of out-running environmental change. That is, OE protagonists (Hannan and Freeman, 1984) see structural forces within firms providing at the start of their operations a selective advantage, but eventually then limiting these firms from being capable of transformative reorganization. While change is seen as possible to a firm's peripheral features, such change is not assumed to be easily achieved across core features of the firm. However, how one determines exactly what is core and what is peripheral from one firm to another remains a contested issue. As a result, OE is criticized strongly (Donaldson, 1995) for as yet not being able to adequately accommodate firm-level adaptive processes into this approach.

It is argued that such problems essentially are a consequence of Hannan and Freeman's desire to adopt a biological population ecology model within which the individual biological entities observed have very little scope to fundamentally change their morphological and/or physiological structures. Thus, it suits OE to insist that individual firms are limited in their ability to respond to environmental change, because that is how many ecologists (Elton, 1927; Hutchinson, 1957; Roughgarden, 1979), from whom they have adapted their ideas, essentially investigated the world. Strategic management theorists hold entirely different assumptions and argue that firms are often inspired to innovate and change their market positioning through innovative behaviours to overcome marketplace disruptions (Christensen, 2000).

FA offers a pragmatic solution to this on-going impasse that isolates OE from genuinely integrating various ideas from other theories of the firm, such as organizational learning. OE defends its structural inertia position from fully embracing organizational learning (Hannan, Polos and Carroll, 2007), suggesting that miscalculations due to opacity will restrict a firm's ability to reorganize firm features and align to changing environmental factors. However, if we reconceptualize what is the actual operational environment experienced by any given firm, we can recast the process of firm adaptation. We can place in front of the manager or entrepreneur an environment that is comprehendible; we can see through the assumed opaque context.

Think about the independent firms that have survived in your local neighborhood, despite the ever-increasing reach of the large (typically franchised) chain stores. Most are not specialists afforded a safe market space due to their unique positioning. Quite often they are generalists, operating on an entirely different scale from the large chain stores, and therefore experiencing a different environment. Their on-going survival is a testament to their adaptive abilities; to deny this would be to ignore the many factors that have changed in their individual operational environments over time. What is of critical importance is that we do not mistakenly over-focus on assumed general progress within an industry at the expense of actual specific focus being made by individual firms (Sahlins and Service, 1973). Yes, observable evolutionary trends do emerge in specific industries, but they frequently do so as the result of ecologically and behaviourally determined factors that occur at the level of the firm. Thus, firms can be viewed as relatively plastic in their abilities to behave differently to other similar firms that also acquire and use similar resources. That is, firms can be expected to demonstrate behaviours aligned to their own local ecology if we view them from a more fine-grained perspective than is common in the OE approach.

The nature of this approach will form the focus of the discussion in Chapter 4.

We step around the problematic theory of structural inertia by expanding our concern from change occurring in the core features of any firm, to placing more concern on shifts in actual behaviour. So, regardless of what features changed or remained the same, it is the actual adaptive behaviour that is crucial. While OE is clearly an approach that has tended to focus on larger firms, FA seeks to be applicable to all types of firms, even those without complex structures, subunits, interlocking directorates and/or joint ventures (see Hannan and Freeman, 1989). It seeks to understand how firms interact with their unique operational environments in specific ways, reliant upon their sensory abilities. It is through the identification of differences in sensory abilities that FA avoids the firm equivalent of the cryptic species problem in understanding species and their diversity (see Paterson, 1993) found in the OE approach (see Freeman and Hannan, 1983), where multiple types of firms are grouped into one category despite observable differences in their environmental interactions.

In summary, OE is an approach based on specific assumptions that create much inflexibility in how we view the adaptive abilities of the firm. The forthcoming chapters will illustrate how FA frees us from such restriction through providing an introduction to the process of environmental matching (Walter and Hengeveld, 2014) through which local firms match local environs through time. To enable such analysis, we must also be mindful and able to explain the nature of environmental modification occurring between any given firm and its unique operational environment. For it is here that local selection events can be seen and understood. The subsequent outcome for all surviving firms is a *fit* that arises from the process of environmental matching. With Martinez and Aldrich (2012) placing great importance on understanding the nature of such a fit, FA allows consideration of its underlying processes and causes to occur at much closer range. While they correctly note the importance of consequences over intentions, FA does not need to assume that the consequences of individual intention will ultimately cascade upwards to affect populations and communities. FA remains focused on local selection events and this is the focus of the next section.

Firm Modification of Operational Environments

From an FA perspective, all individual firms are capable of changing important aspects of their operational environment. That is not to say that the intentions of the entrepreneur or manager to alter aspects of their operational environment will underwrite their continual survival. All that is being stated is that at least certain aspects of any given firm's operational environment are open to manipulation in some form or another. A multitude of factors, local and/or otherwise will ultimately combine to determine the degree of fit between any firm and its operational environment.

What matters is that FA does not place conditions on firm size regarding who is big or strong enough to effect such manipulation. Operating at lower ecological scales enables FA to observe environmental complexity at a level where first-hand observations are more concrete. Rather than assuming that firms belong to populations and/or communities that are subject to a relatively homogeneous selection landscape, FA seeks to understand environmental heterogeneity and how firms respond to that. The assertion that individual firms have limited resources and therefore cannot affect the environment, assumed to relate to an entire population within a common competitive environment (Martinez and Aldrich, 2012), is predicated upon the presence of an actual population of firms. As will be discussed in the following chapter, this assertion is inconsistent with the foundational principles of autecology. For now, let's consider the idea that firms can alter aspects of their environment.

From the FA perspective, the nature of interaction between firm and its operational environment represents a constant process of interpenetration between firm and environment. Such interpenetration can be viewed as the process of acquiring resources (e.g. inputs and revenue) and providing resources (e.g. products and services) to other stakeholders in its operational environment. In contrast to the prevailing logic of OE (see Hannan and Carroll, 1992), FA assumes that while individual firms are subject to environmental selection forces, those very firms are capable of also altering such selection processes through modifying aspects of their own operational environments.

Strangely, little research has explicitly examined such a process of modification (although see Jones, 2009 and Luksha, 2008), despite there being no shortage of confidence that firms do modify their environments (see March, 1994; Winter, 1990; Scott, 1987; Popper, 1972; Rumelt, 1979; Winter, 1964). However, most recent work in this area is from a co-evolutionary perspective, either attributing such modification to collective behaviour, or large corporations, not small individual firms (see Child, Tse and Rodrigues, 2013).

FA is assumed not to be naturally related to the various co-evolutionary approaches operationalized in organizational studies research (e.g. Baum and Singh, 1994, Murmann, 2003; Child, Tse and Rodrigues, 2013; Abatecola, 2014; Breslin, 2014; Geels, 2014). It sees firms as often isolated from population density-dependent (competitive) factors, and quite likely to be impacted by a broader range of environmental variables, such as unique local events and/or processes. There is however room in an autecological approach to accommodate aspects of co-evolution, of the *symmetrical* kind described by Child, Tse and Rodrigues (2013), but not so *asymmetrical* co-evolution that essentially denies firms of *all* sizes the ability to significantly shape their environments. Herein lies a major difference between the FA and the more traditional OE approach. FA is focused upon individual firms and their unique operational environments. Thus, the average firm can be expected to shape many factors in its operational environment, despite not being expected to be able to modify its external (or macro) environment. The works of Child and others link together macro, meso and micro environments in such a manner that the process through which each individual firm scales its actual operational environment, is lost in the shadows of the several layers of relatively homogenous environments that are home to various populations and communities of firms.

Drawing upon the work Odling-Smee, Laland and Feldman (2003: 41) and Lewontin (1983), Jones (2009) and Luksha (2008) positioned the investigation of adaptive change relative to the on-going reciprocal interaction between the firm, the firm's behaviour and its environment. Rather than merely being on the receiving end of competitive selection, as per the OE approach, firms both modify and are adapted as a consequence of interaction with their environment. Such thinking remains consistent with the seminal arguments of Darwin's (1881) that arose from his observation that worms not only change the soil they inhabit, but also ensure a process of ecological (as well as genetic) inheritance that consequently benefits the future survival of the environment modifying worms as well as their eventual off-spring. Thus, FA in highlighting the process of environmental modification extends a focus to specific generative mechanisms through which empirical explanations of *how* firms might alter their environments may be crafted. The FA researcher seeks to understand how individual firms modify the feature–factor relationship between firm and operational environment. What is sought is evidence of firms changing one or more of the factors of its operational environment, 'either by physically perturbing factors at its current location in time and space, or by relocating to a different space-time address, thereby exposing itself to different factors'.

From the standard evolutionary perspective, populations of firms transmit information (routines, cultures and organizational structures) from one generation to the next, under the direction of natural selection. However, enfolding the process of environmental modification into the FA approach enables direct consideration of how individual firms may modify their operational environments. From this approach, each firm (and/or those very similar) may inherit both information and a legacy of modified selection pressures (i.e. ecological inheritance) from incumbent firms. Problems encountered may not require the deliberate attempts to alter organizational routines. Rather, altering aspects of the operational environment may sufficiently lessen or remove the problem.

To recap, there have always existed differing views within the current literature as to whether or not *individual* firms are capable of altering their environments (Winter, 1964; Aldrich, 1979; Rumelt, 1979; McKelvey, 1982; Scott, 1987). Such differences of opinion are not assisted by the paucity of empirical studies addressing this fundamental issue. Introducing the idea of environmental modification, as explained above and addressed more fully in Chapter 4, offers a new window through which to consider *how* and under *what* conditions firms may alter their operational environments, and potentially those of other firms. Most importantly, we can lessen our concern of causal ambiguity (Martinez and Aldrich, 2012) whereby firms are assumed unable to determine the basis for successful performance in a given industry. Focusing upon the interaction between firm and operational environment brings the researcher face-to-face with the specific types of selection impacting upon any individual firm.

Taken together, these three issues (accounting for ecological interactions, the ability of firms to change their mode of operation and the ability of firms to modify aspects of their operational environment) represent an alternate ecological approach to the study of firm. From an FA perspective, the past development of these three issues in OE is highly problematic. The following section considers how the primary assumptions of FA, as described above, relate to the primary assumptions of other popular and related theories of the firm. The aim is to enable you to understand how FA might be used in conjunction with other common approaches. Further, to highlight why FA is either difficult to use and/or inappropriate to use with existing ecological approaches due to conflicting underlying assumptions.

RELATING FA TO OTHER THEORIES OF THE FIRM

Theories of the firm typically have two components in common: they focus on firms, and in one way or another, the environments they are held to operate in. Whether these firms are aggregated together or viewed individually, each approach is underpinned by important assumptions that provide a logic to each approach. It has been argued above that the logic upon which OE has developed is often misunderstood. As a result, OE is often interpreted too broadly as being the only way to view firms ecologically. While there have been attempts to genuinely integrate OE with the strategic management literature (Durand, 2006), doing so tends to rely on bending the original assumptions that informed the initial development of OE. Conversely, FA is argued to naturally achieve integration with several other theories of the firm. Let us first consider those other theories where there would appear to be opportunities for integration, starting with the best fit.

Firm-level Theories

The resource dependence theory of Pfeffer and Salancik (1978: 12) provides many similarities to FA, as described above. The unit of analysis is the same, that being the firm and its environment. There is a far greater acceptance of strategic choice (Child, 1972) than permitted in OE, simply because many firms are in reality observed to overcome the constraints they encounter. However, although there is a tight focus on the firm and its environment, this is where there are important differences also. Resource dependence theory views the environment initially as 'every event in the world which has any effect on the activities or outcomes of' firms. However, firms are not expected to understand all aspects of this environment as they are either buffered from them or ignorant of them. In this sense the environment is largely something to be known, something that can be negotiated through changing exchange relationships (Poole and Van de Ven, 2004). As organizations try to alter aspects of their environment to overcome constraints, they are likely to become subject to different constraints, and will ultimately evolve through a process of constraint avoidance. Those firms that survive are assumed to hold more power due to their interdependence and location in social space relative to other related firms. Thus all firms are not equal in terms of the abilities to alter aspects of their environment. This is an important difference with FA, given the assumption in FA that all firms can potentially alter aspects of their operational environment to adapt through time. It is through this issue where the greatest difference is, that of how the environment of each individual firm is defined. Whereas resource dependence theory sees firms located within inter-firm relationships, power constellations and other power relations, FA does not make these initial assumptions. Due to its narrower environmental focus, FA importantly grants firms greater abilities to alter aspects of their environments.

The behavioural theory of the firm (Cyert and March, 1963) places great emphasis upon organizational learning, or the ability to solve problems present within the environment, very consistent with FA. However, as originally formulated, firms are expected to negotiate their external environment through sharing in the learning of other related firms, adopting best practice to better adapt to a relatively common external environment. The environment is also assumed to produce external shocks that are uncontrollable. In this respect, the behavioural theory of the firm places far less concern on the micro-environment of the individual firm and more concern on interaction within the broader external environment and thus, organizational learning is seen to occur in a deeper industry context.

In a similar way, the strategic choice approach of Child (1972) also views the environment as highly complex, emerging from product and factor markets, technology, politics and socio-cultural factors. Again, these factors are seen to exist independently of any individual firm, but can be overcome through the agency that exists within firms. While this approach is interested (like FA) in the permeation between firms and their environments, there is an inevitable default to sociological ideas whereby power relations ultimately are seen to mediate interaction between the firm and its environment.

Other Theories of the Firm

Most other prominent theories either focus below the level of the firm, or above, in terms of the unit of analysis. The OE approach has been discussed above, and so will not be discussed any further at this time. Institutional theory (Meyer and Rowan, 1977; DiMaggio and Powell, 1983) sees homogeneity where FA sees heterogeneity. It also views the environment from an institutional perspective and assumes the presence of isomorphic processes that produce homogeneous firm types. Thus, firms are not seen to typically change their environment, but rather, to be changed by it, in ways that provide them with the legitimacy to survive.

Evolutionary economics (Nelson and Winter, 1982) provides an interesting approach within which a firm's routines act as mechanisms that guide local searches that ultimately produce incremental improvements in its routines. Here there is clearly a similarity with FA, which also assumes that the stability of firm routines provides a conduit for firm adaptation to occur. FA enrols the process of autopoiesis (Rose, 1997) to consider how an individual firm may *be* and *become* through precise delineation of firm boundaries (see Radosavljevic, 2008) and environment interaction. However, the conceptualization of the business environment in evolutionary economics is far broader than FA where firm adaptation is also seen to be possible without any specific change to firm routines.

Finally, the resource-based view of the firm (Penrose, 1959; Barney, 1991) is similar to the extent that it sees each individual firm as being potentially unique, due to resource heterogeneity. However, FA does not place great emphasis on the idea of a competitive advantage being obtained and/or lost due to environmental turbulence. Firms that survive, from an FA perspective, are successful regardless of their comparative resource strengths/weaknesses due to their ability to match their interacting elements with the nature of the operational environment experience and shape.

In summary, the FA approach does not claim to displace any of the approaches discussed above. It merely seeks to establish the importance of a different set of questions. As noted previously (Alvarez, 2003: 260), each current theory of the firm has been 'developed to address a particular set of characteristics and behaviours of interest'. FA places unique emphasis upon the ability of individual firms to alter the unique operating environment they interact with. Firms can be observed doing so due to the fine-grained analysis common to autecological studies (Walter and Hengeveld, 2014). Rather than assuming that firms directly experience what is commonly called an *external* environment, the actual manner in which any firm scales its environment is first considered. This produces the discovery of the firm's *operational* environment, or, all environmental phenomena *observed* to have *operational relations* with any firm. Once we are operating at this level of analysis we are able to witness first-hand the likely process of environmental modification. From this field of view, new observations, research questions and knowledge are possible to the researcher of firms.

THE PROMISE OF ANOTHER THEORY OF THE FIRM

This chapter has introduced an alternative ecological theory of the firm and its environment. It has been claimed that this alternative approach differs from the traditional OE approach in how it accounts for the interactions between firms and the environments they experience. Further, unlike OE, the FA approach accepts the ability of firms to change their mode of operations to better match the requirements of their operational environment. Finally, and most importantly, the FA approach promotes the ability of firms to modify aspects of their operational environment in ways that alter the nature of selection they experience. These three specific differences do more than merely distinguish FA from the traditional OE approach; they also provide an exciting pathway to connect FA to many common assumptions held within other theories of the firm.

For example, FA as proposed fully embraces all aspects of the organizational learning literature. In doing so it focuses upon the specific learning processes of the firm doing the learning. Rather than requiring the process of learning to be illustrated across time in longitudinal studies or at multi-levels of analysis, we can be content with observing the learning that most influences the feature–factor relationship between firm and operational environment (see Poole and Van de Ven, 2004). The nature of generalization possible through FA lends itself to such simple, yet potentially broad observations. FA expects to find complex patterns of learning across different types of firms. It uses heuristic generalizations to guide such investigation of firm–environment interaction. Thus, there are no assumed laws related to firm learning that firms would be expected universally to comply to.

FA makes it possible to connect the field of organizational studies to the current renaissance of autecological thinking (see Walter and Hegeveld, 2014). It also enables an explicit focus on adaptive mechanisms, sensory abilities, and the process through which firms modify their interactive elements (see Jones, 2005) to better match the requirements of their operational environment. Interestingly, FA draws upon Rose's (1997) idea of a *lifeline* to also explicitly consider the nature of environmental matching occurring across the different phases of a firm's lifeline. The operational environment is therefore directed, timed, ordered and spaced by and across the lifeline of a given firm.

The next chapter consider the question, what is a firm? It will be argued that neither routines nor firms can be seen as isolated from their own operational environments, as they constantly interpenetrate each other. It will be argued that every firm has, in its organization, a range of sustenance activities, these being organized regularly and enduring activities aimed at supporting firm survival (see Gibbs and Martin, 1959). So while various aspects of the firm must change to facilitate continual adaptation, order must remain within the firm's sustenance activities to allow the firm to both *be* and *become*.

PART II

The Firm and its Environment

2.   What is a firm?

Life inevitably diversifies. It does so because it is perpetuated by reproduction and inheritance, so that adaptive changes are transmitted only in lines of descent. (Sahlins and Service, 1973: 13)

Firms that survive do so by continually adapting to their surroundings in unique ways. They operate in environs that most certainly differ from their neighbours in ways that are mostly confidential, even secret. Such differences may be small or large, but they are ever-present, and this inevitably leads to observable differences in the firms we see across the world, but one may have to look closely enough. This chapter is about firms and the unique relations they maintain with their operational environments to ensure their survival. To build the arguments necessary to support the development of an autecological theory of the firm and its environment, we must first be very clear what it is that constitutes a firm. Clearly, if we fail at this task, any attempt to elucidate the precise nature of relations between a given firm and its operational environment will be nigh on impossible.

Classifying firms ecologically from an autecological approach, while challenging and time-consuming, is an unavoidable task. Kimberly and Miles (1980: 142) noted that asking 'why are there so many different kinds of organizations within each of the many kinds of populations?' was a logical question to ask. This is a question worth asking, but not one this book will dwell on, other than to note the propensity of firms to increasingly become different from one another, rather than converging on a common structure, form and/or behaviour. It is convenient within the OE approach to envisage selection as acting upon the differences that firms exhibit. But again, that assumes the presence of a common environment, something not expected in FA. Therefore, we are free to observe as much variety as is on offer. As such, we can move beyond the challenge of domain/category classifications (Hannan, Polos and Carroll, 2007) and instead focus on what is common to all firms when defining what is a firm. Several questions arise here. What is common to firms considered to belong to a particular type? Is there such a thing as a particular type? Could it be arbitrary, like a family or genus in biology? In the next section we introduce the precision required to address such questions.

WHAT IS A FIRM?

From an FA perspective, a firm is a *non-autonomous entity, located in an operational environment, and is socially constructed, goal-directed, boundary maintaining and maintained through sustenance activities*. This definition draws upon the sociological work of Aldrich (1999) to identify three accepted common elements (being socially constructed, goal-directed and boundary maintaining). Further, it adds the ecological ideas of Mason and Langenheim (1957) to place the firm into a very specific context, that of its own operational environment. Finally, acknowledging that firms that exist through time must constantly engage in activities that support survival, we enrol Gibbs and Martin's (1973: 31) observation that 'organization for sustenance is one of man's most effective ways of adjusting to his environment'.

Importantly, the word *organization* is used here in ways not interchangeable with the word *firm*. While others, such as Aldrich (1999) have referred to firms as organizations, we restrict the use of the word organization to refer to organization occurring within firms, rather than firms being organizations. Further, implicit in this definition is a claim that at every moment of the firm's existence it is locked into a process of both *being* and *becoming*. By including the process of autopoiesis (Rose, 1997), or self-organization (Maturana and Varela, 1980), we can directly address the issue of what features of a firm are regularly subject to change (through self-organization) and those that are not. Further, we can construct a definition of the firm that is both time-based and environmentally embedded.

As previously proposed (see Jones, 2005), what constitutes a firm is illustrated in Figure 2.1 below. Combinations of interaction elements that are delivered by humans and technologies, actual products and services, and the identity of the firm, provide the means to reconcile the firm's operational environment in terms of operational relations that are deemed to be reconcilable via a baseline. The notion of a baseline was proposed by Knudsen (2002) to enable both sides of the selection–adaptation argument to be reconciled. The baseline idea suggests that feedback from the firm's interacting elements is available to the decision-makers in the firm and they can replicate what works and modify that which does not. The ellipse that features in Figure 2.1 represents the boundary constructed by the firm's activities that separate the firm's operational environment from its external environment. Thus, the baseline highlights that aspect of the environmental conditions from which interaction and subsequent feedback is possible.

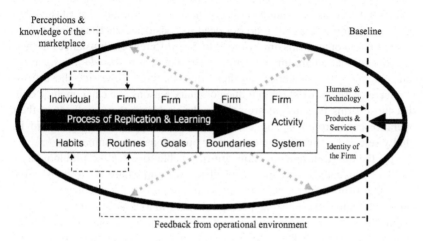

Figure 2.1 The firm, its environment and its sustenance activities

Through a process feedback, the perceptions and knowledge held in the firm are subject to change through learning that is related directly to the perceived performance of its interacting elements. Importantly, these perceptions are held to be fallible (Langlois, 1997). As such, the process of change at the firm level is one considered conditional upon misperceptions and trial-and-error learning through which firms attempt to limit the degrees of maladjustment between themselves and their operating environment. Rather than assuming the firm is bound by inertia, we see the process of replication as maintaining internal order. However, the firm is free to attempt to adjust its routines, goals, boundaries, activity system and ultimately its interacting elements in order to survive. In reality, firms do not change radically overnight; they tend to replicate much of their goals, systems, culture and interacting elements to ensure order is maintained in the operations. Over time, firms that survive do so by accumulating many small and large changes into their pre-existing order.

Nevertheless, no guarantees emerge from this process of interaction. While allowance has been made (in the far right) in Figure 2.1 for the firm to exert influence upon phenomena in the firm's operational environment, no assumptions are made as to the eventual success of any such *future* interventions. All that can be said is that the existence of the firm indicates that *past* efforts in shaping aspects of its operational environment have not been unsuccessful.

WHY DO FIRMS PERSIST?

Following the logic of Haukioja (1982), firms (like organisms) are considered successful if at a given moment of evaluation they are observed to maintain their existence. We do not need to consider their fitness relative to other firms as other firms are assumed to face different circumstances in their own operational environments. Our primary concern is *why do firms persist*, rather than are they superior to other firms. Putting to one side those firms that have ceased to exist for genuine voluntary reasons, we can conclude only that those firms that persist are solving the problems they confront in their operational environment above a threshold level at which they would be fatally selected against by factors in their operational environment.

Still the question remains, how are firms able to solve the problems they face? As illustrated in Figure 2.1, feedback is assumed always to be possible from the firm's interacting elements. Importantly, this feedback can be balanced against the existing perceptions and marketplace knowledge held within the firm's stock of working knowledge. We argue that firms are able to use this imperfect knowledge to bring about different types of change. First, the firm's existing goals, boundaries and activity system can be subject to change. Second, the firm's interacting elements can be altered in an attempt to achieve better alignment to stakeholder and public expectations. Third, the firm can attempt to modify aspects of its operational environment to increase awareness/acceptance or lessen external selection processes upon its interacting elements. In reality, we would expect to see various combinations of these three approaches used. Critically, the degree of actual trial-and-error learning relied upon will be directly related to the *sensory abilities* of the firm, or the ability to track and rise to the challenges found within their operational environment.

Logically, firms that exist through time can be assumed to acquire the ability to navigate adaptive behaviours using a baseline that potentially limits the degree of change due to its direct relationship to the firm's operations and the environment where interaction occurs. However, none of the variables here are expected to remain stable. The problem of making decisions against a changing baseline, shifted by unpredictable environmental change, introduces limitations. Under such conditions, it is challenging to envisage how a meaningful evaluation of positive or negative outcomes associated with internally driven change could be completed in confidence.

Veblen (1922: 191) felt that the firms of today represent some form of adaptation to 'past circumstances, and are therefore never in full accord with the requirements of the present'. The challenge of survival depends upon the minimization of the maladjustment between the firm's interacting elements (i.e. its activities, products and services, and identity) and its operational environment. Clearly, the firm's learning capabilities are critical to enabling continual safe passage through the environment's corridor of persistence. Referred to previously as a corridor of fitness (Jones, 2004), we refer here to the degrees of freedom afforded to the firm's activities, products and services and identity by the operational environment.

The proposition is quite simple: there is no identifiable equilibrium position possible in reality, but rather the relative degree of environmental stability determines the breadth of a buffer zone within which degrees of fitness are achieved. Bruderer and Singh (1996) suggest that instead of assuming an either/or equilibrium position exists, firms are guided by continual feedback through which they adjust their interacting elements to best match the requirements of the local environment. Thus, they tend to be located to either side of a hypothetical, and ever-changing equilibrium position that is akin to the Holy Grail. In reality, from an autecological position, we can disregard the notion of such hypothetical equilibriums, staying focused rather on the actual persistence of firms.

From this perspective, marketplace feedback provides guidance to the adaptive behaviours of the firm. A process of internal selection (Aldrich, 1999), a function of the habits and routines present within the firm, is ultimately judged by key stakeholder acceptance of the firm's interacting elements. Hopefully, you are sufficiently convinced of the plausibility of the ecological explanation unfolding thus far. However, given the obvious importance of the proposed areas of interaction, in makes sense to consider them in more detail.

Understanding Interaction

The firm's three areas of interaction are: 1) human and technological controlled activities; 2) the products and services produced; and 3) the actual identity of the firm. This first element relates to all contact points through which the firm and its agents interact with all external stakeholder groups. The actual services and products the firm provides (2, above) should require no further explanation as an element through which firm/stakeholder interaction occurs. Identity though is somewhat less clear-cut. It has previously been considered an interactor (Knudsen, 2002: 461) with regard 'the personal and professional identity of team members'. However, the proposed role of identity considered here also includes the firm itself. The literature tends to use the phrase *corporate identity* (Stuart, 1998) to describe corporate personality, which is based upon corporate strategy. Here, the term *corporate* will be used interchangeably with *firm* to reflect a broader application. The identity of a firm embodies its culture and personality, as recognizable by both internal and external stakeholders. Therefore, a function of its interaction with external stakeholders is the firm's image. This image also influences the firm's fitness within its operational environment.

Any such changes are managed through the balancing of the firm's features relative to the environment's factors, which is known as the feature–factor relationship in evolutionary biology (Odling-Smee, Laland and Feldman, 2003). Of particular interest in this respect is when firms are able to change the balance of this relationship to their advantage. This process will be discussed in detail in Chapter 4.

Inertia and Adaptation

The central thesis of this book is that firms can and do adapt to their local environment through modifying the features of their structural/strategic organization and/or modification of factors in their operational environment (or influencing them). This constant process of matching between the firm's features and environmental variables, the adjusting of inner relations to outer relations, constitutes the lifeline of any given firm. The on-going existence of any firm indicates a capacity 'simultaneously to *be* and *become*', as it is for individual organisms (Rose, 1997: 142). Most aspects of this statement shouldn't be too controversial. The ability of firms to modify the aspects of their organization is well accepted (Cyert and March, 1963; Child, 1969), as is the presence of selection produced by environmental change (Nelson and Winter, 1982) that prompt firm-level changes to restore a fit between a firm and its environment. What may be more controversial are the following related assumptions that also accompany the statement above.

Many firms are expected to adjust to their operational environment without achieving any noticeable evolutionary progress and/or with perhaps, even losing degrees of their past complexity. What matters is the degree of ecological versatility (Mac Nally, 1995) achieved by each individual firm. Put simply, the extent to which any firm can fully exploit the resources in their operational environment matters most. From an autecological perspective, adaptive improvements are relative to the environmental problems encountered. Autecology allows the researcher to view evolution from two distinct (but related) perspectives, they being, *specific* and *general* evolution. Sahlins and Service (1960: 13) note that 'specific and general evolution are not different concrete realities; they are rather aspects of the same process, which is also to say, two contexts in which we may place the same evolutionary things and events'. We can look at either the *specific* nature of adaptation occurring, or from the perspective of *general evolution*, overall change. Given the FA approach being developed in this book, preference is given to understanding the nature of *specific* evolution.

Such a focus on *specific* evolution is central to the autecology approach, which sees individual firms operating in and adapting to environments defined in relation to the particularities of their operations. From this perspective, we are freed from the default OE position of assuming that evolution will proceed through a process of natural selection, or differential selection across similar firms occurring within a common environment. Instead, we can entertain the possibility of environmental selection (Brandon, 1990), rather than natural selection, as a means for explaining the survival of firms. So, rather than assuming that differences in firm fitness are derived from the sorting of firms in common environments, the actual heterogeneity of the environment is highlighted to enable firm adaptedness to also be viewed as a property-in-an-environment. This is because the adaptedness of the firm is only observed relative to its specific operational environment, more on this in Chapter 3.

Firms may appear from specific vantage points to be quite inert across many metrics, but may have subtly adjusted aspects of the feature-factor relationship that ultimately define each firm and its operational environment. For example, a private process to gain more access to a particular resource may have proved rewarding, significantly altering the feature–factor relationship, but may well remain unknown to all other stakeholders. While the firm appears relatively inert, it has managed to improve the feature–factor relationship in its favour, and that matters more that having made noticeable changes elsewhere.

Why Firms and Not Populations of Firms?

Hopefully by now sufficient logic is emerging to make the case for the ecological study of firms as individual entities. This is what most differentiates FA from OE. It is our concern for the individual firm and of its members' interests that motivates us. Populations of firms, however defined, are viewed as epiphenomena, or simply the side-effect of many individual firms interacting with their operational environments whilst engaged in sustenance activities.

The forensic focus on each firm's operational environment fundamentally changes the way in which firms can be studied ecologically. FA dismantles the revered status of competition, a key component of population thinking (Andrewartha, 1984). Gone are assumptions about upper and lower population limits to which firms would be expected to conform. Instead, a problem-solving logic of control is proposed. Simply stated, the extent to which any individual firm can solve the problems that exist in its operational environment determines the ultimate control that particular firm has over its continued existence. So we can still contemplate resource thresholds, but at the level of the firm and its unique operational environment, rather than at higher population and community levels.

Traditionally, ecological approaches have ignored the motivations and interests of the actors that manage firms (Kasarda and Bidwell, 1984), because the only control they were envisaged to experience was that exerted on them by population-level factors. While such downward causation is not ruled out, for example, anti-competitive behaviours, it is not expected to be the norm either. What matters more is that we are able to correctly identify types of firms and gain an understanding of the general behaviour associated with their existence.

TYPES OF FIRMS

In the OE approach, firms in an industry (or sharing classification codes) are typically assigned to a population, and then perhaps divided into categories like specialist or generalists. For example, when Freeman and Hannan (1983) studied the environmental effects upon California restaurants they collapsed 33 restaurant types into three types: specialists, fast food and generalists. Alternatively, in the FA approach individual firms' differences are preserved and membership in a restricted group, such as a population, is not assumed. For example, when Jones (2009) studied the survival of restaurants he retained all 23 restaurant formats observed as distinct types of firms. In fact, given his specific focus on Pizza firms, he actually identified six sub-types of Pizza firms. Rather than a process of category convergence, as in the OE example, a process of category divergence emerged.

Indeed, if the entire 23 restaurant types were studied to the same depths as the Pizza firms, many more sub-types of firms would certainly have been identified. To illustrate, consider the nature of the six sub-types of Pizza firms.

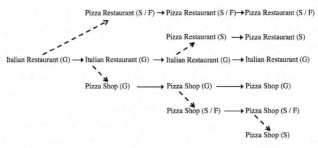

Note: G = Generalist, S = Specialist, F = Franchised Operator.

Figure 2.2   Simple categorization of Pizza firms

When the nature of relations between Pizza firms and their operating environments was studied, Jones (2009) observed significant morphological (form and structure) and physiological (functions and activities) adjustments that developed over time in the Pizza industries studied. Put simply, distinctly different types of Pizza firms operated in ways that were not reducible to a single form, or type of firm. A brief explanation of each type illustrated in Figure 2.2 should demonstrate the importance of this observation.

Initially, most areas were serviced by a single family-run Italian restaurant that included pizza on its menu, along with many other Italian dishes. Thus, they appealed to a broad range of customers in a generalist sense. Eventually, franchised firms entered local areas offering low-cost Italian food with an emphasis on pizza, to replicate this traditional format. They could be considered specialists given their narrower menu and focused target market, which was shaped primarily by affordability. The increasing legitimacy of pizza thus increased and local Pizza shops increasingly became popular for consumers in the night-time economy. They operated in a generalist manner with pizza being served alongside kebabs, chicken, and fish and chips. By this time, upmarket Pizza restaurants also became popular, also operating as specialists through their narrow focus on pizza alone, but aiming at consumers looking for a higher-level restaurant experience. A second form of franchised firm entered the market, offering only delivery of pizza, without any provision for sit-down dining; they also operated also as specialists. The final type of Pizza firm was the local Pizza shop that focused solely on pizza, either as café dining or delivery/pickup. These firms typically operated as specialists outside the delivery zones of franchised firms located in higher density population areas.

Aggregating all six types into a category for pizza, or worse still, into a single larger category of restaurants ignores the unique feature–factor relationship that each sub-type maintains with their respective operational environments. Within the OE approach, the unique feature–factor relationship is not focused on at all, so this aggregation issue does not exist. However, an FA approach requires of the researcher to eliminate, as in biology (Paterson, 1993) the potential for cryptic species to be conflated inappropriately. We can recognize the above six sub-types of Pizza firms as belonging to a cryptic *firm* complex. Each type is a *true* firm, with a unique and identifiable ecology, but which is associated with morphological (form and structure) and physiological (functions and activities) differences.

We argue that in the social sciences this issues matters as much as it does in mainstream ecological research, in terms of research design. More importantly, we predict the prevalence of the cryptic species problem to be more common in the social sciences than in the natural sciences. Our reasoning is based upon a simple comparison of the mechanisms for information storage and transmission operating in both contexts, as follows.

In the natural world information required to enable the replication of any form of life is stored with high accuracy and transmitted with equally high accuracy. This results in future generations of any given species being potentially able to preserve into the future. Alternatively, the average firm does not maintain highly accurate stores of information from which to ensure its replication. When such replication is attempted, the fallible processes of learning and imitation are used to transmit information from one firm context to another. We would therefore expect to observe a tendency towards diversity to increase during this evolutionary process (McShea and Brandon, 2010).

Consequently, in any given industry, over time, we expect to see multiple forms of *firm-types* emerge. The challenge will always be to ensure that the ecology of such firm types is observed and understood before engaging in the process of categorization. This issue becomes highly visible when we next consider the mechanisms by which firms seek to maintain their existence.

MECHANISMS OF SURVIVAL

One of the challenges that organizational studies researchers face is accounting for how firms survive with equal reference to both firm-level change and environmental factors (Dobrev, van Witteloostuijn and Baum, 2010). The remainder of the chapter will not explore this process given that it will be fully addressed in Chapter 4. Rather, this section will outline the mechanisms assumed to facilitate the process of firm survival. In this regard, we further develop our thinking on the presence of sustenance activities.

Sustenance activities can be considered regular, organized and enduring activities aimed at supporting firm survival (Gibbs and Martin, 1959). These activities can be observed in firms operated by one person or thousands of employees. Simultaneously, we are concerned with the process of converting resources efficiently to support on-going persistence, equivalent to the process of ecological versatility (Mac Nally, 1995). So we have firms engaged in sustenance activities, through which they seek to acquire and exploit resources in their operational environment to continue their survival.

The third element to the discussion in this section is Rose's (1997) notion, for organisms, of a lifeline. Enrolling Rose's lifeline into conception of the firm adds several dimensions to any consideration of firm survival. Firms are acknowledged to develop in tandem with their operational environment, making different demands and displaying differing abilities to shape aspects of their operational environment, over time. Time is the key aspect focused upon here as the firm is seen as being required to solve many environmental related problems to survive; these are problems that vary across the development of the firm from start to finish.

So, we have firms viewed as likely to be different from one another, in some respect, operating in their own unique operational environments, and exhibiting different trajectories based on the problems they have solved over time. Whereas Hawley (1950: 67) determined explicitly that such an autecological investigation was not within the domain of human ecology, we argue the opposite because FA focuses on the functional relationship between firms and their immediate local environment, it deals directly with the subject matter. So let us further explore these three component mechanisms of our explanation.

The Process of Sustenance Activities

Any observation of a firm engaged in sustenance activities tells us neither that the firm will survive nor fail in the short-term. Likewise, when an organism engages in a process of foraging (Stephens and Krebs, 1987) it neither ensures its survival nor demise. What matters is the efficiency of the process vis-à-vis the energy/resources spent relative to the energy/resources gained. With direct reference to the process of optimal foraging, Jones (2009) observed a survival advantage associated with the optimal foraging activities of certain types of Pizza firms; hence the suggested importance of ecological versatility. The inclusion of ecological versatility provides the means to question the relative efficiency and *effectiveness* of a firm's sustenance activities. When we observe optimal foraging in conjunction with the firm demonstrating learning capabilities sufficient to solve problems/exploit opportunities, we should expect firms to persist in the short-term.

One of the reasons we can look no further than the short-term is that without knowing in advance the developmental trajectory of any given firm, we cannot be sure of its lifeline, and therefore the changing nature of the feature–factor relationship it seeks to maintain within its operational environment. So neither the firm nor its operational environment is preferred. Either can exert influence upon the other, both can test the limits of the other. The relationship is dialogic in the purest of interpretations of Bruyat and Julien's (2001) meaning; that is, one cannot be understood without direct reference to the other.

So whilst there should be celebration that firm learning is fully supported in an autecological study of the firm and its environment, it is tempered by: 1) the recognition of the fallible perceptions (Langlois, 1997) that such learning is based upon; and 2) recognition that problems in the operational environment may prove impossible to solve. What matters is that firms are deemed capable of learning. We are more optimistic than Tosi (2009) about the value of combining adaptation and selection processes, because the dialogic relationship that exists between the firm and its environment already combines them. While not proposing firms as being omniscient, we are also more optimistic than Cyert and March (1992) given that we afford the firm more scope to positively influence the environment within which it interacts.

LEARNING AS SURVIVING

Reconciling learning and survival is perhaps the greatest challenge in developing an autecological theory of the firm and its environment. We can never assume that those firms that survive were better learners than those that failed; this would introduce an unwanted tautology. We confidently say that firms of all sizes and shapes will be tested by events and elements occurring in their operational environment. Further, we can say confidently that firms need to rely on their learning capabilities to solve such challenges. But what we cannot say is that Firm A is better at learning than Firm B, therefore Firm A has a higher probability of surviving than Firm B. There are two main reasons.

First, at any given time along the lifeline of a firm, environmental challenges can be viewed from multiple perspectives. Further, the eventual outcome of the decisions taken cannot be viewed with absolute precision, for 'many other outcomes were equally probable' (Aldrich, 1999: 33). Second, 'adaptive improvement is relative to the adaptive problem' (Sahlins and Service, 1960: 15), and given that we assume firms experience unique operational environments, we also assume firms will face different challenges from one another.

Therefore, great care is required not to commit what Aldrich (1999: 33) terms a retrospective fallacy whereby earlier events are viewed as if 'they were controlled by their subsequent outcomes'. Thus, we are mindful of the indeterminacy of outcomes when contemplating the process of firm-level learning and its potential impact upon firm survival. We expect to see firm-level strategies and abilities used to positively influence the feature–factor relationship between the firm and its operational environment. We are neither pessimistic nor optimistic about any given firm's ability to solve the challenges they face; we remain possibilists.

We see firms interlinked with their operational environment. A dynamic relationship mediates such situations, given the stochastic structuring of the environment and the fact the firm's activities may also shape the structure of the environment. Nevertheless, firms cannot know in advance how suitable future conditions will be. Therefore, it is reasonable to conclude that those firms that extend their lifeline do so by demonstrating adaptive qualities. The degree to which these qualities vary from one firm to another matter little. What matters is that any given firm's adaptive qualities are sufficient to overcome the specific challenges to be found in their operational environment. This is a distinguishing feature of FA, and sharply contrasts the approach from both the traditional OE approach and recent strategic management approaches, such as dynamic capabilities (King and Tucci, 2002).

REIMAGINING FIRM ADAPTATION

Adaptive qualities can accumulate over time but this is no guarantee of their value when employed against unique problems. We do not see firms as constantly chasing a sustainable competitive advantage (Teece, Pisano and Shuen, 1997). In this regard, we see firms as largely ignorant of such ambitions, more concerned with the day-to-day challenges in their operational environment. Jones (2009) noted that despite their relative geographical proximity, the six sub-types of Pizza firms frequently existed in strategic isolation to one another. For example, both major franchised operators claimed not to consider the other as a competitor, nor did they express concern about the operations of local independents. Conversely, the local independents, while conscious of the presence of the larger franchised firms, tended to operate in a manner that underwrote their co-existence.

This again emphasizes a stark difference in the autecological approach. FA sees ignorance as a first-order firm problem, whereas OE sees inertia as (eventually) a first-order firm problem. Within the FA approach, firms can be ignorant of other firms so long as they do not contribute to problems and/or shape their operational environment. Holding an assumed sustainable competitive advantage over ecologically irrelevant firms counts for nothing. However, this is all a matter of conceptions of what actually constitutes the firm's environment.

While this issue is discussed in great detail in the following chapter, what is important with regard to our conception of the firm is that the presence of a common environment is not assumed typical in FA. This is a game-changer when understanding the behaviour of any given firm. Merely copying the actions of others firms will not improve fitness if both firms operate in different environments. Different environmental challenges require different firm responses. Under such circumstances, each firm is relatively alone in solving their problems, be they related to overcoming threats or exploiting perceived opportunities.

Importantly this means that surveying assumed core or peripheral elements of firms may be pointless, given that the morphology (form and structure) and physiology (functions and activities) of each firm is: 1) changing across its own distinct lifeline; and 2) of varying importance vis-à-vis the actual challenges encountered by each firm. From this perspective, we do not assume a process of external selection optimizing certain features of the firm (relative to other firms) to explain increasing fitness. Instead, we expect to see firms persisting through time, demonstrating an ability to solve the challenges they confront daily in their operational environment.

We expect to see evidence of order that has been maintained through which other change is possible. In this sense, we define adaptation at the level of the firm, and relate it to the persistence (Haukioja, 1982, Wake, Roth and Wake, 1983) that is achieved via a process of environmental matching (Walter and Hengeveld, 2014) in which the firm's sensory abilities enable it to track and rise to the challenges found within their operational environment. As will be demonstrated in the following chapter, we have greatly simplified the complexity of firm–environment relations by viewing them at a firm-specific ecological scale. Thus, our level of investigation has the *extent* and *grain* (Wiens, 1989) determined by the behaviour of the firms under investigation, rather than by parameters convenient to, or preferenced by, the researcher.

Being mindful of *extent* and *grain* ensures FA identifies the operational environment at the correct ecological scale. The operational environment is therefore temporally correlated to the firms investigated, and it is spatially related to each firm's operations. This increases the probability that FA will avoid the problem of producing research findings that have unwanted pseudopredictability (Wiens, 1989) due to incorrect temporal and spatial scaling.

The final explanation of firm behaviour relates to the specifics of what aspects of the firm may be altered to support persistence. We are more optimistic than others (Hannan and Freeman, 1984) in this regard. This is in large part because we are not viewing the world through the lens of community and population structures and laws. We are interested in types of firms that are identifiable by specific forms of behaviour and environmental relations. Such relations, viewed intimately, and as ordered by the behaviour of individual firms, are confirmed through observation rather than inference. This final section of the chapter brings us full circle, returning to the many assumptions contained within Figure 2.1.

ACCOUNTING FOR PLASTICITY

That firms can alter aspects of their form and structure and/or their functions and activities is not doubted by anyone. What remains in doubt to some OE researchers is the extent to which such change would be expected to enable regular adaptation to changing environments. We have outlined above that part of the difficultly here is that the environment is conceptualized at such a high level in OE that is rendered highly complex. FA is largely freed from these concerns due to its greater precision as to what is an environment; we see no problem in firms being able to adjust to environmental change guided by a process of learning and relying on sensory input, be that precise or from trial and error, or combinations of both.

We hope that the development of FA will unite those researchers curious about ecological relations and organizational learning. Whilst FA is inspired by and developed through the importation of ecological theories and concepts, our social context is truly unique. Most animals and plants have less ability to influence their operational environments. Most animals and plants achieve fortuitous adaptation over generations, not within a single lifeline. Most animals and plants are ignorant to the process of adaptation occurring around them on a daily basis, for they are all neatly woven into Darwin's (1859) entangled bank. These essential differences have long been recognized (McKenzie, 1934a).

The firms we choose to study do have remarkable abilities to alter many aspects of their local environment. They are capable of achieving significant adaptation within their specific existence, and they are capable of observing the nature of change occurring around them across a range of contexts. Therefore, in terms of ecological theory, firms represent almost the opposite of Maynard Smith's (1958) fruitflies. We do not need access to multiple generations of offspring to understand the process of information transfer. We need access to single firms who have persisted through time, adjusting to their environment and shaping the environs as they go. FA is more interested in information *use* in firms than it is in information *transfer* between generations of firms. Our focus is on firm persistence, not population or community persistence.

Therefore, while FA is guided by many sources of ecological and evolutionary theorizing, it also explicitly recognizes that firms do not equate to plants and animals in terms of information acquisition, use and transfer. This is an important point because it frees FA from many of the restrictive ecological law-like generalizations that restrict OE from seeing the wonder of individual firms and their adaptive qualities.

The Lifeline of No Return

Enrolling Rose's (1997) notion of a lifeline introduces a line of no return. As we previously stated, firms are acknowledged to develop in tandem with their operational environment, making different demands and displaying differing abilities to shape aspects of their operational environment, over time. Such change can be viewed as the maturation of the firm's sustenance activities. So, to the line of no return. We face two explanations. First, firms are imprinted from day one with an ontogenetic blueprint that, subject to environmental shocks, will determine their eventual development. This explanation is much like the journey of the caterpillar becoming a butterfly, it was preordained from the very start, and no amount of learning could have halted the process.

The second and more believable explanation is that firms start with a purpose, specific resources and seek to realize their aims. Across time, firms have choices about changing and/or expanding their purpose and resource acquisition/usage. The process of change across time is accompanied by learning that may prove beneficial or not. This explanation appears to fit well for the Finnish company Nokia, founded in 1865 as a pulp mill, would eventually morph into a producer of electricity, rubber products and electrical cables. Operating in electronics and radio industries it would ultimately become a pioneer in the mobile telecommunications world, and only the process of firm-level learning could have produced such incredible evolution during the past 150 years. In this approach, we accept the presence of detectable and predictable changes in the operational environments of firms that can be both understood and influenced by firms.

The use of the lifeline concept brings with it an acceptance that the firm and its operational environment constantly interpenetrate each other constantly across the lifeline of the firm. The result of this constant interaction is highly variable given the unpredictable nature of the environment, the fallibility of our reading of the environment, the myriad of choices we have in responding to environmental stimuli, and finally, the numerous events that could have resulted from any action taken. Is it any wonder the entrepreneur is less noted for his or her precision and more praised for their resilience?

Nevertheless, and despite the vagaries of human learning and decision-making, both processes are central to the process of firm adaptation. Returning to Figure 2.1, we posit that firms are created by individuals who have perceptions and knowledge of the environment/industry they choose to enter. We acknowledge the value of such perceptions and knowledge to vary in quality and value across the entire lifeline of the firm. Nevertheless, these cognitive abilities give rise to the form, structure, functions and activities that the firm initially relies upon to survive its initial entry in its chosen industry. Over time the firm makes decisions related to growth ambitions and the breadth of its operations, all influenced by its sense of its surroundings and what it perceives to be required to maintain its existence. How it organizes those regular and enduring sustenance activities are central to maintaining the *order* that can be relied upon to ensure stability.

However, the operational environment of the firm is typically awash with change, some of which may be insignificant, some of which may require action to maintain a positive feature–factor relationship between the firm and its operational environment. At any point the firm is able to receive information about its interacting elements and their degree of acceptance by external stakeholders. Whilst this information may be difficult to interpret, it is nevertheless generally available.

Firms are generally able to receive information related to when and how they should exchange resources with stakeholders, how many resources they need to acquire to stay viable and to whom they should promote themselves and/or what to protect their operations from. Table 2.1 illustrates the challenge of trying to neatly explain the process of learning vis-à-vis information availability.

Table 2.1 Classification of informational interactions

Firm response	Information from the environment	
	Related information	Unrelated information
Adaptive	Useful information	Serendipitous opportunity
Maladaptive	Lost opportunity	Harmful distraction

The firm may produce an adaptive response using related information, assumed to be *useful*, from the firm's operational environment. However, the firm may also produce an adaptive response using information related to a *serendipitous opportunity*. This information can be viewed as being part of the firm's potential environment, as will be explained in the following chapter. Alternatively, the firm may produce a maladaptive response through misinterpreting and/or failing to organize an appropriate response to related information, thus *losing an opportunity*. Finally, the firm may also produce a maladaptive response by wasting time and resources on *harmful distractions* by interacting with unrelated information of no actual value to the firm.

At any moment the firm may be interacting with various combinations of related and unrelated information. As a result, many different outcomes are possible through which fitness could be positively or negatively impacted.

There is nothing linear associated with this process of learning, only an iterative process of navigating a corridor of persistence in which confirmations are experienced alongside confusion. From these mixed signals, the challenge lies in pursuing a never-ending adjustment of inner relations to outer relations (Veblen, 1922).

A Caveat

Two insightful passages remind us of the paradox that every firm confronts on a daily basis. Just because a firm believes it knows what it needs to do to persist, does not mean it does know or can act in ways to achieve such desired fitness. Veblen (1922: 192–193) argued, at some length, that:

> The readjustment of institutions and habitual views to an altered environment is made in response to pressure from without; it is of the nature of response to stimulus. Freedom and facility of readjustment, that is to say the capacity for growth in social structure, therefore depends in great measure on the degree of freedom with which the situation at any given time acts upon the individual members of the community – the degree of exposure of the individual members to the constraining forces of the environment. If any portion or class of society is sheltered from the action of the environment in any essential respect; it will in so far tend to retard the process of social transformation.

Sumner (1902: 67) also observed that:

> The observation that motives and purposes have nothing to do with consequences is a criterion for distinguishing between the science of society and the views, whims, ideals, and fads which are current in regard to social matters. Motives and purposes are in the brain and heart of man. Consequences are in the world of fact. The former are infected by human ignorance, folly, self-deception, and passion; the latter are sequences of cause and effect dependent upon the nature of the forces at work.

Worse still, if the firm remains unaware of what needs to be done, it eventually will become aware, but perhaps after the opportunity to act has passed. So while learning and problem solving is central to our conception of persistence of the firm, these are not viewed as simple and obvious processes that firms can rely upon to maintain their existence. Rather, they are seen as essential capabilities, the validity of which are constantly examined by unpredictable environment phenomena.

NATURE LOVES TO HIDE

Imagine yourself driving down the main street where you live. As you pass by the many firms located on each side of the road, are you also aware of the invisible firms increasingly located in the ether, perhaps also seeking your attention. Consider for a moment the full breadth of sustenance activities required to enable each one of these unique firms to persist. As ecologists, we remain forever challenged by Sears (1935) to go beyond merely seeing *what is there*, and to understand *what is happening there*. Since the dawn of civilization, it has been recognized that nature loves to hide; herein lies our collective challenge.

The ideas advanced here may appear to increase the degrees of complexity one is required to encounter to research firms. Metaphorically speaking, we can imagine the autecologist walking into a multiplex cinema, surrounded by different genres, languages and starting times, being left confused. Alternatively, we can envisage the autecologist having developed a very detailed appreciation of a specific genre and arriving on time to experience the film. In this latter sense, nature is not hidden; its complexity is reduced to the time and place of the observations made. Yes there are many other things happening around us, but we have left Hutchinson's (1965) expansive ecological theatre, choosing a more intimate setting where nature is observable and potentially comprehendible; this is the operational environment of the firm.

Rather than looking down upon the world, we are aiming to view the world through the eyes and ears of the firms we investigate. In doing so, we see the harsh realities of firm's attempting to learn around their surrounds. We see firms deliberately and accidently shaping aspects of their operational environments. We also see other firms' actions deliberately and accidently shaping the operational environments of other firms. We can sense the invisibility the surrounds many environmental variables, many of which come into sight too late to be addressed. But most importantly, we have achieved a vantage point through which our focus seemingly has the power to slow down the interactions we observe; such is the potential power of our focus.

What is a Firm?

The aim of the chapter was explain how a firm could be viewed as a *non-autonomous entity, located in an operational environment, that is socially constructed, goal-directed, boundary maintaining and maintained through sustenance activities.* We believe we have partly made that case. The following chapter explains the nature of the environment that is deeply embedded in this definition of the firm. Chapter 4 will further explain the nature of the sustenance activities that enable firms to persist through time. For now, let us summarize the key issues discussed in the chapter.

Previous attempts to define firms range from contemplating what they have in common (Aldrich, 1999) to the way in which they can be grouped into very specific domain classifications (Hannan, Polos and Carroll, 2007). Our approach embraces the ideas of Aldrich, but moves away from the need to group firms based on arbitrary methods. We remain open that for the purposes of investigation, *types* of firms may be observed. We also accept that we may observe firms to be so unique in their morphological form/structure and/or physiological functions/activities and/or temporal/spatial positioning, that they are difficult, if not impossible to group.

We see firms reconciled to their unique operational environments through a baseline that potentially enables learning to be informed by feedback related to the firm's interacting elements. Although we do not assume that firms simply have or do not have learning capabilities through which their persistence will always be explainable. There are too many other factors that may influence such survival outcomes. We can comprehend ignorant firms surviving whilst clever firms fail. Such unintuitive outcomes rest on our acceptance that not all firms face the same environmental tests. We see problem solving occurring, but occurring in complex ways that are difficult to compare. For example, the Pizza firms studied by Jones (2009) faced many different problems, but few faced the same problems. Whereas large franchised firms grapple with technological opportunities to be more efficient, small independent firms were not observed to.

The Corridor of Persistence

Our position regarding what is a firm is largely derived from visualizing firms operating in their own unique corridors of persistence. The lifeline of each firm is particular to it, as are the problems it needs to solve. As MacIver (1917: 361) observed, 'every difference whatever of life from life involves a difference of environment from environment'. It is around this very issue that Bews (1935: 7) argued that any such classification of man's activities must 'be based differences in the mode of life of different types'.

Returning to your journey down the main street of where you live, it would be foolish to assume that such a street metaphorically represents a corridor of persistence; for each firm must solve different types of problems. Our firms are commonly studied in aggregates, thus implying a common corridor of persistence that all such firms must pass through. Such approaches employ assumptions of a common environment. We do not, as will be explained in the following chapter.

Our firms are capable of adjusting to the changing nature of their environments, but not guaranteed to do so. In comparison to the firms studied ecologically in the OE approach, our firms are not restricted by inertia, but rather capable of changing most aspects of their operations. Whether such change proves beneficial largely depends on both internal and external factors. Internally, the sensory abilities of firms to track and rise to the challenges found within their operational environment are critically important. Externally, different types of environmental change may prove insurmountable to overcome; other environmental change may fortuitously benefit firms.

The failures of our firms matter greatly to us because our firms do not exist as a source of routines for future generations of firms. Our firms exist to satisfy the aspirations and daily needs of the owners and their staff. Our firms are not represented in datasets as a number, but rather are known by their unique histories and the personalities of those that operate them.

Summary

Everyday, firms engage in sustenance activities to ensure their persistence. These activities vary greatly from firm-to-firm, industry-to-industry, location-to-location and from one time period to another time period. These activities, when intertwined with a firm's ability to sense its surrounds, learn about the problems it needs to solve underwrite the firm's persistence. Using the logic of Haukioja (1982), every firm we see operating are, to some degree, successful at that moment in time. This is what separates our firm's from most others studied. Our firms are deemed to be doing something right by virtue of their persistence. Our aim is to understand the adaptive mechanisms of the firm relative to the environmental factors it maintains operational relations with. Unlike most other ecological phenomena, our firms have a history they can describe in detail; details that we can verify with other data. They have present day operations that can be studied in situ. These firms also hold aspirations for the immediate future based upon their reading of their current and future environmental conditions. Our firms are ecologically unique in that they can communicate with those that wish to research them, and typically, they have left behind detailed artefacts of their historical operations. The next chapter considers the actual environmental context of each firm, a context so germane to demonstrating the uniqueness of our firms.

3.　What is an environment?

Environment is infinitely complex, never quite the same for any two living creatures; it is ever present, never to be entirely known or estimated; it is modified by the beings whom it modifies, in an endless and never wholly calculable reciprocity. (MacIver, 1917: 364–365)

Environment is highly complex and integrated, but this should not be a matter for despair, for environments are probably still less complex than organisms! (Daubenmire, 1947: 342)

Before we begin, it is worth taking the time to read each of the above selected quotes again, for within them lay hidden the essential logic of this book. These two quotes capture a recognition that the environment surroundings can be understood, if only imperfectly as with all understanding of our surrounds and ourselves, and that we can quantify the operation of entities within a given, known environment. In discussing the nature of what is a firm in Chapter 2, constant reference was made to the operational environment of firms. Within this chapter the nature of what is an environment, how it relates to any given firm and the dynamic interaction that connects both will be explained.

This chapter represents the heart of the book. It is here that this work differs so markedly from existing concepts and theorizing about the firm. Our conceptualization of the environment is not entirely new, rather, it is novel and narrow in its application to the domain of the social sciences. It is premised upon acceptance of the following syllogism.

In reality, the firms we study are expected to vary considerably in terms of the form, structures, functions and activities used to maintain their existence.

Further, the firms we study are not assumed to experience a common or homogeneous environment.

Therefore, any conception of the firm's environment must be firm-centred to reveal the true nature of its operational relations to environmental phenomena.

From an FA perspective, we define the operational environment (as illustrated in Figure 3.1) as *all observable environmental phenomena that are operationally related, directed, timed, ordered and spaced by and across the lifeline of a particular firm.* This definition draws upon the specific works of Mason and Langenheim (1957), Spomer (1973) and Rose (1997). We will draw upon many other ideas to explain our conception of environment, remaining true to the assumptions that underpin an autecological approach. Our challenge is not to criticize the assumption choices others make, but rather, to explain the logic of the choices we have made in outlining our approach, and to justify them. This process of explanation begins with our discussion of our schema illustrated in Figure 3.1 below.

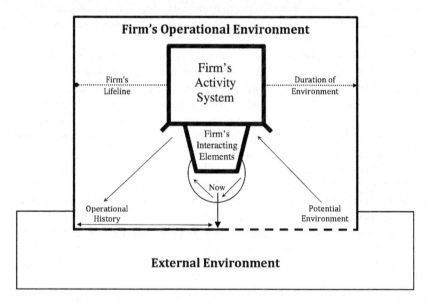

Figure 3.1 The firm's operational environment

As in the last chapter, we have presented our definition at the beginning of the chapter. We do so to focus your thoughts, as we will shortly present the data that will evidence our thinking with regards to the assumptions concerning the spatiotemporal dynamics of socioeconomic environments. This is a critically important issue given the inherent complexity we maintain exists in our research contexts. We are deliberately interested in understanding the idiosyncratic *noise* that is all too often averaged away through the process of aggregation. For it is within this noise that the stories of individual firms are to be found and understood; such noise in reality is the substance we seek to understand.

Within Figure 3.1 we have illustrated our definition of the environment of a firm (and it is readily adapted to any specific type of firm), not an environment of firms (plural). Typical approaches to defining the environment of firms assumes homogeneity (Hannan and Freeman, 1977) and/or, where environmental textures are suggested (Emery and Trist, 1965), they are still expected to be experienced by all firms in a population at any given moment. Our observations lead us to believe that firms will differ in terms of the form, structures, functions and activities used to maintain their existence. As a consequence, each will maintain different operational relations with its environment. They will also most likely experience different types and degrees of dynamic environmental relations. The composition of such operational environments, drawn from structured, but stochastically influenced and unpredictable surrounds, defines the nature and existence of each firm.

We begin by identifying those specific factors through which we can identify the parameters of the operational environment. Once again, *all observable environmental phenomena that are operationally related, directed, timed, ordered and spaced by and across the lifeline of a particular firm*. So lets start with the issue of *observable environmental phenomena that are operationally related*. Identification of a firm and its operational environment demarcates what environmental phenomena the firm is immediately and directly operationally significant to (the operational environment), not yet operationally related to (the potential environment), or which phenomena it is not now or ever likely to be related to (the external environment).

Mason and Langenheim (1957) first proposed the idea of the potential environment to ensure time was included when defining the environment. This conceptualization provides, for FA, a firm-centred means of reconciling today's resource use with tomorrow's similar or different resource use on a firm-by-firm basis. It also draws attention to phenomena in the external environment that has the potential to be operationalized by a firm. The key determinant in making these judgments is to stay firm-centred and thus be freed from the confusion and ambiguity that typically surrounds analyses that focus research attention at higher levels of aggregation.

It is in this sense that we say that the environment is firm *directed*. The firm's *lifeline* is also highlighted within Figure 3.1. We recognize that each firm will make different demands upon its environment as it develops naturally over time. These demands will be influenced by both knowledge inside the firm and other factors (including changing markets and geography) external to the firm. What matters, is we recognize that any such alteration of the feature–factor relationship will be *timed, ordered and spaced by a particular firm and across the lifeline of that firm*. It is for these reasons that the environment is defined at the same time as the firm is observed so that it can be understood.

FACTORING IN HETEROGENEITY

The above discussion has briefly explained the basic construction of our schema in Figure 3.1. Before we proceed further with this explanation, we need to explain further the nature of our key assumptions. The first issue is that of the constant variability of the environmental context of particular firms and, thus, our subject matter. To demonstrate our concerns, we draw upon the logic of Møller and Jennions (2002) to highlight problematic factors.

First, the contexts we choose to study are not perfect; there are lags between events and selection and between selection pressures and responses that precede eventual selection (for or against). For example, the advent of Amazon.com did not produce the same effect in local bookseller markets globally, nor does it provoke similar responses from affected local booksellers. Second, there is inherent randomness in the contexts we study. That is, the environmental variables relevant to firms are not the same across towns, cities or states. Third, there are so many possible responses that firms can attempt in response to perceived environmental change, yet typically only a few are focused upon. This leaves space for confounding variables to create sufficient noise to blur the assumed relationship between other variables. Fourth, the behaviours of many firms vary considerably across time and space and are therefore difficult to measure. Fifth, it is difficult to capture the evolutionary past of all firms being studied. Thus, the capacity of each firm to respond differently is difficult to explain. Last, the actions of one firm can alter (negatively or positively) the outcomes of other firms, a difficult dynamic to observe. Rather than bundling such actions into a category called competition, we must take care to fully explain the nature of coactions (Haskell, 1949) actually occurring.

We believe firms do indeed experience unique operational environments that can be understood only at the level of the firm. In drawing upon the logic of autecology to conduct fine-grained exploration of such contexts, it was inevitable that we would cross paths with other assumptions made about these contexts. For example, in the OE approach (Hannan and Freeman, 1989) the researcher is deemed more capable of understanding the process of selection under investigation than those who are actually operating the firms. Alternatively, the FA approach argues that firms exist through time by negating to some degree, and/or influencing environmental variables in ways that we as researchers need to discover. In the former, firms experience a common environment; 'selection processes have general properties that hold across historical periods' (Hannan and Freeman, 1989: 20) and are knowable by the researcher at the level of the population. In the latter, firms are not expected to experience a common environment; environmental variables vary across historical periods and must be discovered by the researcher at the level of the firm. Thus we see people controlling firms in response to internal and external variables and influences. OE sees people as being controlled by a laissez-faire environment that exerts its invisible influence through competitive selection processes. In this sense, OE is dehumanising.

In the above example, we have removed the assumption of firms experiencing a common environment. Thus, FA is radically different from OE in the primary assumptions upon which it is developed. The flow on effect of adopting this position is that we no longer call upon the process of natural selection to act upon the random presence of different types of firms in ways that rewards those most efficient at acquiring and using scarce resources. We see the presence of different types of firms in society as evidence that firms, different from one another at their inception, have developed their own lifeline to remain adapted to their unique surroundings.

NATURAL SELECTION AS NOT GIVEN

In the OE approach, it is selection that is said to be delivered from a given or common environment vis-à-vis an identifiable population. Firm survival is based upon having the right structural form to ensure access to the required resources from the environment (Carroll and Hannan, 2000: 385), that is, 'forms differ in how well they align with a given environment'. The assumption being made is that while the environment is different from one population to another, it is common to all firms within any particular population. As such, a homogeneous selection process acts upon differences in structural form and identify to remove ill-adapted firms and thus shape the form of surviving firms. In this approach, adaptedness is a *property of the firm*, based on its structural form and/or identity. That is because we are essentially comparing survival outcomes of many firms within a given environment.

A different set of assumptions is used in FA. We do not start with the presumption that firms based in an industry experience a common environment. We therefore do not believe it is possible to consider the selection of individual firms from the perspective of an assumed homogenous selection mechanism that sorts firms based on individual differences. The actual structuring process within firms, a human-driven response to perceptions of the environment, is entirely different in a socio-economic context than it is in nature. Therefore, we see firms as related to environments operationally in unique and historical ways. As a result, we do not need to enrol the process of natural selection to explain evolutionary outcomes within industry contexts. Instead, we confine ourselves to ecological scales consistent with the firms we investigate and rely upon heuristic generalizations to guide our investigations of firm–environment interaction, as is the focus in ecology/autecology (Walter, 2013).

This is why our definition of a firm and its environment is so critically important to FA. We perhaps should have combined the chapters on what is a firm and what is an environment to symbolically communicate this importance. Our definition of an environment is firm-centred and precise. In OE, the environment is defined relative to a population and/or community with little optimism that its elements can be accurately identified (see Hawley, 1950), such is its assumed complexity. It is essentially assumed to be primarily competitive. For FA, we cannot understand the environment if we do not first understand the mode of operation of the firm, and/or a specific type of firm. Therefore, the classification of any type of firm must depend on precise knowledge of the operational relations a given firm has with its environment, relations based on sustenance activities.

As a result of these alternative assumptions, FA proceeds with the initial guidance of heuristic generalizations to guide questions, investigation and interpretation. It does so in such a manner that the environment, despite its unpredictability, can be known relative to any firm worthy of study. The challenge of such precision requires that the environment of every firm can be identified and compared if necessary to other related or unrelated firms. To achieve this, we enrol several ideas rarely used in the social sciences.

THE COMPONENTS OF THE ENVIRONMENT

As illustrated in Figure 3.1, we draw upon the ideas of Mason and Langenheim (1957: 335) and Spomer (1973) to develop the idea of the operational environment in FA. There are some potential limitations in the development of Mason and Langenheim's conceptualization of the operational environment. They propose the idea of the non-environment, or the elimination of 'all other … [unrelated] … phenomena traditionally associated with environment, even though near or surrounding the organism' from the concept of environment. In transferring this idea to the social domain, we believe it important to appreciate that firms may be required to widen the scope of their environmental relations more than an animal or plant. That is to say, plants and animals might be expected to be conditioned to react to a narrower set of phenomena than might a firm across their respective individual lifelines.

In essence, we see an individual firm as being capable of changing their form, structure, functions and activities to a greater degree than an individual animal or plant could within their respective lifelines. As a result, we need to be more pragmatic in viewing the possibility of unrelated external phenomena subsequently being conditioned by firms in the future as they react to environmental change and stochastic events. For example, in the previous chapter we discussed different types of Pizza firms (see Figure 2.2). During the course of the evolution of these six types of Pizza firms, their potential environments have altered quite significantly. Whereas the franchised firms have drawn more heavily upon the environment for technological resources, other more traditional Pizza restaurants have not.

Consequently, we link the firm's operational environment to the broader external environment, connecting them both with Mason and Langenheim's (1957) potential environment. Whereas they left the external environment as an undefined empty space for the potential environment to relate to, we do not totally ignore the cacophony arising from the mishmash of unrelated environmental phenomena. We remain mindful of its temporal unrelatedness, but it has potential as a source of new resources for the firm's future operations. This does, however, require that we are specific about what the external environment of the firm actually is. At all times, the operational environment is a discrete sub-set of phenomena found in the external environment. Movement of phenomena from the external environment to the operational environment occurs through the firm's potential environment. The potential environment is just a potential future state of the operational environment, just as the operational history depicted in Figure 3.1 represents a past state of the firm's environmental relations.

The External Environment

The work of Brandon (1990) further helps us to understand how to identify the external environment. He suggests three specific environmental dimensions related to the ecological interactions of any entity, in our context, firms. First, the external environment typically refers to the sum total of all factors external to the firm that may potentially influence its survival. However, this overarching view of the environment does little to highlight which specific phenomena actually previously were, currently are, or potentially will be operationally important to one firm or another. It essentially relates to the factors that all firms in all industries may be exposed to (for example, high interest rates), regardless of their overall importance to actual firm survival. Importantly, the external environment can exist independently of any individual firm, and most individual firms could not significantly alter it. That is, what we view as the external environment of Firm A and Firm B would remain for Firm A even if Firm B ceased operations.

Inside the Operational Environment

We can reconcile Brandon's two other environmental dimensions within the operational environment, given they are also only identifiable relative to the entity under investigation. Thus, they have the same dependence upon an ecological lifeline. The second dimension is the *ecological*, which is a narrowing down of focus. Now we are only concerned with those phenomena that are operationally related and of primary importance to the firm's sustenance activities, or the on-going recoupment of the resources required for survival.

Brandon's third environmental dimension is the *selective*, which is related to those phenomena (for example, consumer taste) that specifically influence the selection for or against an individual firm's interacting elements (such as their products and services (see Jones, 2005)). We can unite the ideas of Brandon (1990) with the central idea of the operational environment in this simple way. Each firm interacts with its own operational environment. This operational environment is comprised of potentially negative and positive factors. That is, the *selective* and *ecological* dimensions that have no existence independent of the firm; and thus they are dimensions of the firm's actual operational environment (Spomer, 1973). Whilst some firms may seemingly share very similar operational environments (for example, two hotels in the same street), there are still many localized factors that prevent them from being identical (for example, one focusing on five star service and the other on budget accommodation), and thus, environmental heterogeneity is an issue that must be accounted for.

Our approach does not shelter us from the intricacy of firm–environment relations; it just reduces that complexity to comprehendible phenomena. It does however provide us with the ability to observe first-hand ecologically scale sensitive modifications of the environment. In this regard, FA shines light on one of the unresolved questions in firm research; can, and/or, in what ways do firms modify their environments? This issue will be discussed in detail in the following chapter. Until then, we return to the issue of environmental heterogeneity.

SEEING HETEROGENEITY

The inclusion of the selective and ecological dimensions within the operational environment provides specific phenomena that can be visualized in any analysis of the firm and its environment. We can ask what specific factors support the survival of specific types of firms, and what factors create selection pressure upon the continuation of such firms. Rather than placing competitive factors at the heart of such analysis, we remain guided by the need to develop autecological knowledge of the specific firms' mode of operational relations. This approach will naturally lead us to discover the nature of environmental heterogeneity.

The findings of Jones (2007; 2009) demonstrated that firms located across 19 geographically related towns experienced vastly different access to resources and selection processes. Further, within each town, the Pizza restaurants clearly existed within an operational environment of their own creation. This is consistent with Andrewartha and Birch's (1954) assertion that resource availability would be expected to vary from one location to another. Using the FA approach, we should not expect an even distribution of resources and/or selective pressures from one firm to another. The challenge for the FA researcher is to understand how individual firms attempt to solve their survival problems, rather than assume that the environment essentially determines such outcomes.

As this analysis unfolds the researcher will increasingly become aware of the ecological data that will be associated with expected heterogeneity. Let us consider an example of how environmental heterogeneity can be identified and analysed. We will first consider environmental heterogeneity at the level of the region, then at street level, and finally inside a shopping centre.

The Case of North Yorkshire/East Riding

In his study of Pizza firms, Jones (2009) used Pianka's (1973) Community Similarity Index to measure the extent to which the varied composition of restaurants in 19 North Yorkshire/East Riding towns differed across towns and through time. The Community Similarity Index is simply X/N, where X is the number of sub-populations (or firm-types) common to two towns and N is the total number of sub-populations occurring in both; thus community similarity equals 1 when two towns are identical, and 0 when they share no sub-populations. The technique was used to safeguard against committing an ecological fallacy (Babbie, 2005) where incorrect inference about individual cases are drawn from observation on the broader group to which they belong. As such, it is important to test the similarity of towns so as to be aware of the degree to which variance may be averaged away through aggregation of the data.

Community similarity values for the North Yorkshire/East Riding guild were low and relatively consistent across time. At the beginning of the study (1975) the value was lowest ($\overline{X}$ = .39, S.E. = .015, s = .248, N = 253), increasing by the mid point of the study (i.e. 1990) ($\overline{X}$ = .47, S.E. = .012, s = .187, N = 253) and essentially holding that degree of similarity ($\overline{X}$ = .48, S.E. = .012, s = .185, N = 253) at the end of the study period in 2004.

To further analyse the nature of dissimilarity observed across towns through time, Canonical Discriminant Analysis was used to identify what specific phenomena were associated with environmental heterogeneity across the study period. Using the individual towns as dependent categorical variables, the relationship between each town and a diverse set of independent variables (for example, several diversity indices, the change in resources, the growth of the guild, and the relative abundance of resources) was studied. We define an ecological guild in our specific context, with reference to Root's (1967) original definition, as a group of firms that seek to exploit the same types of resources in similar ways.

Figure 3.2 illustrate the nature of inter-town variance observed in 19 North Yorkshire towns in 1975. The nature of this variance remained constant across each year of the 30-year period under investigation. Simply stated, statistically, there is a highly significant difference between the examined towns across a combination (or discriminant functions) of the following variables: Guild change, Resource abundance, Margalef index, FisherALPHA index, and Resource change. These variables (illustrated in Table 3.1) provide insights into the varied composition of the operational environments of the Pizza firms under investigation. Table 3.2 highlights that while nearly all of the variance of the model is explained by the first two discriminant functions (i.e. 1 and 2), the Wilks' Lambda values indicate that all five variables are useful within the model. The association between the discriminant scores and the towns is strongly correlated, as evidenced by the values all equalling 1. The very low value of the Wilks' Lambda (Table 3.3) indicates greater discriminatory ability of the function. The incorporated chi-square statistic tests the extent that the means of the functions used are equal across the towns investigated. The small significance value indicates that the discriminant function does better than chance at separating the towns.

Canonical Discriminant Functions

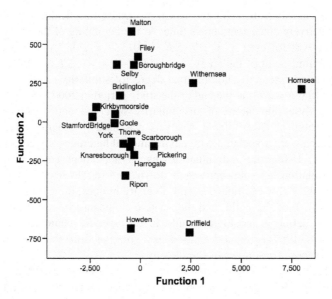

Figure 3.2   Inter-town variance in North Yorkshire towns in 1975

Table 3.1   Stucture matrix

	Function				
	1	2	3	4	5
Guild Change	-.006	-.192	.080	.699*	.684
Resource Abundance	.005	-.076	-.329	-.233	.912*
Margalef	.017	-.037	.575	-.090	.812*
Exit Rate[a]	.017	-.037	.575	-.090	.812*
FisherALPHA	.295	-.077	.528	-.161	.776*
Resource Change	-.020	.608	.347	-.151	.698*

Notes: Pooled within-groups correlations between discriminating variables and standardized canonical discriminant functions.

Variables ordered by absolute size of correlation within function.

* Largest absolute correlation between each variable and any discriminant.

[a] This variable not used in the analysis.

Table 3.2 Eigenvalues

Function	Eigenvalue	% of Variance	Cumulative %	Canonical Correlation
1	10081329[a]	97.3	97.3	1.000
2	227962.961[a]	2.2	99.5	1.000
3	27937.184[a]	.3	99.8	1.000
4	16796.263[a]	.2	100.0	1.000
5	3111.860[a]	.0	100.0	1.000

Note: [a] First 5 canonical discriminant functions were used in analysis.

Table 3.3 Wilks' Lambda

Test of Functions(s)	Wilks' Lambda	Chi-square	df	Sig.
1 through 5	.000	1411.739	90	.000
2 through 5	.000	1008.584	68	.000
3 through 5	.000	700.161	48	.000
4 through 5	.000	444.307	30	.000
5	.000	201.082	14	.000

From the analysis above, the Pizza firms operating in this region obviously do not experience a common environment from one town to the next. Given that we have already identified (see Figure 2.2) that different multiple types of Pizza shops have evolved across the industry's lifespan, the challenge is to also explain the nature of environmental heterogeneity at the level of the firm. To achieve this, we now consider the operations of many seemingly similar shops operating in the Philippines.

The Case of Dumalag, Philippines

Any visitor to South-East Asian countries will be familiar with the plethora of almost identical looking convenience stores that operate by the hundreds from one town to the next. In the Philippines they are called sari sari stores, literally meaning *variety* store. These stores are generally located within homes and are street facing. They tend to sell essentially the same staple items such food items, coffee, shampoo and toothpaste sachets, beverages, ice cream, plastic containers and phone cards.

The town of Dumalag is in the Capiz region of Panay, the sixth largest of the 7000 islands that comprise the Philippines. Surrounding agriculture primarily supports the population of 30,000. The main street of the town depicted in Figure 3.3 is about 1000 metres long, supporting many sari sari stores.

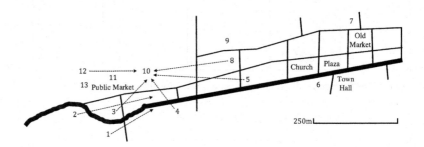

Figure 3.3 Dumalag main street

At one end of the main street is the public market area where market day occurs on Wednesday and Sunday. On all other days the public market area is empty with minimal foot traffic. The main street is constantly busy all week with continuous foot, cycle and motor traffic past the church, plaza and town hall. The locations of 13 sari sari stores are noted in Figure 3.3 and an arrow indicates their preferred location. Six of the stores prefer their current locations and the other seven would like to locate to be closer to either the public market area or the main road.

To discern the nature of the environment within which each store operate, a series of questions (see Appendix 1) were asked of each operator. The answers revealed a great deal about the specific factors that, on a temporal or spatial basis impact upon the sustenance activities of each of these firms. Despite all of the stores having numerous common items available for sale, each reported a reliance on unique products to produce most of their income. For example, store 13, capitalising on its marketplace location, sold mostly vegetables, noodles and oils. While they where open for business seven days a week, 90 percent of the income was received on market days. Alternatively, store 12 focused on onions, spices, hotdogs and chickens, with most sales occurring on market days.

In contrast, stores 3 and 4 sold mainly alcohol, with the latter working long hours seven days a week to gain an advantage over the former. Store 8 specialized in dried fish, store 9 in charcoal and special rices. Store 7 did not specialize in anything in particular, but opened the store around the times daily mass was held at the church. Likewise, store 6 focused her restaurant food on local workers at the town hall and on students. All proprietors reported that the common products they sold indeed made the stores similar to one another, but noted too that their areas of specialization and/or regular custom from friends or churchgoers made them different.

In combination, these factors translate into observable phenomena through which the feature–factor relationship between each firm and their environments can be understood. The average age of the stores was 10 to 20 years, with family succession common. The sensory abilities of each storeowner to solve *local* problems in their *operational* environment were quite evident. Their explanations in this regard were easy to connect to their observed longevity. However, when asked to nominate a preferred place of operation, the logic expressed by those who wished to be closer to the market/main road (stores 1, 2, 3, 4, 5, 8 and 12) seemed to ignore other competitor-related issues that would risk the very factors that support their current sustenance activities.

We can confidently conclude that the stores did indeed operate in unique operational environments that they had, in part, co-created. These stores were clearly adept at solving the problems they encountered in their operational environment, but were naïve of the potential factors related to operating their business just a few hundred metres away. They were all however able to identify those environmental factors that contributed to or detracted from their aspirations to survive and/or grow.

The Case of Gaisano Shopping Mall, Roxas, Philippines

To explore further the nature of how a firm's unique operating environment can be discerned, the same research questions used in the main street of Dumalag were used in a shopping mall in the city of Roxas, an hours drive north of Dumalag. The shopping centre could be described as small by western standards – 25 shops that varied from being national brands to local operations surround one large anchor tenet, a national supermarket/department store. In between these shop are located another 20 to 30 firms whose operations are limited in size by their glass cabinets, generally to around four square metres.

These firms either sell phone accessories, watches or other tourist-related items. Within the context of this study, it was those 11 firms selling phone accessories that were of direct interest. They all looked the same, with seemingly identical products and services. Their glass top cabinets were also identical, having been supplied by centre management. So this context represented a real challenge with respect to the questions asked of the storeowners in Dumalag.

While six of the firms identified themselves as providing phone accessories, only two carried out repairs. In terms of their perceptions of the external environmental factors they encountered, all six firms noted the variability in weather and crop production as being factors that influenced floor traffic in the centre. In terms of why they may do better than the other ten similar firms in the centre, all located within 100 metres of each other, their responses highlighted the nature of the environmental heterogeneity they encountered.

Only one of the six firms wished to remain in its current location. The other five firms would have preferred to relocate nearer to the front entrance or closer to the grocery section. Each believed that a different type of change was required to make them more profitable. While one store wanted to sell phones, others wanted to have more store space, have more modern looking store space, have more products to sell, have more than one location in the centre and finally, also to sell food. Each of the six firms clearly perceived opportunities and threats differently from one another in this small space. This was related to the type of customer they tended to attract and also their location in the centre. Thus, even in a small shopping centre, firms selling seemingly similar products define their environment differently. They perceive opportunities related to their environments differently and therefore react to their environment differently.

Summary of the Three Cases

When we look closely at the nature of the environment that Pizza firms in North Yorkshire/East Riding experience, we can see great variance, both temporally and spatially, related to factors that would be expected to shape the operational environment of individual firms. When we drill down further to the level of a main street in a town in the Philippines, we see even more heterogeneity. There, we are able to discern not only environmental heterogeneity, but also the corresponding diversity of firm structures, form and/or behaviour. At this relatively micro-level, firms that would be typically grouped together as common types of firms demonstrated that they interacted differently with, and shaped, the operational relations they held to their environments.

Extending this experiment even further, to the context of a small shopping centre, did little to challenge the view that firms can in fact be observed to operate in unique environments. While some factors, such as the volume of floor traffic, were quite constant for all 11 firms selling phone accessories, a range of other environmental factors did vary enough for the uniqueness of each firms' operations to be identified. The key issue here is that both environmental heterogeneity and firm differences in structure, form and/or behaviour were observable. Indeed, such differences were observed to be interrelated and an outcome of the feature–factor relations that exists between the firm and its environment. As such, the OE approach and its underlying assumptions could not be used to explain the adaptive behaviour of these small firms.

USING HETEROGENEITY

Our approach is different from past and existing determinations of both the environment and how firms interact with their environments. For quite some time (see Aldrich, 1979) the environment of the firm has conveniently been defined through membership in an industry or specific grouping of firms, and continues to be (Hannan, Polos and Carroll, 2007). Clearly we see this approach as ignoring the vital individuality of each firm and its lifeline. For us, understanding the problem-solving abilities of each firm is ecologically important. We see sufficient diversity in such problem-solving processes to know that firms cannot be prematurely grouped on the basis of industry codes and then assumed to behave in common ways.

We see the positions adopted in the current literature regarding firm adaptation as highly problematic from an autecological approach. Some see increased competition and/or technological change as decreasing the time individual firms have to adapt to their surrounds (Teece, 2016). Further, firm inertia is considered (Hannan and Freeman, 1984) to prevent aging firms from successful adaptive behaviours, leaving them at the mercy of younger, more agile, new entrants (Teece, 2016). Such thinking is standard in the organizational studies literature and is premised upon many assumptions, most of which are inconsistent with observations on the autecology of firms, as well as the premises of FA.

One of the limiting assumptions in the literature relates to how firms can (or can not) alter their environments. The extant literature in the domains of sociology, economics and organizational studies appears to offer little empirical evidence on how firms might be able to alter their environments. Rather, opinions are essentially divided as to whether such a process is possible. A point of difference would appear to relate to the strength apportioned to the environment with respect to the operation of firms. The prominent heterodox economist Hodgson (1993) provides an argument in favour of cooperative firm behaviours altering the environment positively, revisiting the classic works of Whitehead (1926), Lewontin (1978) and Sober (1984). Alternatively, those that hold the view that the environment–firm interaction is mostly based on competitive forces (Hannan and Carroll, 1992) give little hope of individual firms altering their environment significantly.

While this issue forms the direct focus of the following chapter, it also is import to this discussion.

Others have questioned the dominant OE perspective on this issue. Scott (1987: 118) for example saw that 'environments shape organizations, but organizations also shape environment'. Aldrich (1979) argued that larger firms have the capacity to alter their environments, whereas McKelvey (1982) suggests otherwise. In an interesting debate regarding the capacity of firms to influence their environment, Rumelt (1979: 3) in addressing Aldrich's (1979) view that only larger firms held such a capacity, contributes the challenge 'that an organization's environment can be altered without altering the environment itself. To change environments one only has to do different things. The change is not simply cognitive, or perceptual, but quite physical'. He goes on to argue that perhaps small firms (due to greater flexibility) have even greater opportunity to do so than larger, less flexible firms. The issue now seems to be the dividing of the environment into what is within the firm's boundaries and what is not changeable beyond such boundaries. While not directly said, Rumelt appears to be recognizing that some aspects of the firm's environment is open to change, and it is possible that while such aspects may seem minor, to the extent that they influence survival, they may also matter most.

Challenging Assumptions

It is through this line of thinking that autecology intersects with the organizational studies literature. Consider, for one moment, a firm that is quite rigid (in terms of its structures, form and/or behaviours), but capable of altering those aspects of its environment that matter most to its survival. Now consider a firm that is quite capable of changing its structure, form and/or behaviour, but not in ways that would enhance its survival chances vis-à-vis altering its operational environment. Under such circumstances we might see a correlation between firms displaying inertia, and the process of firm adaptation.

The process of contemplating such an ecological explanation of firm survival requires one to challenge many ingrained assumptions present in the literature regarding firm survival. Figure 3.4 illustrates the key differences in the autecological approach (from the traditional OE Approach) to defining and investigating a firm's environment.

The relationships drawn in Figure 3.4 are designed to be provocative. In the context of the traditional approach, we are encouraged to adopt one of two arguments, both relying on extreme positions. The first is that firms can demonstrate ambidexterity (O'Reilly and Tushman, 2004), using their dynamic capabilities to 'act strategically, embrace new opportunities, and even shape the business environment' (Teece, 2016: 203). The central argument is that environments change and/or new opportunities emerge, firms with sufficiently developed capability can avoid a position of maladaptation by remaining or becoming better adapted. FA is indeed sympathetic to this logic.

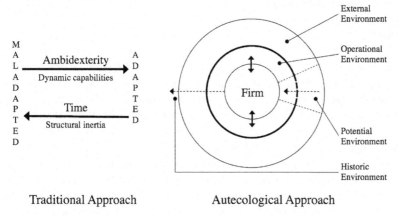

Traditional Approach   Autecological Approach

Figure 3.4 Visualizing the firm's environment

Alternatively, the OE approach suggests that as time passes, older firms are increasingly likely to become structurally inert, are in danger of becoming maladapted to their environment. While both sets of logic have their supporters, neither approach offers the researcher simple direction on how to test such logic vis-à-vis the survival of any individual firm. When the focus is on an individual firm, the environment related to the all-important process of adaptation is defined relative to the industry to which that individual firm is assumed to belong.

Given the obvious presence of environmental heterogeneity and our desire to remain fascinated by the individual differences firms exhibit, the OE perspective is untenable. Therefore, we propose an alternative autecological approach to visualising the firm and its environment. As illustrated in Figure 3.4, the nature of the operational environment can be located alongside the sum of all operational processes that each firm uses to maintain its survival. This relationship is shown by the double-ended arrows that indicate the exchange of resources and information in both directions between firm and operational environment. The operational environment is connected to the broader external environment by the potential environment. Through the potential environment, phenomena, present now or in a future external environment, may eventually come to enter the operational environment of the firm.

Through this approach we can be very clear as to what environmental phenomena matter when investigating a firm and what do not. Importantly, we can be more focused when investigating such matters historically as to what would have constituted the firm's operational environment previously, therefore avoiding the trap of attributing meaning to unrelated past environmental phenomena.

Summary

In closing, we have outlined a very different way of defining the environment of an individual firm. Having done so, we are now ready to consider the dynamic relationship between firm and environment. Before doing so, we redirect your attention back to the wise words upon which this chapter was developed. We hope we have convinced you of the environment being infinitely complex and never quite the same for two firms, as MacIver (1917) noted so long ago. We hope, in conjunction with Chapter 2, that we have convinced you that despite the complexity of any environment, it is most likely no more complex than any firm under investigation, and like plant ecologist Daubenmire (1947), we believe both sides of the equation deserve equal attention. Finally, having demonstrated the prevalence and importance of environmental heterogeneity and firm diversity, we hope to be rid of simplistic notions of selection occurring through a process of natural selection.

The environments we seek to understand are home to a myriad of ecological interactions (Boucher, 1985), as well as deliberate and unplanned responses that shape the processes of selection. We are confident that our approach can help the field not only to understand better what happens in the black box of the firm, but also appreciate the complexity of the environments our firms both encounter and co-create. We recognize the controversies surrounding these issues and have deliberately avoided becoming mired by endless debate. Like others confronting similar ecological scholarly challenges elsewhere (Strong, Simberloff, Abele and Thistle, 1984) we also believe the key to resolving these philosophical, conceptual and methodological issues is through evidence. However, prior to working with such evidence in Chapter 5, we still need to explain the operational nature of firm–environment relations and the subsequent process of firm adaptation.

4. Modification and matching

Organizations pursue intelligence. It is not a trivial goal. Its realization is imperfect, and the pursuit is endless. Every day there are failures to temper any successes. (March, 2010: 1)

Adaptive improvement is relative to the adaptive problem; it is so to be judged. (Sahlins and Service, 1960: 15)

The term adaptation is all too often used in the literature as a verb, suggesting it is something firms do, rather than become, that is adapted. Here we prefer to use the term adaptation to refer to the end-product of multiple ecological processes acting upon firms that maintain their existence across time in a particular operational environment. We do so very mindful that unlike animals and plants, firms uniquely influence the nature of these ecological processes and environments in deliberate ways, but often also unintentionally so. This chapter focuses on the specific processes through which firms alter aspects of their operating environment. Further, this chapter will explain how firms rely upon their daily sustenance activities to maintain a match with their environment through time, using their sensory abilities.

At this point, it is worth remembering that when we talk of firms, we do so in relation to all types of firms, large and small, physical and virtual, manufacturers and service providers, and public and private. There are no caveats to the application of our ideas; they are universally applicable to all firms. The primary reason for such confidence is our development of and reliance upon heuristic generalizations to guide our investigation of the behaviour of firms generally. Our continual acceptance of the presence of multiple coactions, different types of ecological processes, and various forms of firm behaviour ensure that only in the presence of evidence does FA offer explanation of ecological events. We are beholden to no laws to which our observations should concur. The lifeline of each firm we investigate autecologically will be reconcilable to established ecological theories and concepts. Consistent with the thinking of Sahlins and Service (1960), we expect the ecological pathway of each firm will always be determined by the nature of the problems they confront during their lifeline.

ENVIRONMENTAL MODIFICATION

Having previously provided a precise definition of both the firm and its environment, it is now possible to discuss the manner in which firms can modify the feature–factor relationship they maintain with their operational environment. Defining the operational environment of a firm frees us from long-held concerns that the environment is too complex to define with precision (Hawley, 1950), merely a creation or enactment of the entrepreneur's mind (Penrose, 1959; Weick, 1979) or just a dispenser of blind selection and/or a source of new variation (Hannan and Freeman, 1977), that may either be related to organizations strongly or weakly (McKelvey, 1982). We can now enrol several well-established ideas to explain how firms modify the nature of their environmental relations.

The idea of environmental modification has previously (Jones, 2016) been explained by drawing upon the niche construction literature of Odling-Smee, Laland and Feldman (2003). We avoid the use of the word *niche* in this discussion to stay true to the underlying core ideas of autecology (see Walter and Hengeveld, 2014). Instead, we focus on the identifiable environmental factors that comprise the operational environment of any given firm. This is critically important, as we do not assume that individual firms can make noticeable changes to the broader external environment to which they are related. Rather, we have reduced our consideration to only those environmental factors that each firm is operationally related to. In doing so, we resurrect the logical observation of McKenzie (1924) that human ecology is distinctly different from animal and plant ecology because of the cognitive abilities of man. Specifically, the institutions created by humans are capable of higher levels of adaptive behaviour.

Stepping back from the obvious intricacy of the external environment that relates in part to all firms across all industries and local communities, we give ourselves a chance to be honest witnesses of a story rarely if ever told. Embracing the notion of specific evolution rather than general evolution (Sahlins and Service, 1960), we are fascinated by the never-ending process of diversification that occurs alongside the process of environmental modification. We see the lifeline of individual firms as diverging, rather than converging, as in general evolution. We see such diversification as the natural by-product of firms matching their environmental conditions by solving local problems and exploiting perceived opportunities. For example, of the six types of Pizza firms noted earlier being such an outcome. We do not expect firms in industries to face the same identical problems or to have been originally formed with the same skills and knowledge. Therefore, we feel that firms are likely to evolve via different lifelines.

The next section draws upon the ideas of Odling-Smee, Laland and Feldman (2003) to explain the process of environmental modification. Once explained, we can further build on these ideas to consider the process of environmental matching in greater detail.

Changing the Feature–Factor Relationship

In Chapter 2 we identified the features of any given firm with reference to its activity system. The activity system is an artefact of the firm's individual habits, firm routines, goals and boundaries. Together, these components produce interacting elements (humans, technology, products, services and the identity of the firm) that collectively are the features of the firm. On a day-to-day basis, it is the firm's sustenance activities that provide the most effective ways of adjusting to the environment (Gibbs and Martin's, 1959). These regular, organized and enduring activities, which are aimed at supporting firm survival, are the features that underpin the ecological versatility (Mac Nally, 1995) of each individual firm.

In Chapter 3 we identified the factors of the operational environment as *all observable environmental phenomena that are operationally related, directed, timed, ordered and spaced by and across the lifeline of a particular firm*. Therefore, the feature–factor relationship between the firm and its operational environment can be envisaged to be changeable through firms altering aspects of their features, firms altering aspects of their operational environment, or stochastic change to the firm's operational environment. Let us now further explore this process in more detail.

We say, and with specific reference to Odling-Smee, Laland and Feldman (2003), that environmental modification occurs when a firm alters the feature–factor relationship that exists between the firm and its operational environment. It does so by changing one or more of the factors in its operational environment either by physically modifying factors at its current location in space and time, or by shifting its operations to a new space–time location, thereby changing the composition of environmental factors to which it is now operationally related. In doing so, each firm has the ability to alter the nature of the selection pressures it experiences, both positively and negatively. What matters here is that, in doing so, the firm not only inherits knowledge, capabilities and ecological relations from one time to the next, but also has the potential to influence the nature of selection forces it inherits from one time to the next. Such a process of inheritance is critically important to understanding how firms, notwithstanding their diversification in format, can survive across time despite not conforming to assumed industry norms.

This line of reasoning assumes that firms that alter factors in their operational environment may also temporarily derive a selective advantage. Further, that firms that employ sustenance activities that demonstrate such awareness may also be capable of repeating this modification process repeatedly, and thus maintain themselves through time. We also acknowledge that some firms may alter aspects of their operational environment in ways that also benefit related or unrelated firms that rely on similar factors in their own operational environments. There are four distinct ways in which we can view the actions of any given firm to engage in the process of environmental modification, as illustrated in Table 4.1.

Table 4.1 Categories of environmental modification

	Internal Adjustment	External Adjustment
Proactive	Firms introduce a change in their operational environment by altering some feature of their sustenance activities.	Firms expose their operations to new environmental factors by expanding their area of operation.
	e.g., Change of advertising.	e.g., Geographic expansion.
Responsive	Firms respond to emergent change in their operational environment by adjusting internal features.	Firms respond to a change in the operational environment by moving or repositioning their activities.
	e.g., Regulation compliance.	e.g., Adopting online sales.

The first two ways that firms can modify environmental factors, and therefore potentially influence their performance relative to actual selection pressures experienced, is by internal and external adjustment. Internal adjustment can occur when a firm deliberately changes a feature of their activity system and/or interacting elements in ways aimed at modifying factors in their operational environment. For example, a firm may seek to educate existing and potential customers about their activities that support the local community. The advertising and/or public relations processes designed to achieve this, do so by changing the perceptions of consumers in the operational environment. In doing so, the firm, for some time, develops a new ecological environment hopefully more favourable to its local presence.

External adjustment can occur when a firm deliberately alters the location and/or time at which they operate. In doing so, the firm is exposed to new environmental factors. This could include different operating regulations or customer behaviour. For example, a firm chooses to operate in a new market area, establishing a physical and online presence to service potential demand. In doing so, the firm has altered the nature of its operational environment. In these two examples, the firm proactively aims to improve the nature of feature–factor relations, typically using both internal and external adjustments to do so.

In addition to being proactive, firms can also be responsive to changes in their operational environment. As noted by March (2010) and Langlois (1997), the search for information, and interpretation of information is quite often imperfect. Therefore, we cannot assume firms can rely entirely on their deliberate, proactive actions to ensure survival. It is important that firms can eventually respond to changes in their operational environment that may have originally been overlooked. In the case of responsive internal adjustment, firms seek to realign their internal features to better match the nature of altered environmental factors. In doing so, they potentially avoid the scrutiny of selection that may threaten their survival. For example, an authority may decide that the employees in certain industries must hold certain qualifications. By assisting their workforce to re-educate, the firm achieves a better match with the requirements of their operational environment.

Finally, firms can engage in responsive external adjustment. In this situation, firms respond to a change in the operational environment by moving or repositioning their activities. For example, accepting that increasing numbers of potential customers are buying a product or service online, a firm may decide to expand their operations into such a virtual marketplace. In doing so, they evade the potential selective scrutiny that non-adopters of new operating processes are likely to face.

In each of these four processes, firms are seeking to alter the feature–factor relationship in their favour. Being proactive can introduce more risk as novel solutions may need experimentation and financing, but does have the potential for greater returns. Being responsive can appear safer, as knowledge associated with the planned response is potentially already disseminated in a market context. However, in contemporary markets characterized by simultaneous technology and consumer change, being a responder to such change may be very difficult. Recent history demonstrates that those firms that successfully exist in new markets do so without sharing the spoils to many imitators, Amazon being a classic example.

More than Change

Whitehead (1926: 139) said, 'the key to the mechanism of evolution is the necessity for the evolution of a favourable environment, conjointly with the evolution of any specific type of enduring organisms of great permanence. Any physical object which by its influence deteriorates its environment, commits suicide'. We acknowledge that in the context of firms, the same logic applies. Firms can engage in positive environmental modification, just as they can achieve negative environmental modification. When viewed as a problem-solving process, responsive internal or external adjustment seeks to enable firms to better align their sustenance activities to altered conditions. When viewed as a value-creating process, proactive environmental modification aims to either enhance the match between firm features and environmental factors and/or decrease the energy used to acquire necessary resources, thus increasing its ecological versatility (Mac Nally, 1995). Having outlined the four essential ways in which firms can engage in environmental modification, we can now turn our attention to the related process of environmental matching.

ENVIRONMENTAL MATCHING

We argue that firms exist in localities where factors in their operational environment satisfy their sustenance activities and do not exceed their tolerances, much as organisms do within their environmental context (Walter and Hengeveld, 2014). This process of environmental matching is fundamental to FA. While we do not discount the likelihood that some firms are simply favoured by environmental conditions from time to time, we also accept we must provide a comprehensive explanation of how firms persist through time. Otherwise, we are stuck with Alchian's (1950: 214) notion that 'there may have been no motivated individual adapting but, instead, only environmental adopting'. Yes, firms get lucky, but no more frequently than they get unlucky. To explain their long-term persistence we need to fully explain how such outcomes can occur.

In doing so, we are not restricted to the non-efficiency arguments that economists enrol when describing imperfect competition (Chamberlin, 1933). We are also not restricted by the idea of evenly distributed competitive pressures (Hannan, Polos and Carroll, 2007), thought to act upon identifiable populations to influence firm survival. The firms we study are *successful* if they maintain their operations at the time of evaluation (as per Haukioja's (1982) definition of success for organisms (as a replacement for fitness)). We take care not to simplistically compare or group the assumed behaviours of individual firms given that we acknowledge the different conditions they have developed operational relations with. Therefore, we do not speak of under-performing firms that persist (DeTienne, Shepherd and De Castro, 2008), but rather of the need to embrace the range of variables, conditions and circumstances (Weick, 1979; Tsoukas and Dooley, 2011) surrounding all firms.

We also draw upon literature that potentially demystifies this complexity related to ecological services (Norgaard, 2010) through which the presence of emergy (Odum, 1996) can be considered. In combination, the positions we take and the ideas we use enable a logical and coherent explanation of firm persistence to be developed. Our aim is never to lose sight of the different stages of each firm's lifeline through which they develop, maintain and shape operational relations with the environment.

The Nature of the Firms we Study

It is obvious that firms neither stay the same nor experience the same environment through time. Figure 4.1 illustrates a likely scenario for three firms in the same industry. Drawing on the idea of the corridor of persistence discussed earlier, and illustrated to demonstrate its dynamics through time, the sphere of operation of each firm is plotted as a solid shape to indicate their operations and that they differ from one another in this respect. We can, on this diagrammatic basis suggest probable evolutionary journeys for each firm.

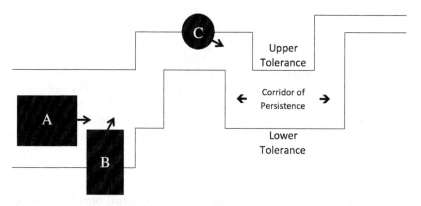

Figure 4.1   Corridor of persistence

Firm A appears well matched to its surrounds, with a clear buffer zone around its operations. Its most likely trajectory is to maintain status quo in terms of its form, structures, functions and activities. That is, until the managers/entrepreneur senses the need to adjust some combination of those features to remain within the upper and lower tolerances of its operational environment. Placed centrally within the corridor of persistence we can be comfortable in thinking that at this moment of observation Firm A is well matched to its local environment.

The same cannot be said of Firm B, which is clearly operating outside the levels of its operational tolerances. Under these conditions Firm B has good possible options for action. If Firm B has sensed this non-alignment with its operational environment, it could attempt to alter its features to better align to the requirements of the operational environment. It could also attempt to change factors in its operational environment so as to rebalance feature–factor relations in the favour of the firm. It could also attempt to simultaneously change both firm features and environmental factors. Remember, 'adaptive improvement is relative to the adaptive problem' (Sahlins and Service, 1960: 15).

As stated earlier, we are neither optimists nor pessimists regarding the ability of firms to engage in such adaptive behaviour; we are possibilists. Everything is possible once we recognize that at the moment of observation the firms we seek to study differ in their features and experience different environmental conditions. Despite the suggestion that the three firms in Figure 4.1 are in a common industry, several firm-specific differences are highlighted. First, the three firms depicted are different from one another in their operations. Second, logically, they all face a different pathway to match the requirements of their operational environment. Third, each firm is spatially and temporally remote to the others. Fourth, while one firm is well matched to its current local environment, the other two firms are not, with different types of tolerance issues being confronted.

Remember, the central thesis of this book, that firms can and do adapt to their local environment through modifying the features of their structural/strategic organization and/or modification of factors in their operational environment (or influencing them). This constant process of matching between the firm's features and environmental variables, the adjusting of inner relations to outer relations, constitutes the lifeline of any given firm (is precisely the same way in which the lifeline of organisms, in nature, is run). The on-going existence of any firm indicates a capacity 'simultaneously to *be* and *become*', as it is for individual organisms (Rose, 1997: 142).

Autopoiesis and the Nature of Firms

Again, we do not need to be pedantic as to the specific feature of one firm or another, this is not our main concern. The sustenance activities that *all* firms rely upon provide the means to develop mechanistic explanations of the survival of firms, within the environmental context relevant to them.

Autonomy and diversity, the maintenance of identity and the origin of variation in the mode in which this identity is maintained, are the basic challenges presented by the phenomenology of living systems to which men have for centuries addressed their curiosity about life. (Maturana and Varela, 1980: 73)

Following the lead of Maturana and Varela (1980), we are also fascinated with that which is common to all firms that persist through time. Just how can firms repeatedly demonstrate the capacity to simultaneously be and become, when other firms fail to do so? Our mechanistic approach requires that we can reformulate the fundamental phenomena of environments and firms to explain the relationships and interactions that support the survival and persistence of firms. Again, it is the organization within the firm that interests us, specifically its ability to self-organize.

We view firms as systems, each with its own form of organization that produces both internal order and the facilitation of external relations. In Figure 2.1 we outlined the manner, through an ecological baseline, in which the interacting elements of a firm provide a potential information flow to support the future regeneration of such interacting elements. This process, while not perfect, is central to the sensory abilities of a firm. Firms that ignore or receive and then misinterpret such information, logically, are likely to have a greater probability of failure. We have previously noted the works of Veblen (1922) and Sumner (1902), who advocated the dangers of being ignorant to changes in the environment (in their case the social/economic). Like animals and plants, firms rely upon environmental response systems to survive, as do organisms each in a species-specific way (Walter and Hengeveld, 2014), whether they acknowledge or understand how such processes work.

In most firms these systems rely upon business acumen and experience. For example, customers in a restaurant can provide instant feedback as to the quality of food and/or the nature of ambience and service. Restaurants that choose to ignore any such negative feedback would be expected to perform worse than those that listen and react to such feedback. For many other larger and more complex firms, deliberate processes are developed to capture data from end-users and other stakeholders to gauge the acceptance, or otherwise, of the firm's interacting elements.

Each firm therefore has the potential to use its activity system to ensure sufficient order exists within the firm, whilst also altering the sustenance activities, if need be, to maintain the acceptance of the firm's interacting elements. In this way, a firm can be viewed as autopoietic in that it maintains its persistence by both *being* and *becoming*. Thus, self-reproduction through time is central to the firm's ability to not wander too far from the requirements of matching its local environment. Conversely, the firm also evolves through time, as modifications to the previous state are future actions of self-reproduction. Therefore, it is not the environment that directly alters the firm, but rather the firm's interactions with the environment and the eventual interpretation of information related to this interaction.

THE SENSORY CHALLENGE

We can contemplate the survival skills that many living organisms inherit as instincts. For example, web building for spiders, pheromone trails for ants and the highly synchronized flying skills of starlings when grouped together. None of these abilities are developed at schools for spiders, ants or starlings. They are inherited genetically and ontogenetically developed during the lifeline of each. Darwin famously made reference to an entangled bank to help us visualize the very breadth and depth of the complex countless relationships required to enable living entities to co-exist. What we as humans tend to overlook is that each living thing in such a context clearly does 'live in different sensory environments, bounded by the properties of their sensory organs' (Stevens, 2013: 3). These ideas can be applied directly to the firms we speak of; the sensory abilities of a firm are likely to govern the degrees of freedom afforded to them in the corridor of persistence.

Within the OE approach there is little reason to draw upon the developing sensory ecology literature given the lack of agency afforded to firms (Aldrich, 1992). By contrast, the opportunity clearly exists in an autecological approach. The one obvious challenge is that humans do not genetically inherit sensory abilities for use in the market or more general societal contexts. We are presumed able to learn theories and frameworks related to environmental scanning and sense making, but history suggests this is questionable, given the consistent presence of high business failure rates.

The challenge would seem to be not that you could know all things, but what you actually know that is relevant to your precise context. Collecting data makes sense only if it is related to the environment and processes of selection a firm is exposed to, the nature of interaction occurring in the firm's operational environment, and/or how a firm might modify such factors to their advantage. In the past, the idea of a firm's absorptive capacity (Cohen and Levinthal, 1990) had be offered as a way of understanding how firms can value, assimilate and apply new knowledge. More recently, Zahra and George (2002) discussed the notion of *potential* and *realized* absorptive capacity, focusing specifically upon the firm routines that make possible such awareness and those other routines used to benefit from such knowledge.

The idea of *potential* and *realized* absorptive capacity serves as a reminder that there is no simple formula for a firm gaining optimal awareness of their surrounds and exploiting any such awareness. Indeed this approach introduces time and conditions as likely factors that may derail the process.

From our perspective it is more important for firms to know what they need to understand, than for them to simply be able to organize for the acquisition and analysis of information. To address this challenge, we propose the adoption of Endsley's (1995; 2015) situation awareness construct to explain the basis upon which the sensory abilities of firms can be viewed from an autecological approach.

Situation Awareness

A motivator in adopting the process of situation awareness is our recognition that all firms are capable of possessing sufficient sensory abilities, regardless of size, complexity or ambition. It is easy to follow the flow of resources between firms and their environments without paying proper attention to the information flows that preceded these resources flows (or did not do so). Just as the ecologist Dusenbery (1992) noted, observing the complex behaviours associated with organisms solving problems is challenging and requires a direct concern for the mechanisms related to information gathering, sense-making and response, so it is with observing firms in action.

Situation awareness is defined as 'the perception of the elements in the environment within a volume of time and space, the comprehension of their meaning and the projection of their status in the near future' (Endsley, 1995: 36). The situation awareness construct is ecological in design (Hancock and Diaz, 2002), and when considered from the perspective of Gibson (1979), offers us an opportunity to understand the behaviour of firms by studying the information in a firm's operational environment, and the related epistemological connections between firm and environment.

Originally formulated in the aviation industry, situation awareness has been applied in domains such as 'business management, chess and science' (Endsley, 2015: 102). As defined, situation awareness provides a theoretical bridge towards understanding how people in firms perceive the elements of their environment, the nature of interaction occurring, and how their future actions may shape the nature of such interactions in their favour.

Drawing upon the environmental interaction framework of Jones (2013), we can visualize several factors in Figure 4.2 of which all firms must be constantly mindful. All firms can be studied in the context of the operational environment to which they are related. All firms rely upon their resource profile (Aldrich, 1999), exploiting social capital (SC), applying human capital (HC) and accessing resources using their financial capital (FC) when constructing their sustenance activities. As a result, there always remains the potential for firms to seek and receive information about the acceptance of their interacting elements (humans, technologies, products, services and their identity, noted as H/T, P/S and I in Figure 4.2) from within the firm's operational environment. This information can inform the firm as to the extent of cognitive and socio-political legitimacy that the interacting elements of the firm hold. That is, to what extent they have *taken for granted status* and/or *approved* by key stakeholders (Aldrich, 1999) in the firm's operational environment.

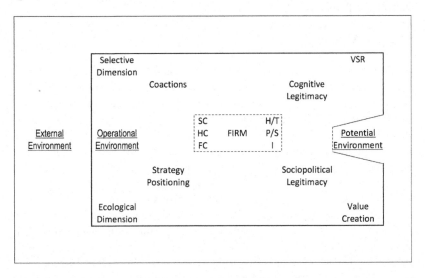

Figure 4.2   Common elements of a firm's operational environment

Firms also need to be able to understand the nature of how best to create and capture value from their interacting elements, be that through value chain, value shops or value networks (Stabell and Fjeldstad, 1998). Further, firms need to understand how change does, or does not occur more broadly in their operational environment. Therefore, firms must know how the process of variation, selection and retention (VSR) plays out within the context of their operational environment. What new ideas fail and which work? Why are certain processes and products/services retained in society when others are rejected?

Firms must be sensitive to the nature of coactions they share with multiple stakeholders throughout their operational environment. They also need to be knowledgeable about how they might improve the nature of such coactions. The strategic position of the firm also needs to be understood and monitored. Is the firm organized strategically for the short-term or long-term? Is the firm positioned seeking to capture a narrow resource type or a broader resource type? Are these positions sustainable or do they need adjustment periodically?

Finally, does the firm fully understand the nature of the selection process operating within its operational environment? That is, to what extent does the operational environment have properties that offer growth/survival assistance (i.e. oligotrophic) or potentially harmful factors (i.e. eutrophic) (Kangas and Risser, 1979) that can be exploited, modified and/or avoided? Further, does the firm understand what phenomena presently in the external environment may soon, through choice or otherwise, become part of the firm's potential environment?

Visualizing Situation Awareness

We can envisage a firm that demonstrates a high degree of situation awareness. This firm, its managers curious by nature, would be closely in tune with the firm's operational environment. They would manage not merely the flows of resources between firm and environment, but also the flows of information required to achieve the ecological versatility (Mac Nally, 1995) necessary to support their on-going persistence. Within the context of their operations, we would imagine this firm would be excellent at *perceiving cues* from the environment regarding all aspects of their interacting elements. This would include an acute appreciation of those factors that matter and those that do not. This appreciation relates to the firm's *comprehension* of the information it deals with on a daily basis and to relate it directly to its operations. This ability represents ecological realism (Flach, 1995), whereby the human mind is neatly synchronized with its environmental surrounds. We can imagine how such capability would increase the ability of such a firm to more accurately *project*, from current events, contemporary information and predictions, actions suitable for future situations. These three abilities, perception, comprehension and projection capture the three levels of situation awareness (Endsley and Garland, 2000).

Our use of situation awareness fits neatly with the logic of the operational environment. Both the presence of awareness and an operational environment are premised upon a volume of time and space that is changing and unpredictable. As such, we do not assume that any firm can be credited with having a high degree of situation awareness at some point in the future simply because they were observed to have such an ability at an earlier time.

However, we do expect one specific type of commensalistic relationship in firms with high degrees of situation awareness. Increasingly the importance of ecological services (Daily, 1997) are being recognized in society. In the natural world these may be processes and conditions through which biodiversity is conserved, providing humans with essential food sources. In the economic world, many ecological services are also possible. Jones (2009) drew attention to the idea of emergy (Odum, 1996) to illustrate how many small Pizza firms gained a significant survival advantage from the widespread advertising of franchised Pizza firms.

Many of these Pizza firms were clearly acutely aware of the benefit they gained from someone else essentially doing their advertising for them. Some, however, were ignorant to the potential benefits to be gained from organizing their operations to take advantage of this ecological service. For example, these firms failed to position their operations so that their interacting elements so they were not in competition with the larger, more scale-efficient franchised operators. Or, they allocated scarce resources to advertising that was not required to attract customers. When the abundance and distribution of these Pizza firms were studied, Jones (2009) concluded that the presence of emergy, or independently produced energy that other entities can use to their advantage, was the primary reason for both the distribution and abundance of independent Pizza firms in the region studied. In this example, a commensalistic relationship exists, as the eventual user of the surplus energy does not harm the producer of the emergy.

SUMMARY

This chapter has outlined the fundamental differences that permit human agency to be central to the autecological investigation of any firms and its operational environment. This acceptance of human agency shines a spotlight on an ecological paradox at the heart of the FA approach. Organisms by and large inherit genetic information germane to their expected environs that Dawkins (2009) labels *survival instructions*. Conversely, humans do not inherit such precise instructions and are required to learn about their constantly changing and unpredictable surrounds continuously through the course of their life. Whereas OE views the application of such learning skills pessimistically vis-à-vis the successful adaptation of firms to changing environmental conditions, we do not. That said, we do not assume the process of learning required for successful adaptation to stochastic environmental change a straightforward practice.

The ecological paradox is that while organisms inherit a survival advantage, its potential value is largely governed by the upper and lower environmental tolerance levels encountered. By contrast, firms, created and managed by humans are gifted no such advantage. However, learning processes within the firm have the potential to shift the nature of upper- and lower-environmental tolerance levels related to firm persistence. Therefore, while firms do not start at an equivalent ecological baseline to organisms, in terms of natural survival advantages, they have a greater potential to adapt to and shape their environs to extend their lifelines. As we have discussed throughout this chapter, the question is not if firms can adapt to and shape their environments, but rather, how? The following chapter provides an example of how an autecological investigation of the mechanisms related to firm survival could be approached.

PART III

Explaining Adaptation

Explaining Adjudication

5. A model of *Transferred Demand*

The way in which knowledge progresses, and especially our scientific knowledge, is by unjustified (and unjustifiable) anticipations, by guesses, by tentative solutions to our problems, by *conjectures*. (Popper, 1963: vii)

This chapter is written in two parts. First, the research of Jones (2009) is presented in first person context. Second, the response of Walter, also in the first person, provides a final comment from the autecologist's perspective. We have chosen this approach to 1) retain the original critical realist prose, and 2) to highlight the views of a practising autecologist presented as pure scientific commentary. One voice highlights the speculative reasoning, or retroduction process through which this research was developed. The other voice is of the seasoned ecologist casting an opinion of the validity and value of the approach, and offers suggestions for employing the autecological approach further in the social sciences.

WHY DO PIZZA FIRMS SURVIVE?

For quite some time, my interest has been in how firms adapt so as to persist. I considered many potential contexts to explore this issue, and eventually settled on the Pizza industry for the following two reasons. First, the rise of the Pizza industry since the late 1960s has been a global phenomenon, data are available from which to reconstruct a census of all participants, and many of the industry's pioneers still exist and/or are available for comment. Second, it is obvious that the industry has experienced tremendous change with respect to operational, technological and marketing practices.

The research pursued may be summarized in terms of, why *some* firms, in the face of increasing *apparent* competition, survive for considerably longer periods when other *apparently* similar types of firms operating under *apparently* similar conditions do not? An immediate challenge in this preliminary question is the assumption of assumed similarity. This question could easily be rephrased as, within a specific industry, during times of apparent increases in competition, to what extent is firm survival determined by differences in the type of firm and/or the presence of generative mechanisms and/or conditions they experienced?

Prior to explaining the details of this research project, I reflect on my experience prior to commencing this research journey. Having developed and managed a large franchise operation in Tasmania for several years, I bring to this study a practical way of thinking about firm survival. Subsequently, I found myself drawn to the works of Aldrich (1999) and others (Hodgson, 2004), who tend to view the socioeconomic world through an evolutionary/ecological lens, for one main reason. Life (and therefore business) is unpredictable and theories that aim to achieve high predictability have never really impressed me. Evolutionary theory on the other hand is used to explain past events, with the explainer being responsible for accommodating the indeterminacy of outcomes. That is, we must avoid at all cost 'viewing earlier events as though they were controlled by their subsequent outcomes' (Aldrich, 1999: 33). The one caveat I have imposed upon my use of such evolutionary or ecological ideas is that I will always attempt to use Hodgson's (2001: 90) principle of consistency, to ensure that 'explanations in one domain have to be consistent with explanations in another, despite examination of different properties and deployment of different concepts'.

The Initial Research Problem

How new organizational forms emerge and how new firms are retained and/or adapted in the genesis of new populations of such forms is a fundamentally important question in the domain of organizational studies (see Aldrich, 1999). The last chapter of Aldrich's now landmark *Organizations Evolving* serves as an invitation for the use of evolutionary theory to further advance our understanding of many issues related to the survival of firms in our local, national and global economies. This research contributes to that invitation by addressing the question, *why do some firms survive for considerably longer periods of time when other apparently similar types of firms operating under apparently similar conditions do not?*

Despite past focus on the subject of firm survival (see Vernon, 1966; Utterback and Abernathy, 1975; Williamson, 1975; Jovanovic, 1982; Abernathy and Clark, 1985; Mata and Portugal, 1994; Audretsch, 1995; Ericson and Pakes, 1995; Klepper, 1996; Caves, 1998; Agarwal and Audretsch, 2001), such simple questions about firm survival remain difficult to answer satisfactorily. These past studies do not inform the reader greatly about how the actions of firms (vis-à-vis firm survival) can be understood from a historical and local perspective with implications transferrable to higher levels (i.e. nationally or globally). Aldrich (1999) implores researchers to address the subject of such social change (or for example, firm survival) in more *encompassing* ways to ensure we develop a greater understanding of how the collective behaviours of firms are accounted for. Currently, the middle ground held by pragmatic researchers (e.g. Haveman, 1992; Amburgey, Kelly and Barnett, 1993; Bruderer and Singh, 1996) is seen to offer the best opportunity to reduce the influence of extreme arguments of either environmental selection (e.g. Hannan and Freeman, 1977; 1989) or firm adaptation (e.g. Tushman and Romanelli, 1985; Levitt and March, 1988). Restated, it is considered that the unifying agenda of Levinthal (1991) provides the means to consider the fullest array of factors associated with the interaction of firm and environment, without assuming the superiority of one over the other.

A related challenge within the domain of organizational studies has been determining the appropriate level/s of analysis to conduct research on firm survival (see Davidsson and Wiklund, 2001). This issue would seem closely related to the challenge of developing an encompassing way to explain all such social phenomena. An immediate challenge is present in trying to side step the extreme arguments of environmental selection (e.g. Hannan and Freeman, 1977; 1989) or firm adaptation (e.g. Tushman and Romanelli, 1985; Levitt and March, 1988) that tend to place too much emphasis on a particular way of viewing the research task. Throughout this research, an attempt will be genuinely made to consider *all* forms of ecological and evolutionary theory so as to reconnect to the past intentions of Young (1988) that any such application of ecological and evolutionary theory in the social domain should be deliberately conducted in an inter-disciplinary manner.

Within the context of this research, it is the individual firm that is of specific interest. Where firms, such as Pizza firms, are observed to co-exist alongside other restaurants, the nature of their diversity is taken into account seriously. While past work in this area has typically debated the importance of the level (or unit) of analysis (see Baum and Singh, 1994; Davidsson and Wiklund, 2001), the issue of the ecological scale (Wiens, 1989) would seem not to have been discussed in such studies. In this research, it is the extent of the firms' operations and their area of overlap that determines the scale of inquiry, not the preferences of the researcher. The restaurants under investigation operate within towns and, therefore, the unit of analysis is the individual firm and the level of investigation is the town within which the individual firms operate and potentially overlap.

The firms are not assumed to belong to a population of firms given their obvious diversity. However, they can be viewed as belonging to a cryptic firm complex, as identified earlier in Chapter 2. Reference to cryptic firm complexes enables firms to be studied as individuals, but with consideration also given to the presence of other similar types of firms operating locally (for example Chinese or Indian restaurants), that are considered capable of influencing the nature of each other's operational environments. Therefore, and consistent with standard practice in the field of landscape ecology (and its direct interest in environmental heterogeneity), the way in which the subject firms *scale* their environment, determines how they are investigated. Put simply, Pizza firms (and other restaurant types) operate in discrete local environs and therefore our observations/measurements must fall within the same domain, acknowledging that these domains may also vary.

OBSERVING THE PHENOMENA

The research process unfolded through three distinct stages. The first stage was entering the field not only to *see* what is there, but also to *understand* what is happening there, as per the challenge of Sears (1935). In this stage, I entered the field without assuming any one overarching theory would adequately explain why some firms would survive where others might fail. The aim was to take full advantage of each individual's ability to articulate their firm's experiences of survival/failure.

Next, using a critical realist approach, a model of firm survival was developed from combining my insights with those of the research subjects and my subsequent engagement with the broader literature. This second stage sought to address the empirical irregularity observed in the first stage through the development of a model of underlying generative mechanisms 'which *if* they were to exist and act in the postulated way would account for the phenomenon in question' (Bhaskar, 1979: 15). Critically, it was not my perceptions that were the explicit focus of the research, but rather my ability to access a reality that lies beyond my initial perceptions (Stake, 1995). This is important given the primary research objective of furthering an account of generative mechanisms that allows for the ascribing of (causal) power or potentiality under a given set of contingent conditions. Especially so, when it is accepted that generative mechanisms 'may either be dormant for a while or they may be counteracted by opposing mechanisms and lead to no events' (Tsoukas, 1989: 553).

The third, and final stage dealt with subjecting the model of firm survival to empirical scrutiny in another context that was a similar, but different context. The North Yorkshire/East Riding restaurant industry was chosen for the following reasons. First, the commencement and development of the industry in Hobart and North Yorkshire were very similar, both temporally and spatially. Second, regional television networks for localized and national advertising serviced both areas. Third, both industries were started by local independent firms, and these were then followed by franchised food chains.

Fourth, in both study areas, Pizza firms commenced as an *exotic* sub-population within an established, yet diverse restaurant/fast food industry. Finally, there is a comprehensive record of all entrants (and therefore entrants, exits and/or survivors) from local telephone directories that are still available.

Past Studies of Restaurants

Over the last 25 years the restaurant/fast food sector has been the subject of many studies concerned with firm survival (e.g. Freeman and Hannan, 1983; O'Neil and Duker, 1986; Muller and Inman, 1994; Muller and Woods, 1994; Shriber, Muller and Inman, 1995; Bates, 1995; English, Josiam, Upchurch and Willems, 1996; Muller, 1997; Hjalager, 1999; Kalnins and Mayer, 2004; Parsa, Self, Njite and King, 2005). Whilst the importance of spatial factors is emerging as a specific issue related to firm survival, it still remains an area primarily examined using extensive research methodologies that, by design, search for regularities across the population of firms, rather than attempting to explain the causal relationships between certain objects or events. Therefore, an opportunity existed to employ intensive research methods that aim to discover and explain any relationships that may exist between spatial factors and any other factors that may influence individual firm survival. Such model development is an appropriate approach given recent concerns regarding the current inability of evolutionary theories to adequately explain firm survival (i.e. population change) in the organizational studies domain (Amburgey and Singh, 2002).

THE HOBART PIZZA INDUSTRY

This section deliberately provides a descriptive, non-theoretical account of the Hobart Pizza industry from 1970 to 2005. The industry provides an excellent context in which to investigate a service- and product-based industry within which environmental change and firm adaptation was observable over a 36-year period. The account provided has been formed from interviews with Pizza shop owners, researcher observations and the examination of historical documents, such as telephone directories and newspapers, from which past behaviours can be observed against a known set of marketplace events. Thus the process relied upon multiple sources of data derived independently from both qualitative and quantitative sources to identify and comprehend the developmental phases within the Hobart market. Thus, a process of analytical generalization (rather than empirical generalization) was used 'to clarify the necessary and contingent relationships between structures' (Danermark et al., 2002: 105). This section concludes with the presentation of a *working* research proposition that provides the initial focus and direction of the research project.

The Phases of the Hobart Pizza Industry

The Hobart Pizza market traces back to the late 1960s and its subsequent developments were influenced by several external events and the involvement of many Italian entrepreneurs. Three distinct epochs are discernable. The first period (1970–1983) relates to those years when no franchised firms operated alongside local independent firms. The second period (1984–1994) relates to those years when local independent firms operated alongside one franchised operator (hereinafter referred to as Franchise 1). The third period (1995–2005) relates to those years when the local independents operated alongside two or more franchised operators. Across all three periods, significant events occurred that were to prove favourable or unfavourable as the case may be to the participating firms.

Italian families typically founded the pioneering firms, with a few exceptions. They introduced not only an alternative food source, but also a passion and flair for food excellence. This pursuit of excellence has clearly motivated and guided the development of the industry during the 36-year period of investigation. The many social trends that have accompanied the industry's growth are perhaps best considered through discussion of each distinct period.

Period One – Pre-Franchise 1

Just as post-war immigrants help to establish an Italian restaurant culture in other Australian cities, Hobart was no different. It would appear that the initial knowledge related to producing pizza was imported and/or inherited by first, second and third generation Italians. Initially, three well-known Italian eating-houses represented the Pizza industry in Hobart; all holding close ties to the local soccer community. The industry was just like many other multicultural offerings that increasingly became apart of Australia's culture. It was not without its own special theatre, with the tossing of the dough considered essential to producing the perfect pizza for example.

An event that had considerable influence on the industry's growth was the introduction of Australia's first casino in Hobart. The Wrest Point Casino benefited from a relaxing of operating hours. As a result, rather than Hobart having the lights turned out at 10pm for those desirous of a beverage, the party continued at the casino. Initially, this had the effect of producing two specific new groups of clientele. Those that had partied until late and those that had served the party until late. Both had similar needs, a place to unwind and eat. This proved to be a windfall for the handful of Pizza restaurants in Hobart. Other more traditional providers of take-away and restaurant food were closed and not looking for any additional business due to their early opening hours. The attraction of the casino acted to draw many patrons, many of whom dispersed back into Hobart throughout the evening. So a new customer base for Pizza restaurants was born and continued to grow; a late night pizza became a regular event for many. As will be discussed during the post-Franchise 1–Pre-Franchise 2 period, the casino also became an important place for Pizza restaurant owners and their staff to meet, relax and share knowledge.

The next event that influenced the industry was the relaxing of hotel trading hours. Coming into effect in August 1977, the Licensing Act of 1976 provided this emergent industry with much impetus. The volume of hungry patrons grew exponentially. Many of the new Pizza restaurants that entered at this time would subsequently remain as Hobart's favourite restaurants. Importantly, these entrants also employed many eventual Pizza restaurant owners. During this period, the demand was so great in the early hours of the morning that many firms needed to turn off the lights to prevent additional patrons from interrupting their cleaning of the premises. The emerging legitimacy of the Pizza industry in Hobart was based upon many different styles of operating formats. From the traditional, to the modern, to the take-away style, pizza was already challenging other forms of restaurant cuisine. The availability of physical locations was also not problematic. At this time, a group of restaurant owners banded together to form the Pizza Owner's Association.

The pioneers all agreed that their success was based on three factors. The first was great food. The pizza had to be made from the best fresh ingredients and cooked to perfection. To a man, it would seem these pizza pioneers were passionate about the end product. Second, excellent service was essential. For many, the concept of service varied from table service alone, to the provision also of a sense of theatre that drew customers into the production process. As the industry began to emerge as a genuine alternative to other types of restaurants, ambience became the third critical factor.

During this early period, many of the more entrepreneurial pioneers experimented with new types of dough mixes, the use of higher quality (mozzarella and ricotta) cheeses, and the sourcing/distribution of fine coffees. Many of these practises were shared amongst friends and became industry norms. The medium of transfer was the weekly socialising activities, such as ten-pin bowling and Sunday nights at the casino. It was common for staff to be part of these get-togethers and this seems to have added to their abilities to eventually leave their employment and start up their own Pizza restaurant.

The fact that these early Pizza restaurants were distributed throughout Hobart's suburbs and not in direct competition seems to explain the ease at which industry-specific information was transferred between the pioneers, with the interesting side note that nine restaurateurs all played for the one soccer team.

Period Two – Post-Franchise 1–Pre-Franchise 2 and 3

The next major event in the industry was the arrival of a national franchise Pizza chain, Franchise 1. Far from being viewed negatively, Franchise 1's presence appears to have benefited incumbents in three specific ways. First, there was a substantial increase in the primary demand for pizza. Franchise 1's entry introduced an array of advertising activities that promoted pizza more generally than it did the Franchise itself. As a result, for the more entrepreneurial pioneers, opportunities were abound. The media used by Franchise 1 (e.g. leaflets, TV, radio, etc) was highly visible and relatively easy to imitate. Those with flair grew with the market to establish a stronger presence, positioned on the basis of their existing orientation towards quality. The last benefit introduced was a by-product of the last two issues. A process of *educating the public* about pizza led to a change in the time that pizza was consumed. Pizza became not solely the domain of late night revellers, but became available earlier, to those about to party, and those thinking about dinner or even lunch. Ultimately, the arrival of Franchise 1 increased the legitimacy of the Pizza industry by assisting incumbents and redefining the *how* and *when* of pizza consumption. By altering the hours during which pizza was consumed, many pioneers were encouraged to remain in the industry. The need to be *on deck* when production was peaking, typically after 10pm, had eased. Owners could now work restaurant hours, returning to a more normal life by leaving a manager in charge to finish the late shift.

The industry experienced a huge increase in foundings after Franchise 1's entry. In 1986, with the industry growing rapidly, an Adelaide-based franchise operator entered the market to introduce the concept of pizza home delivery. This change is credited with increasing turnover threefold in many well-established Pizza firms. Many local restaurateurs responded by setting up their own home delivery capabilities. New systems and staffing arrangements needed to be developed to deliver a new form of service that was unique to pizza. Franchise 1 again became the hero of many local restaurants. Their TV advertisements, while clearly aimed at creating primary demand for Franchise 1's product, had a spillover effect. It was common for everybody else's phone to start ringing as soon as Franchise 1 advertisements had been shown, such was the impact of Franchise 1 on primary demand throughout Hobart. However, in reality, consumers remained loyal to their existing local Pizza restaurants whose focus on quality was typically the most influential determinant on their intention to purchase pizza.

Even so, there were calls from incumbents for market regulation. An early pioneer feared the market (at this stage 26 firms) was on the verge of saturation. Another also felt that each area should have a limited number of Pizza shops. The owner of the Adelaide-based franchise felt, by contrast, that with their mainland backing it was best to let the market decide. For another stalwart, who entered in 1973, these changes meant the end of his once thriving business. This operator worked alone, but spoke little English, and was unable to continue his operations given the need to receive phone orders. While demand was still strong, fewer customers physically entered his shop to choose from a menu board on a shop wall.

Adding to this new trend was the increasing acceptance of the random breath testing laws enacted in 1983. Fewer consumers were out driving around at night and the whole concept of having pizza delivered was becoming a normal way of acquiring a pizza. By now, additional customer segments had emerged. Taxi drivers not only became loyal customers at many Pizza restaurants, but also became a source of recommendation for many of their passengers. Many of the police who manned the random breath testing stations also became regular customers.

During this period of rapid change, the significance of the casino in providing a steady flow of hungry patrons had lessened. Many alternative nightclub venues had emerged and the competition between existing Pizza restaurants had now seemingly intensified. The market was moving towards one based on higher volume and lower margins. Many sought to take advantage of technological innovations to increase their advantage. For example, steel trays gave way to smaller and cheaper aluminium trays; traditional deep ovens were sometimes replaced with purpose built four-deck ovens. Computerized systems that enabled the processing of wages and stocktaking were adopted. Software that recognized the caller phone numbers and recalled past preferences and delivery addresses also became popular with the larger operators. Many operators were increasingly influenced by the preferences of their customers who sought variations, leading to development of gourmet pizzas and in some instances, woodfired pizzas. In 1989, the market for home deliveries was consolidated with Franchise 1's acquisition of all of the Adelaide-based franchise sites. Without the market power and resources of Franchise 1, many of the pioneers of the Hobart market used existing friendships to embark upon joint ventures aimed at capturing a larger slice of the growing market.

In 1990, the Australia economy became dominated by recession. However, this downturn in general market conditions proved a bonus for the Pizza industry. A combination of pizza no longer being perceived as a luxury good and the downward pressure on pizza prices resulted in demand for pizza increasing during such hard times. While fewer families could afford to dine out at even moderately expensive restaurants, the price bundling of a family pizza meal complete with assorted accessories became increasingly popular. This occurred despite the introduction of other successful global franchise operations in related food categories around this time.

Perhaps the most contentious innovation was the conveyor belt oven. Introduced during the early 1990s, its impact is viewed differently by many restaurateurs. For many, the conveyor belt oven introduced increased efficiency. Employee burn rates decreased, and so too with burnt pizzas. They were cheaper to run in comparison to conventional pizza ovens, did not suffer temperature fluctuations from continual monitoring of pizzas, required fewer kitchen staff and enabled peak times to be managed better. For others though the conveyor pizza oven (initially around $20,000 compared to about $2,500–$4,000 for a traditional oven) introduced potential decreases in effectiveness and quality. Some argued that the simplicity of its operation encouraged the hiring of less skilled labour whose knowledge of the intricacies of dough lead to pizzas being merely toasted and not cooked. It would seem however that in skilled hands, the conveyor belt oven introduced efficiencies. Alternatively, in the hands of the unskilled, they represented a potentially ineffective means of making pizza. Whatever the perspective held, to the smaller operator, many of the potential efficiencies associated with conveyor belt ovens were unattainable due to the initial investment required to acquire one.

This factor was perhaps dependent upon the physical size of operations. For instance, if there was a separation between the staff that served customers who *dined in* from those who cooked, then the use of less skilled kitchen staff perhaps only impacted upon pizza quality. Whereas, in smaller operations, it is possible that the use of less skilled staff to cook pizza and serve customers may have put at risk attainment of the three success factors (i.e. great food, great service and great ambience) discussed earlier. As the industry emerged as a direct competitor to others sections of the restaurant market, these three factors became more important, enabling operators to compete on the basis of quality rather than price, thereby avoiding direct competition. The number of operators peaked at 48 in 1994, the same year that the next franchise chain operator, Franchise 2, would enter the market.

Period Three – Post-Franchise 2

Franchise 2 entered the market, introducing a *fastest gun in the west* approach to pricing and promoting pizza. Franchise 2 appeared more intent on capturing market share than on promoting the industry as a whole. This view of their intentions was commonly held by independent shop owners and was largely based on the perception they were more interested in selling franchises than pizzas. The pricing-led strategies of Franchise 2 appear to have had a very significant impact on independent Pizza operators. During the five years prior to Franchise 2's entry (1989 to 1993), the number of firms in the industry grew by 47 percent; this despite the presence of the recession, and the introduction of other significant franchise-based competitors in related food categories. During the five years after Franchise 2's entry (1995 to 1999), the Pizza industry experienced a decline of 46.5 percent, despite the recession having increased profitability from the adoption of various efficiency-related technologies.

The predatory behaviour of Franchise 2 was seen by most as the reason for this decline. Firms that were unable to maintain prerequisite levels of great food, service, and ambience were in the direct line of fire. Market forces that had assisted them previously, now worked against them. It would seem that while many firms had adapted to their operating environments through a quality baseline, other firms unable to deliver (or develop in time) these three success factors were susceptible to competing upon a price dependent baseline.

There was clear evidence that new Pizza entrants had entered the market and succeeded with an approach based on quality. Two new restaurants in particular provide such evidence. Both are positioned for high-quality food, encourage bring-your-own and have extensive wine lists designed to cater to their middle/upper class target markets. Both avoid trying to compete for the price-conscious customer. They rely upon word of mouth to stimulate demand. They prefer to seek other more profitable opportunities within their marketplace. For example, catering to organizations, thereby maximizing the output of their physical assets. It would seem that while pizza has been elevated from a meal fit for the court jester to one fit for royalty, both customer types still exist.

While the franchise operators could satisfy the court jester's needs, it takes an entirely different type of business model to compete within the quality end of the market. The middle ground would appear to be the most dangerous path travelled. If the time period that covers the two years prior to and after Franchise 2's entry (1992 to 1996) is considered, survival was clearly a tough assignment for new entrants. Of the 23 new entrants during this period, only five survived to 2005. The survivors are all linked by previous industry experience, good locations and a focus on quality. Other seasoned operators sold pizza by the slice, thereby avoiding head-to-head competition with other price-based competitors. Quality and innovation were still the drivers of success.

The last significant change in the external environment was the introduction of a Goods and Service Tax (GST) in 2000 by the Australian Federal Government. It is unclear to what degree this caused problems to existing operators given that well-established operators have continued through its introduction until the present. For the franchised operators, their market segments are contested through continual product innovation and pricing strategies. At the other end of the market, the passionate pursuit of quality, service and ambience remain the success factors. The middle ground still remains for wily operators to traverse; getting it right in the middle is not as easy as it was when the market was booming in the late 70s and 80s. Those that have survived the past 30 years in this industry have done so through an ability to exploit their own strengths and through the adoption of different organizational forms and production and marketing processes.

Notable Issues

Several issues arise from this discussion of the Hobart Pizza market. It seems obvious that cooperative actions on the part of the independent Pizza firms aided their long-term survival. However, survival also appears to have been influenced by external factors, rather than from factors directly related to the actors themselves. A distinct lack of competitive relations between the independent firms was very obvious until such time that home delivery of pizza changed the operating boundaries of most firms. In fact, not even the arrival of Franchise 1 could alter this level of cooperative interaction. Post home delivery, the arrival of Franchise 3 intensified the eventual (positive and negative) influence the franchised firms had on selection pressures within the market, an influence that was largely determined by the marketplace positioning of the independent firms. Perhaps of most interest was the observation that the *environment* as observed was highly fragmented and was experienced in distinctly different ways by apparently similar types of independent firms. Let us consider these emergent issues in more detail.

The nature of environmental pressures appears to have not occurred with any sense of uniformity within and across the life course of the industry. The behaviour of Franchise 1 actually even benefited many firms throughout the industry's life course (and could ultimately have been detrimental to their own marketplace positioning). For example, the advertising practises of Franchise 1 were both very effective and relatively easy for even small independent Pizza firms to emulate. It would seem that certain types of (normal) firm-level behaviour have altered the nature and process of environmental selection, an observation that goes beyond assuming adaptation by individual firms to observable environmental forces. Or, specific firms have survived due to the nature of their adaptive responses to a changing environment. For example, despite the relatively small geographical area conversely of the Hobart Pizza market, observable differences in the nature of environmental pressures were evident. The three metropolitan areas, the cities of Hobart, Glenorchy and Bellerive are within 10km of each other. In between the metropolitan areas are many suburban areas, and beyond each of them are a number of smaller regional areas.

In Period 1, environmental conditions provided favourable conditions for firms closer to the metropolitan areas, whilst not favouring firms in any of the outlying regional areas. There is nothing unusual about such a situation, given the lack of awareness of pizza during this time. However, environmental pressures and their intensity across the next two periods did not occur in any predicable manner. After the arrival of Franchise 1, regional pizzerias were increasingly favoured. The survival of regional Pizza shops after the entrance of Franchise 3 is quite obvious. Many operators claimed that the increased advertising used by the franchised firms acted as a driver of demand into all areas of the Hobart market. It would appear that in attempting to gain increased market share of their metropolitan areas, the franchised firms actually increased the profitability and therefore survival of regional (and to a lesser degree, suburban) firms. What is apparent is that the nature of selection operating on firms has not occurred evenly across space, despite the relatively small area of the market. Overall, the location of firms has been most strongly related to survival and little evidence relates success to any particular type of firm, say specialist or generalist.

Franchise 1's Unintentional Altruistic Behaviour

A form of unintentional altruistic behaviour by Franchise 1 seems ultimately to have proved detrimental to their fitness. When Franchise 1 was the lone franchised firm in the market, the independent firms saw the presence of the former as positive. Their marketing activities not only increased demand, they were also relatively easy for the more entrepreneurial independents to imitate. However, on face value, it would seem that Franchise 1's behaviour painted them into a corner where the firm was neither sufficiently different nor similar to the independent firms. The arrival of Franchise 2 and then Franchise 3 appears to have resulted in Franchise 1 having to defend a market position that it had never really claimed as its own. As a consequence, they were neither able to be positioned at the quality end of the market or as the kings of cheap pizza. Several of the Franchise 1 restaurant style stores and take-away sites were closed. The remaining presence of Franchise 1 in the Hobart market then focused on the take-away segment, complete with a new corporate market image. It would seem that despite the dominance of Franchise 1 prior to Franchise 3's entrance, the firm had failed to own any specific market segment through its (most likely unintentional) willingness to share the Hobart market with the independents.

Firm Behaviour Changing the Nature of Environmental Pressure

As would be expected, there is evidence of the process of selection and adaptation related to market change. But, perhaps the most interesting feature of the Hobart Pizza industry would appear to be the influence upon selective pressure across time and space by individual firms. In the first instance, it would appear that Franchise 1's marketing activities proved beneficial to virtually all incumbent and future entrants. Potential selection pressures related to assumed increased competition, rapid market change, technological change and economic downturn appear not to have materialized by the ability of Franchise 1 to increase the primary demand for pizza. The arrival of Franchise 3 appears to be associated with demand no longer being transferred (and therefore increased selection pressure) to those specialist (price-focused) firms operating in the metropolitan area of the environment. In strongly positioning itself as the dominant take-away Pizza operator it would seem that Franchise 3 sharpened consumer perception with respect to the now apparent quality–price dichotomy.

In doing so, Franchise 3 appears to have partially reversed Franchise 1's positive influence within the overall market. After their arrival, the occurrence of demand being transferred was clearly a temporary phenomenon for those specialist (price-focused) metropolitan firms. A weakened or *quality dependent* benefit was evident for some suburban firms, and a *blanket* benefit for all regional operators persisted. Interestingly, for those metropolitan and suburban independents positioned more as generalist (quality-focused) providers, the arrival of Franchise 3 and Franchise 4 appears typically not to be associated with any negative outcomes. These operators appear to be favoured solely by consumer appreciation of quality food, service and ambience.

Emergent Themes

Several important themes can now be considered in more detail. In the Hobart Pizza industry, an apparent process of *Transferred Demand* beneficial to the survival of independent Pizza firms was clearly observed. The presence of this phenomenon has been proposed to relate to independent Pizza operations in: 1) a positive way during the early to mid part of the markets' development, and 2) in a positive/negative way during the latter part of the market's development dependent upon the form of resource and/or space usage. The degree of landscape fragmentation with the smaller and/or larger populated areas that may remain stable or experience seasonal fluctuations may also impact on the presence and influence of the proposed process of *Transferred Demand*. The role of strategic adaptation to environmental change does not appear to be as strong a factor in firm survival as does the pre-existing propensity towards quality and/or occupation of relatively uncontested market space. That said, it would seem that during the mid period of the industry many pioneers developed an additional presence in regional locations that have remained viable to this day. However, little evidence has been found as yet to suggest any specific strategic foresight accompanied such action.

The franchise operators appear to have impacted their local environments, both stimulating demand and restricting the availability of resources through direct competition. The franchised operators have, through their day-to-day activities, dramatically changed the environment experienced by both themselves and the independent operators. They have also altered their surrounding external environment and that of independent operators located beyond their operational concern, with the franchise operators seemingly unaware of the largely positive impact on independent firms. Certain types of *normal* behaviour related to the development: of 1) the individual franchiser's presence, and 2) the market, produce different (unintended) survival outcomes for the independent Pizza operators. Further, an inherent disposition towards quality seems to provide one type of survival buffer, as does operating in an isolated landscape where relatively stable consumer preferences are potentially influenced by television advertising.

To summarize, the preliminary process of investigating the development of the Hobart Pizza industry has revealed the presence of significant environmental heterogeneity. Further, this heterogeneity is influenced (and therefore experienced) by the Pizza firms themselves across both time and space. Also, the nature of competition in the industries was as varied as the heterogeneity associated with their operating environments. It would seem that competition within each (metropolitan, suburban or regional) area ranged from extreme, to weak, to non-existent, but was seldom the dominant influence in the environment of Pizza firms. In addition to the context of time and space, other factors such as customer type and opening hours have contributed to the nature (or lack) of competition and overall survival in the industries.

The nature of environmental selection processes has been increasingly influenced, both positively and negatively, by the seemingly normal operating practices of the franchised firms. Practices that, regardless of their intentionality appear to have resulted in the demand for pizza being indiscriminately transferred to independent Pizza firms that they neither compete directly with, or which are located within their zones of operation.

As such, the relationship between firm survival and other obvious factors (e.g. advertising, exposure to competition, and localized economic challenges) appear to be mediated by the presence of an invisible force or an unappreciated influence.

Conceiving Components and Boundaries

At this point, it would seem perfectly reasonable to suggest that a model of (independent) firm survival in the Hobart Pizza market must incorporate an invisible force, or generative mechanism, that has the capacity to act in such a way as to alter the normal impact of economic challenges and environmental selection. The model's operation would also need to relate to different environmental conditions that vary considerably across small geographic distances. The capacity of any individual firm to alter their operating environment so as to increase or decrease the magnitude of the assumed invisible force must also be accounted for to ensure the model can adequately explain differential survival outcomes. Let us consider what has emerged from the forgoing discussion.

Firstly, it would seem that a critical factor to emerge from the above discussion is the frequency of *non-harmful relations* occurring alongside apparent increased independent firm survival. Despite the obvious market power of the franchised operators, under a range of different conditions, independent and franchised firms *co-exist* in a manner that is seemingly benign to the franchised firms, yet beneficial to the many independent firms.

Secondly, despite the relatively small size of the industry investigated, a patchwork of *different environmental factors* was clearly observed. Firms within just a few kilometres of each other experienced very different operating conditions. Clearly, the flow of resources and exposure to selection pressures was not equally distributed across the areas investigated.

Thirdly, there is little doubt that the franchised firms have *changed the environment* experienced by independent firms in a variety of positive and negative ways. Put simply, the flow of vital resources (i.e. consumer spending) has been increased by the normal development of the various franchised operations. An additional consequence of this increase in demand has been the increased presence of both competitive and non-competitive relations determined by marketplace positioning and/or location.

Lastly, it would seem of critical importance to this discussion that the presence of an *invisible force* is factored into future explanations of firm survival. Many industry participants described the way in which the advertising of the franchised firms positively influencing localized demand for pizza. In summary, this section has identified several factors believed to comprise the foundational elements of a model of *Transferred Demand*, defined (in the context of a *preliminary* research proposition, vis-à-vis this study) at this point as: *Transferred Demand is a force capable of altering the local environment of independent Pizza firms, potentially enhancing survival, and its influence is determined by the interaction between franchised and local independent firms and elements of the environment they share across time and space.*

BUILDING A MODEL OF *TRANSFERRED DEMAND*

The initial aims of this section are two-fold. Firstly, to identify, interpret and redescribe the components (of the model) identified in the previous section. Secondly, various theoretical frameworks and/or interpretations will be used to provide new insights into the proposed notion of *Transferred Demand*. The initial starting point will centre on the following (previously discussed) themes, or components: 1) the presence of harmful (i.e. competitive) and non-harmful relations; 2) environmental heterogeneity as it relates to differential resource availability and/or selective pressures; 3) the capacity of firms to alter the environment in both negative and positive ways; 4) the presence of an invisible force from which energy transfer is possible; and 5) consideration of past studies of firm survival in the restaurant and fast food industries. Along the way, several postulates will be developed for the purpose of identifying specific areas of empirical investigation that are aligned to the proposed presence of *Transferred Demand*.

Postulate Development

At the heart of the approach undertaken here is a realization that 'scientifically significant generality does not lie on the face of the world, but in the hidden essence of things' (Bhaskar, 1979: 227). To unearth this hidden essence, a process of theoretical redescription (Danermark et al. 2002: 77) is employed to consider the transfactual conditions at play in this research; or 'the more or less universal preconditions for an object to be what it is'. So the components noted above form a starting point, and the aim of this process is to identify from the literature support for the *preliminary* research proposition and to develop a series of related postulates through which to subject the model of *Transferred Demand* to empirical scrutiny.

The nature of the research task (i.e. investigating the possible presence of a generative mechanism that is presumed to have directly influenced firm survival) is challenging. In essence, this study attempts to develop a plausible and valid explanation of past events that relate to the operation (and/or suppression) of a generative mechanism that is not directly observable by the researcher but assumed to positively influence firm survival. Mahoney (2003) argues that given that the explanation to be developed relates to an outcome that has already occurred (and therefore cannot be tested); the challenge is to develop a set of testable postulates that can tease out the presence of (unobservable) generative mechanisms.

As will be explained in more detail shortly, an epistemology drawn from the realist paradigm (Bhaskar, 1975) has been used. This is in line with my ontological position that the world 'consists of abstract things that are born of people's minds but exist independently of any one person' (Healy and Perry, 2000: 120). Therefore, it is not my perceptions that are the explicit focus of the research, but rather the need to access a reality that lay beyond my perceptions (Stake, 1995). This is important given the primary research objective of furthering an account of generative mechanisms that allows for the ascribing of (causal) power or potentiality under a given set of contingent conditions. Especially when it is accepted that generative mechanisms 'may either be dormant for a while or they may be counteracted by opposing mechanisms and lead to no events' (Tsoukas, 1989: 553).

The following section will enable the reader to contemplate the nature of the *transfactual conditions* that could relate to the proposed process of *Transferred Demand*. In doing so, the proposed limitations of the extant organizational studies literature will be revealed and new theoretical perspectives from other ecological bases introduced. The first major limitation within the domain of the organizational studies literature relates to Aldrich's (1999) framework of relations between organizational populations. It will be argued that this framework does not allow adequate evaluation of harmful and non-harmful relations between firms and/or in this situation, within cryptic firm complexes.

HARMFUL AND NON-HARMFUL RELATIONS

Firms in the Hobart Pizza industry experienced an apparent lack of competition throughout much of their industry's history. Competition was observed as it related to the proximity of similar types of firms attempting to acquire similar resources. Overall, it appeared that few firms throughout the industry's history shared both location and the simultaneous pursuit of similar resources. Thus, it appeared that non-competitive forms in interaction between the firms were more commonplace. Within the context of studies of the firm, let us first consider how the term *competition* is commonly used.

Hunt (2000: 135) argues that 'competition is the struggle among firms for comparative advantage in resources that will yield marketplace positions of competitive advantage for some market segment(s) and, thereby, superior performance'. Like many organizational theorists, his notion of competition is viewed as a selection process. For Metcalf (1998), the issue relates to process- or product-based competition, and to a lesser degree pricing competition. Frequently in the organizational studies literature, an ecological perspective is invoked when defining competition. Barnett and Amburgey (1990: 80) associate competition with any attempts by any entity to survive. They argue that despite larger firms having potential scale advantages, ultimately it is a process that occurs when 'two parties vie for the sanction of a third'. However, they note the potential disconnect between large firms and other firms due to environmental heterogeneity. Along these lines, Hannan and Freeman (1986) note five factors (i.e. technology, the nature of transaction costs, fixed social networks, association memberships and institutional constraints) that isolate the availability of vital resources to all firms, thereby providing the means to account for the boundaries that separate firm forms.

For McKelvey (1982) competition is a form of stimuli directly connected to the environment that shape voluntary (and non-voluntary) business decisions that impact future survival. Alternatively, it is also suggested that in times of resource abundance little competition (or selection) may occur (Perrow, 1986). This latter view is more in line with the influential work of Hawley (1950). Perrow, citing Hawley's work, notes the importance of social and political forces (rather than economic) that account for functional interdependencies through which symbiotic relationships between community members buffer firms from environmental competition.

However, Hawley was clear in his concern that 'the significance of competition is often emphasized to the exclusion of the mutual support like organisms ... [in this context, firms] ... render one another' (Hawley, 1950: 40). Despite his even handling of competitive and mutualistic relations, it would seem that the original contribution of Hawley, which included specific reference to Kropotkin's (1902) theory of mutual aid, has not been consistently applied in shaping the role and relative importance of all the variables that influence firms (and not exclusively competition) in the organizational studies literature. Confusion over the meaning of the term commensalism may well be at the heart of this problem. To explore this important issue, there is a need to reconnect current important works (Aldrich, 1999) to the ideas of Hawley and to their antecedents.

Commensalism as a Descriptor of Competitive Relations

Within the organizational studies literature, commensalism is a descriptor for a *range of competitive relations* (see Aldrich, 1999). Alternatively, in every other domain of the broader ecological literature, it is clear that the term commensalism is used to account for *one discrete type of relation* in which one entity benefits and the other remains unharmed (see van Beneden, 1869). The specific reasons for such apparent misuse of this significant ecological concept by sociologists has been explained earlier in this book. Hawley's particular use of the term commensalism seems to be the source of the problem, and this legacy, unchallenged by subsequent contributors, confers an inability to account for the actual nature of harmful and non-harmful relations occurring between entities in an ecological consistent manner. For Hawley, 'the most elementary and yet salient expression of commensalism in nature is competition' (1950: 39). Within the domain of organizational studies the assumption that commensalism is a form of competitive relation continues unchallenged. So a sociological interpretation based on translation mistakes continues to deny organizational theorists the correct tools to investigate harmful and non-harmful relations between firms. The solution to this problem would seem to be a return to the original formulation of coaction theory proposed by Haskell (1949), which after slight modification by Burkholder (1952) has been used in standard ecological textbooks ever since Odum's (1959) classic text.

Table 5.1 Commensalism as a non-harmful coaction

	0		Indicates no significant interaction		
	+		Indicates growth, survival, or other population attribute benefited		
	–		Indicates population growth or other attribute inhibited		

Haskell (1949)			**Burkholder** (1952)			General Nature of Interaction
	Species			Species		
Interaction	1	2	Interaction	1	2	
1. Neutrality	0	0	1. Neutralism	0	0	Neither population affects the other
2. Synnecrosis	–	–	2. Competition	–	–	Direct inhibition of each species by the other
			3. Competition	–	–	Indirect inhibition when common resource is in short supply
3. Allotrophy	0	+				Feeding the other
4. Amensalism	–	0	4. Amensalism	–	0	Population 1 inhibited, 2 not affected
5. Parasitism	+	–	5. Parasitism	+	–	Population 1, the parasite, generally smaller than 2, the host
6. Predation*	–	+	6. Predation	+	–	Population 1, the predator, generally larger than 2, the prey
7. Commensalism	+	0	7. Commensalism	+	0	Population 1 benefits while 2, the host, is not affected
			8. Photocooperation	+	+	Interaction favorable to both (but not obligatory)
8. Symbiosis	+	+	9. Mutualism	+	+	Interaction favorable to both (and obligatory)
9. Allolimy	0	–				Starving the other

Note: * Haskell's Predation is the same, he is just attributing the role of predator to species 1.

From Haskell's original theory of coaction we can reconnect the broader organizational studies literature to the original meaning of commensalism and all other forms of coaction. The value of Haskell's coaction theory is that we can now account for all forms of coaction in a manner consistent with ecological theory, which typically relate to 'the study of the interrelationships among organisms and between organisms and between them and all aspects ... of their environment' (Attiwill and Wilson, 2003: 570). This is critical given Haskell's assertion that the major properties of any society vary with coaction.

Haskell's theory of coaction sought to separate diversely powerful individuals into the *weak* and the *strong*. Essentially, Haskell (1949: 46) observed that weak and strong 'classes can only have nine, and only nine, qualitatively different [coaction] relations toward each other'. In Table 5.1, the initial classification scheme of Haskell and its later adaptation by Burkholder (1952) are presented alongside each other. Despite some changes, Burkholder abides by Haskell's usage and meaning of the term commensalism, in that it represents coactions in which the weak benefit and the strong are unaffected.

Contrast this position with Aldrich's (1999) position in which commensalism accounts for six coactions (of eight possible ones): 1) –/– full competition; 2) –/0 partial competition; 3) +/– predatory competition; 4) 0/0 neutrality; 5) +/0 partial mutualism; and 6) +/+ full mutualism. When commensalism is allowed to account for all coactions other than those that are symbiotic (see Rao, 2002), then the opportunity to understand and investigate how firms operate is decreased through the inability to correctly account for relations that are predator, parasitic, mutualistic or based on commensalism. It would seem that a return to Haskell's (1949) nine qualitatively different coactions would resolve this issue.

The correct assumption that any such interaction is reducible to observable pairs of species is another problem in ecology (Tilman, 1987). Bender, Case and Gilpin (1984: 11) argue that 'in practice, no community ecologist can measure the density of every potentially interacting species in a community, yet once some species are neglected and others are lumped in composite categories, there is a real danger that indirect effects can confuse and confound the interpretation of the results'. This reasoning perhaps explains the difficulty of researchers to reproduce the past findings of Freeman and Hannan (1983), who reduced diverse types of firms to two arbitrary types, specialists and generalists. This issue of premature aggregation leads to consideration of another concept directly related to the issue of competition, that of resource partitioning. Again issues of consistency of usage vis-à-vis organizational studies and the broader ecological literature emerge.

Resource Partitioning – A New or Old Term?

In developing his resource partitioning theory, Carroll (1984) acknowledges organizational ecology as an intellectual descendant of Hawley's (1950, 1968) human ecology. Not surprisingly, Carroll (1985: 1278) relates his notion of resource portioning to Hawley's description of competitive social processes claiming they both 'predict a shift from competitive to symbiotic relations between organizational forms'. Carroll's model is widely interpreted (e.g. Baum and Amburgey, 2002; 312) as predicting 'that increasing market concentration increases the failure rate of generalists and lowers the failure rate of specialists'. Evidence arising from the Hobart Pizza industry suggests a process similar to Carroll's resource partitioning, but with generalists favoured as market concentration occurs. A review of all literature related to the term resource partitioning again reveals an apparent disconnect between its usage in the natural and social sciences.

The term resource partitioning was originally coined by Schoener (1968) and further articulated in his later works, most notably in his 1974 classic paper titled *Resource Partitioning in Ecological Communities*. While the idea of resource partitioning 'is intuitively understood, it is not necessarily straightforward to decide what does and does not qualify as a case of resource partitioning ... at one extreme, ... [resource] ... partitioning may be defined as any difference in the resource utilization among species' (Tokeshi, 1999: 162). It is commonly defined as 'the differential use by organisms of resources' (Begon, Harper and Townsend, 1996: 967). Pianka (1969) produced a major work that identified three specific areas of resource partitioning; habitat, food and time. Clearly food (i.e. revenue, is the primary resource firms require) and time feature in the observations of the Hobart Pizza industry discussed previously, as does place (or habitat).

However, the assumption by Carroll (1984) that competition must drive the process is inconsistent with the development of resource partitioning in the natural sciences where other forms of coaction are taken into account. The above discussion suggests a different trajectory of thinking that has accompanied the development of the concept in organizational studies literature than within the broader ecological literature. When considering the presence of competition, we must do better than simply assuming competition is the primary organizing mechanism. For example, Hannan and Carroll (1992: 30) in acknowledging the difficulty of observing competition within populations of firms, argue that increasing a focus on intra-specific competition simplifies the problem 'because one can safely assume that members of the same population have very nearly the same fundamental niche'.

Contrast that with Milne's (1961: 60) definition of competition in an ecological setting, 'competition is the endeavour of two (or more) animals to gain the same particular thing, or to gain the measure each wants from the supply of a thing when that supply is not sufficient for both (or all)'. A complete focus on the type of coaction, on the type of resource usage, time of consumption, specific location and mechanism of interaction is missing from current notions of competition within the organizational studies literature. Carroll's (1985) strict notion of resource partitioning does not lend itself to explaining the observations of firm behaviour in the Hobart Pizza industry. Further, there where coactions observed that fall neatly under the natural science notion of commensalism, but are difficult to relate to the social science interpretation. It is worth noting that Brown and Wilson's (1956) theory of character displacement also has not been used in the social sciences to explain how firms adopt or reject particular forms of organization to avoid competition. This is despite its centrality in the further developing resource partitioning in the natural sciences. Another concept common within the broader ecological literature, but rarely considered in the organizational studies literature, is that of facilitation.

Facilitation

Building on the previous consideration of non-harmful (or positive) relations, the concept of facilitation has the potential to explain the events observed in the Hobart Pizza industry. Only in recent times has serious consideration (see Schoener, 1982) been given to the role of positive coactions in shaping community outcomes in ecology. Such interest in the broader ecological literature seems not to have spilled over into the organizational studies literature. However, perhaps this is not surprising, given Bruno, Stachowicz and Bertness's (2003: 119) contention that 'it is time to bring ecological theory up to date by including facilitation. This process will not be painless because it will fundamentally change many basic predictions and will challenge some of our most cherished paradigms. But, ultimately, revising ecological theory will lead to a more accurate and inclusive understanding of natural communities'. In reality, if ecologists cannot agree on such matters, perhaps it is optimistic to expect such new ideas to have already crossed over into the social sciences.

Nevertheless, Rathcke (1983: 306) uses the term 'facilitation to connote positive interactions due to resource sharing within a' cryptic firm complex. Rathcke, an ecologist studying plant-pollinator systems, notes that 'both plants and pollinators act as resource *users* as well as *resources*', as do restaurants/fast food outlets and consumers. Consistent with Rathcke, within this book Pizza restaurants will be considered to be *users*. The idea of facilitation allows us to ask: do overt competitive behaviours associated with attempting to achieve resource ownership occur between and within Pizza operators in the Hobart Pizza industry? The observations previously stated would suggest no. Given the discrete nature of environments that the individual firms experienced, the notion that survival outcomes may be explained without reference to assumed competition seems to have merit.

Further, such thinking does not dismiss the possibility of many different types of coactions simultaneously occurring that may generate harmful relations. Nevertheless, the net effect (or positive coactions > negative coactions) of all coactions can result in facilitation (Holzapfel and Mahall, 1999). Interestingly, plant ecologist Grime (1979) also notes that in ecosystems with low productivity, competition may be less intense, giving rise to the opportunity for facilitative relations to occur. Given the discreet nature of the areas observed in the Hobart Pizza industry, such an idea may have merit. Figure 5.1 illustrates an adaptation of Rathcke's (1983) model to suit the events observed in the Hobart Pizza industry.

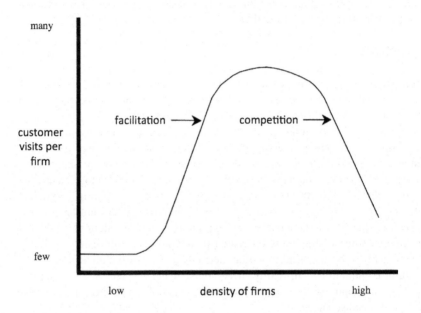

Figure 5.1   A model of facilitation

The density–visitation curve illustrated in Figure 5.1 indicates visitation by customers as the density of firms increase. Interactions are proposed to be facilitative to the left of the maximum point on the visitation axis and competitive to the right as the density of firms increase. Given the lack of observed competitive relations in the Pizza industry, this model of facilitation potentially offers a new means of considering how non-harmful (facilitative) relations may be vital to ensuring the on-going survival of independent Pizza firms. The adaptation of Rathcke's (1983) model still accommodates a focus on a cryptic firm complex, rather than a single population. This is seen as important given the need to examine the assumed survival advantage of independent Pizza firms empirically against other food providers in the broader take-away/restaurant industry.

Summary and Postulate Development

Whilst successful theories have been developed – for example Porter's Five Forces (Porter, 1980; 1985; 1990) – without forensically defining what *is* competition or the environment, the challenge nevertheless remains here to clearly and succinctly describe the nature of harmful and non-harmful relations occurring between firms. This section has highlighted the lack of adequate frameworks within the organizational studies literature as contrasted with the existence of developed theories that might assist in the ecological literature.

The next stage of the research process relates to the development of postulates. As previously noted, this research investigates events that have previously occurred, and is focused on unobservable entities which are also likely to be related to these past events. Mahoney (2003) argues for the use of a particular case study method to develop an outcomes-based explanation, as illustrated in Figure 5.2.

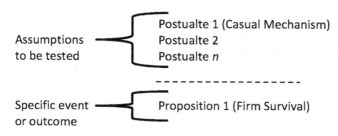

Figure 5.2   The outcomes-based explanation

Rather than the traditional testing of a research proposition, we are required to investigate a series of postulates empirically; postulates that have been developed to capture the various dimensions of the hypothesized explanation of the outcome. Where empirical support is gained for the postulates, confidence in the logic of the research proposition is increased. The primary reason Mahoney (2003) argues for this type of outcomes-based approach is that the events under investigation have already occurred and therefore cannot be tested in the empirical domain (Bhaskar, 1975).

The development of the following postulates is aimed at a more precise determination of the nature of harmful and non-harmful relations vis-à-vis independent firms operating in the Pizza industry. The use of Haskell's coaction theory enables us to move beyond assumptions of competition as the predominant organizing process related to firm survival. Coaction theory allows us to consider a range of positive, negative and neutral relations that may occur due to resource partitioning determined by accounting for the type of resources pursued (the customer type), time of consumption (the firm's opening hours) and the specific location of each firm. To the extent that non-harmful relations are assumed to occur, we may also use the concept of facilitation to explain how non-harmful relations may best contribute an explanation of firm survival, therefore:

Postulate 1: *The degree of competition experienced by independent firms in the Pizza industry will be explainable by accounting for the type of resource, time of consumption, and specific location vis-à-vis each firm.*

A key issue that most determines the presence of facilitation is the willingness of firms in a cryptic firm complex to share the specific resource most required to determine survival. From the perspective of this study, the pollinator would be the customer. Therefore, identifying differences in the willingness to share customers rather than own customers should help to determine variances in competitive relations.

Postulate 2: *The degree of competition experienced by independent firms in the Pizza industry can be inferred from the demonstrated endeavour of individual firms to acquire customers.*

Therefore, and following on from the logic of Postulate 2:

Postulate 3: *A lack of competitive behaviours associated with attempting to achieve resource ownership may indicate the presence of facilitative interactions.*

ENVIRONMENTAL HETEROGENEITY

Having accounted for harmful and non-harmful relations as a component within the proposed model of *Transferred Demand*, the next section is focused on what constitutes environmental heterogeneity vis-à-vis differential resource availability and/or selective pressures. Again, a difficulty in applying current organizational theory leads to the necessity to again explore other domains for theory that can help to shine light on the transfactual conditions that may be associated with the proposed mechanism, *Transferred Demand*.

In Chapter 3, a detailed discussion of what constitutes the firm's operational external environments was presented. In this section we will briefly recap on the specific aspects of that discussion, as they are germane to the development of the postulates regarding our investigation of the environment. Drawing upon the ideas of Mason and Langenheim (1957) and Spomer (1973), the specific nature of the firm's operational environment and relationship, past, current and future to its external environment were discussed. The ideas of Brandon (1990) further help us to understand how to identify the operational environment. Brandon's notion of a selective and ecological dimensions, once included in the operational environment, enable both the process of selection and resource exchange to be considered at the level of the individual firm. As noted earlier, this approach does not ignore the complexity of firm–environment relations; it just reduces the complexity down to comprehensible phenomena. This enables specific postulates to be developed through which to tease out expected environmental complexity at the level of the firm. The aim, therefore, is the development of autecological knowledge of specific firms' operational relations, and this approach is designed to increase the precision and realism missing in other ecological studies of the firm (see Baum and Shipilov, 2006).

Summary and Postulate Development

Discerning the composition of the firms' environments would enable a greater understanding of the cryptic firm complex within which Pizza firms operate (vis-à-vis sources of available energy and/or threats), therefore allowing the factors that drive survival to be better understood. Indeed, environmental heterogeneity is a central assumption of the proposed model of *Transferred Demand*, therefore:

Postulate 4: *Identification of the operational and external environments relating to specific firms will inform the degree of harmful or non-harmful relations between independent firms in the Pizza industry.*

An important consequence arising from the above discussion is that it may not be possible to compare survival outcomes meaningfully across the entire *extent* of the study. This is simply because assumptions of differential survival must relate to firms pertaining to: 1) the same population, and 2) experiencing a common (or operational) environment. If, as was indicated in Chapter 3, firms are apparently experiencing different environs, it is a requirement of the researcher to determine how and to what extent they operate in individuated environments (Brandon, 1990), therefore:

Postulate 5: *The external environment experienced by one or more independent firms in the Pizza industry is an identifiable feature that can be reconciled to their existence.*

Likewise, the nature of available sustenance-related inputs are expected to vary from one town/area to another. Clearly, within the proposed model of *Transferred Demand* it is important to know to what extent the local environment has properties that offer growth/survival assistance (i.e. oligotrophic) or tends to be malignant (i.e. eutrophic) (Kangas and Risser, 1979), therefore:

Postulate 6: *The operational environment experienced by one or more independent firms across time and space in the Pizza industry has an ecological dimension that is an identifiable feature that can be reconciled to their survival/demise.*

Following immediately on from the above logic, it should also be possible to identify different forms of firm-level behaviour that indicate the presence of adverse selection pressures. From Chapter 3, it could be also expected that spatial and temporal factors will help to identify the presence of any such factors, therefore:

Postulate 7: *The operational environment experienced by one or more independent firms across time and space in the Pizza industry has a selective dimension that is an identifiable feature that can be reconciled to their survival/demise.*

The proposed model of *Transferred Demand* assumes the presence of complex and changing (harmful and non-harmful) relations between local firms. Where firms are located within proximity to a common local area, it is still quite likely that the process of resource partitioning and/or facilitation could prevent competitive relations, therefore:

Postulate 8: *Whilst a group of independent firms in the Pizza industry may exist in a local area, each individual firm may experience/create different operational environments.*

Having accounted for harmful and non-harmful relations and environmental heterogeneity as components within the proposed model of *Transferred Demand*, the next task is to address the issue of how firms might alter the environment in both negative and positive ways. Again, as discussed in Chapter 4, the extant organizational studies literature offers little to inform our understanding of this issue. However, two ecological theories provide much food for thought, providing a novel way of contemplating how firms may influence the environment in both positive and negative ways.

ENVIRONMENTAL MODIFICATION

There is a need to draw upon alternative theories to ensure the proposed generative mechanism is subject to empirical scrutiny. The most obvious theories being those of niche construction (Odling-Smee, Laland and Feldman, 2003) and ecosystem engineering (Jones, Lawton and Shachak, 1994). As explained in Chapter 4, both theories do not fit FA perfectly, due to the decreased emphasis upon the notion of niche in FA. Nevertheless, the underlying idea that firms can modify aspects of their operational and perhaps even their external environments in both negative and positive ways is accepted. Reference will be made to *environmental modification* when employing these ideas within FA. The consequence of enrolling these ideas is that it is also accepted that other firms may deliberately or unknowingly influence the operational relations other firms hold with their environments.

Summary and Postulate Development

To recap, there are differing views within the current organizational studies literature as to whether firms are capable of altering their environments, and if so, to what extent. Such differences in opinion are not assisted by the paucity of empirical studies addressing this fundamental issue. The recent development of niche construction and ecosystem engineering theories offer a new window through which to consider *how* and under *what* conditions firms may alter their environments, and those of other firms. Drawing upon the niche construction and ecosystem engineering theories from biology and ecology provides the means to address the possible causal mechanism assumed to alter the transfactual conditions associated with the proposed model of *Transferred Demand*, therefore:

Postulate 9: *The natural development of franchised Pizza firms in the Pizza industry will significantly alter the nature of the operational environments experienced by other associated firms.*

Evidence of environmental modification should also be reconcilable to the differential survival outcomes experienced by local independent Pizza firms (relative to all other similar types of firms), therefore:

Postulate 10: *Evidence of environmental modification in the Pizza industry should highlight which specific firms have (and have not) benefited due to change in their respective operational environments.*

A basic premise of environmental modification is that of ecological inheritance. Evidence of this process should highlight the presence of favourable local environments within which certain firms can more safely commence operations vis-à-vis other similar firms, therefore:

Postulate 11: *Evidence of environmental modification in the Pizza industry may indicate the possibility that certain types of firms should inherit a survival advantage relative to other types of firms.*

Having accounted for harmful and non-harmful relations, environmental heterogeneity and specific mechanism of environmental influence as components within the proposed model of *Transferred Demand*, the next section considers the presence of an invisible force from which energy transfer is possible.

GENERATIVE MECHANISMS

> Generative mechanisms are (usually) unobservable processes, that realists believe are nevertheless real, at higher or lower levels of analysis that cause behavior at a given level of analysis and, thus, are the bases of scientific explanation. (McKelvey, 2002: 891)

McKelvey's (2002) definition highlights the nature of the ontological shadow cast over the concept of a *generative mechanism*. The inference drawn from observations of the Hobart Pizza industry was that a force (a process or mechanism), independent of the actions of most independent Pizza firms observed, was acting to favour certain Pizza firms under particular conditions. Bennett and George (2003) argue that generative mechanisms are ultimately unobservable social, physical, psychological processes that under specific conditions have the potential to transfer energy, information or matter to other entities. A major challenge in accepting the idea of what are generative mechanisms is accepting that while they may shape certain outcomes, they may also be shaped by other processes and/or outcomes. Either way, the 'exact course of events will depend on the relative strength of the different mechanisms at work' (Elster, 1998: 60–61). Therefore, it is considered paramount that specific research methods are employed to gain a careful appreciation of temporal and contextual factors that together form contingent (or transfactual) conditions under which generative mechanisms activate their tendencies to influence contingently related objects (Tsoukas, 1989).

Connecting the notion of *Transferred Demand* to the concept of a generative mechanism requires 'the construction of an explanation for ... some identified phenomenon ... [and] ... will involve the building of a model, utilizing such cognitive materials and operating under the control of something like a logic of analogy and metaphor, of a mechanism, which *if* it were to exist and act in the postulated way would account for the phenomenon in question' (Bhaskar, 1979: 15).   Bhaskar (1975: 56) also argues that such proposed mechanisms may indeed become established as real in the on-going activity of science. Importantly, from the perspective of critical realism, 'generative mechanisms of nature must exist and act independently of the conditions that allow men access to them'. Several postulates emerge from this section.

Summary and Postulate Development

The literature supports the notion that a mechanism can be assumed to exist through which energy transfer is plausible. The challenge for the researcher is to identify the specific conditions that relate to the presence (or operation) of the assumed mechanism. In this instance, it is assumed that the advertising of the franchised firms is directly related to the presence of any such energy transfer, therefore:

Postulate 12: *In Pizza markets featuring both franchised and independent firms, an invisible force capable of altering discrete operational environments is plausible, and its presence would be determined by the interaction of franchised and independent Pizza firms occurring across time and space.*

Further, there should be no such evidence of an invisible force prior to the entry of franchised Pizza firms into the markets under investigation, therefore:

Postulate 13: *The presence of an invisible force will have identifiable transfactual conditions that relate to its tendencies to positively influence independent Pizza firm survival.*

However, the assumed presence of environmental heterogeneity would be expected to interfere with (or suppress) the operation of any such invisible force across time and space, therefore:

Postulate 14: *The contingent conditions related to the tendencies of any such invisible force are explainable by understanding the variance occurring in the operational environments experienced by individual Pizza firms.*

Having accounted for harmful and non-harmful relations, environmental heterogeneity, specific mechanism of environmental influence, and the possibility of a generative mechanism as components of the proposed model of *Transferred Demand*, the next issue relates to past research focused upon firm survival in the restaurant and fast food industry.

RESTAURANT SURVIVAL

Over the past three decades there have been many studies examining firm survival within the restaurant and fast food industries. One of the first was Freeman and Hannan's (1983) investigation of specialist/generalist restaurant survival across 18 California cities. Their study challenged the previously held assumption that generalist firms would be favoured during times of environmental instability. However, the OE approach employed by Freeman and Hannan has been the subject of much academic debate (see Young, 1988; Zucker, 1989), especially as to the validity of the approach developed and employed. A specific limitation of the study was the assumption that environmental variation could be reduced solely to seasonal changes.

An investigation by O'Neil and Duker (1986) failed to find a positive relationship between marketing expenditure and firm survival. Instead, they found that the efficient use of marketing expenditure was more important than the total amount spent vis-à-vis survival. Inspired in part by Freeman and Hannan's OE approach, Muller and Inman (1994) devised a new approach to restaurant management that incorporated spatial analysis. Differentiating between restaurants located in hamlets, villages, towns, cities and a metropolis, they argued that distance and transportation are key factors related to restaurant survival. A related study by Shriber, Muller and Inman (1995) confirmed the importance of accounting for spatial variation when predicting restaurant performance outcomes. Indeed, rather than advocating the collapsing of various restaurant forms into two types (i.e. specialists and generalists), Muller and Woods (1994) proposed a typology of restaurant forms (i.e. quick service, moderate upscale, upscale and business dining), each with a distinctive set of related competencies required to achieve optimal performance.

The growing impact of franchised entrants in the restaurant and fast food industry was examined by Bates (1995). Across a relatively short time span (1984 to 1987), Bates found that despite higher levels of turnover, franchised firms during the study period were less profitable than independent firms due to higher upfront establishment costs and the increased likelihood of competing in overcrowded markets. English et al. (1996), drawing inspiration from Michael Porter's strategic planning model, also found an inverse relationship between the initial start-up investment and eventual success. However, they found that franchised restaurants held a survival advantage over independent restaurants. During this period, Muller (1997) noted the (somewhat obvious) food-service price distributions between the various types of firms operating in the restaurant and fast food industry, highlighting the lack of direct competition between many marketplace offerings.

The survival of Danish restaurants was also explored by Hjalager (1999), employing theoretical perspectives from OE. Like Muller and Inman (1994) before her, she placed specific emphasis upon spatial variation, accounting for metropolitan areas, large cities, towns, villages and rural areas. Her findings suggested lower levels of rural survival related to increased levels of rapid change in a relatively homogenous regional business environment. More recently, Kalnins and Mayer (2004) investigated the survival of Pizza restaurants in Texas. They found that local knowledge was more related to firm survival than distantly gained experience. Their findings argue for the increased consideration of the importance of local knowledge at lower levels of analysis (i.e. towns and villages). Finally, Parsa et al. (2005) used a mixed-method approach to develop a model of restaurant viability. Their model was derived from the identification of 12 elements of success and 21 elements of failure. Importantly, they could not pinpoint restaurant success or failure to any specific factor/s.

Summary and Postulate Development

Overall, the literature related to firm survival in the restaurant and fast food industry reveals some underlying trends. For example, the incorporation of spatial analysis, different theoretical perspectives and the use of various research method has failed to identify any common specific (or dominant) factors related to firm survival. Much of the past findings reported in the studies noted above are drawn from the identification of correlations of various independent variables with survival outcomes as a dependent variable. The Hobart Pizza study differs in that the focus is not upon the relationship between any predetermined number of independent variables and firm survival as a dependent variable. The focus is upon a generative mechanism (or an invisible force) that alters the probability of independent firm survival accounting for spatial and temporal heterogeneity, therefore:

Postulate 15: *The degree to which an invisible force capable of influencing independent firm survival in the Pizza industry will be directly related to (or explainable by an understanding of) the operational environments experienced by individual firms.*

Accordingly, evidence of resource partitioning and/or facilitation as a response by independent firms should form a central element of any explanation of *Transferred Demand*, therefore:

Postulate 16: *Differential independent firm survival in the Pizza industry will therefore be related to differences observed in firm type and location.*

Any alternative explanation should be comparable to existing explanations for comparison. The relationship between specialists and generalists is well accepted within the literature (vis-à-vis survival outcomes) and therefore serves as an appropriate accepted explanation against which to compare the findings of this study, therefore:

Postulate 17: *Collapsing firms into specialists and generalists will not give rise to as satisfactory explanation of the differential survival outcomes of similar types of firms operating in the restaurant and fast food cryptic firm complex in the North Yorkshire/East Riding region, as compared to that developed to explain the assumed presence of Transferred Demand.*

Throughout this section, the components of the proposed model of *Transferred Demand* have been discussed vis-à-vis the organizational studies literature and the broader ecological literature. This section has also highlighted several inconsistencies between the organizational studies literature and the broader ecological literature. The desirable development of FA should adhere to Hodgson's (2001) Principle of Consistency. As a result, this section has paid careful attention to the importation of several ideas that enable a fine-grained investigation of Pizza firms and the environments they experience and quite likely modify.

Throughout the interaction with the literature, 17 postulates emerged. As will be explained in the next section, the proposed generative mechanism (of *Transferred Demand*) is argued to be an unobservable process, hence the need to search for empirical support (or otherwise) for the related postulates. The degree to which the postulates are supported will provide confidence (or otherwise) for the following research proposition: *Transferred Demand is a force capable of positively altering operational environments, thereby enhancing survival, and its influence is determined by the interaction between franchised and independent Pizza firms and elements of the external environment they share across time and space*. The next section explains the nature of the research methodology used to submit the postulates to empirical scrutiny, and thus address the underlying research proposition.

BACK TO THE FIELD

As discussed previously, the main purpose of the study is to *confirm* or *disconfirm* the presence of an invisible force assumed to provide a survival advantage to independent local Pizza firms. Importantly, this study does not aim to test theory or directly extend past theory. Given the lack of fit between the researcher's observations of the Hobart Pizza industry and the theoretical solutions available to explain these observations (from within the organizational studies literature), this study seeks to propose a new model of firm survival. Therefore, a *specific epistemology* is required through which the researcher's observations and knowledge of the world can be used to develop a new explanation of firm survival while at the same time ensuring such cognitive contribution can be empirically confirmed or disconfirmed.

At present, few studies of firm survival attempt to account for *generative mechanisms* that might be responsible for firm survival outcomes, let alone account for the *contingent conditions* (Tsoukas, 1989) under which such mechanisms might operate and/or be suppressed. Given the explicit aims of this study, an epistemology that emphasizes theory development is required (Bhaskar, 1979; Wollin, 1995). The next section provides a brief overview of the research method used, but see Jones (2009) for a more comprehensive and complete explanation.

A Critical Realist Approach

The research *design* is modelled on Bhaskar's (1975) transcendental realism and utilizes the process of retroduction, not to be confused with the process of *retroduction* as described by Van De Ven and Poole (2002). Transcendental realism (Bhaskar, 1975) extends the past notion of Kant's transcendental idealism from what is imagined to empirical confirmation of what is real (Danermark et al. 2002). Transcendental realism holds that what we observe empirically (within the domain of the empirical) is produced by events (in the domain of the actual) that are in turn generated by mechanisms (in the domain of the real).

Table 5.2   Bhaskar's three overlapping domains of reality

	Domain of Real	Domain of Actual	Domain of Empirical
Mechanisms	✔		
Events	✔	✔	
Experiences	✔	✔	✔

Bhaskar proposed a stratified reality, illustrated in Table 5.2, in which knowledge of the empirical world is possible, but only imperfectly, because of our limited access to such reality. 'Whether a particular causal power is exercised, and whether it manifests itself in the actual and/or empirical domain depends on the ambient contingent conditions' (Tsoukas, 1989: 553). So the aim of the researcher is 'to develop real knowledge of the world by naming and describing the generative mechanisms that result in the events that may be observed' (Wollin, 1995: 80). Importantly, the knowledge while considered real is still held to be fallible. Realism holds that it may not be possible to observe every permutation relating to the generative mechanism. Therefore, the developed theory must account for the generative mechanism, the events caused under which contingent conditions and other mechanisms or conditions that may counteract or decrease the expected (or potential) influence of the focal mechanism under investigation.

Organizing the Process

To facilitate this endeavour, the process of retroduction is employed. Danermark et al. (2002: 96) noted that 'retroduction is about advancing from one thing (empirical observations or events) and arriving at something different (a conceptualization of transfactual conditions)'. The process of retroduction typically proceeds through six stages. First, prepare a description of the phenomenon making use of the actors' accounts and data from a variety of sources. This was achieved with reference to the events of the Hobart Pizza industry. Second, distinguish the various components, aspects or dimensions of the phenomenon and establish (tentative) boundaries to the components studies. This was achieved through the development of a research proposition that isolated focus upon non-harmful relations, environmental heterogeneity, environmental modification, the assumed presence of an invisible force and firm survival itself. Third, interpret and redescribe the different components applying contrasting theoretical frameworks and interpretations in order to provide new insights. This was achieved through engagement with different literature bases. Fourth, for each component, seek to identify basic, or transfactual conditions, including structures, causal powers and mechanisms, that make the phenomenon possible. This is partially achieved through the development of 17 postulates. Fifth, elaborate and estimate the explanatory power of the structures, causal powers and mechanisms that have been identified during stages three and four. This will be achieved through the collection of data from the North Yorkshire/East Riding area in the United Kingdom. Sixth, examine how the structures, causal powers and mechanisms manifest themselves in different conditions. This will be achieved through analysis of the data collected in the North Yorkshire/East Riding area.

The process of retroduction is used to allow the researcher to access a reality that is likely to not be directly obvious in the domain of the empirical reality. Thus, the process of transcendental realism naturally lends itself to a mixed-methods approach (see Creswell, 2003) enabling the events under investigation to be described and viewed from multiple perspectives. Unlike transcendental idealism where (conceptual) knowledge development is possible, Bhaskar's (1975) transcendental realism requires of the researcher to confirm (or disconfirm) the existence of the proposed mechanism in reality as well. That is, the postulated mechanism must be empirically confirmed/disconfirmed. In summary, transcendental realism requires the researcher to understand and account for the different levels of reality that exist in society and therefore confirm their presence using suitable research methods. It represents an approach that is in accord with the fundamental requirements of ecology given its capacity to enable the researcher to access the 'real life' (Clarke, 1967: 21) of the entities under investigation.

Case Selection

The North Yorkshire/East Riding case was chosen using the same logic as used in the Hobart Pizza industry. That is, a preliminary inspection of the Yellow Pages directories revealed that the food industry had undergone a similar transformation from no Pizza operators in the late 1960s to a boom throughout the 1980s and 1990s; that the first franchised operator arrived in the mid 1980s and the second in the early to mid 1990s; that the Yellow Pages data were available for a comparable length of time; and that the geographical features of the landscape included all the various features of the Hobart Pizza industry (i.e. metropolitan, suburban and regional towns) and the region was serviced by a local TV network. A key challenge in the second phase of the research was to collect sufficient data to also compare Pizza firm survival across all other restaurant types. In this way, any observed survival *advantage* for pizza could be compared to all other restaurant types.

Consistent with the methods used in Australia, the Yellow Pages data were collected and coded with the *event* of survival or non-survival as the dependent variable. A large number of independent variables were included to account for the diversity of sub-populations investigated and the nature of the spatial heterogeneity of the study region. In addition, regional statistics were obtained from the UK's Office for National Statistics that enabled detailed demographic, social and economic statistics across the entire region and for each individual town included in the study. Between 2006 and 2008, seven visits were made to the study region. During these visits, interviews with 9 pizzeria owners (or staff) were conducted. An extensive catalogue of photographic evidence of the location of each pizzeria was collected. Also, the operating hours and marketplace positioning of the majority of Pizza firms was determined. In excess of 35 informal interviews with local residents (for example, taxi drivers, students, hospitality workers, and other known and unknown persons) were conducted.

Data Collection and Analysis

In total, 2440 firms were identified for the period 1975 to 2004 across a total of 24 restaurant types (see Appendix 1). Further stratification of the data to 23 specific towns reduced the dataset size (see Appendix 2 for a summary of the characteristics of the data analysed at the different stages of this study). A common problem for researchers using Survival Analysis is to account for left and right censoring, or the presence of missing data (Jones and Rocke, 2002). From the data collected it is not possible to know when firms commenced prior to 1975. To overcome this issue (or left-censoring), the dataset was reduced to only those *new entrants* that commenced in 1976 or later (a reduction of 412 firms). Given that the study period ends in 2004, we also have the problem of right censoring. That is, we could not know if the survivors in 2004 continued to be survivors in 2005 and onwards. A check of the status of the 2004 survivors in the 2005 and 2006 Yellow Pages directories was made to reduce the possibility of overstating the degree of survivorship within the dataset. Of the 119 surviving Pizza firms in 2004 only three firms did not survive until 2006. Thus, in this study a concerted effort has been made to account for both left and right censoring.

Despite the fact that logistical regression is a commonly used statistical tool in many firm survival studies, the required stratification of the dataset prevented the use of such regression processes. The stratification process created many small sub-sets with insufficient cases to work with the large number of variables used within this study (see Morgan, Leech, Gloecker and Barrett, 2004). However, other statistical approaches were appropriate to use.

For example, *Canonical Discriminant Analysis* was used to build a quantitative model of town similarity based upon observable characteristics.

Two processes, new to firm survival studies (in the organizational studies literature) were developed in this study. The first was the adaptation of Pianka's (1973) Community Similarity Index to determine the qualitative similarity of the towns within this study. This index was created by using the same logic and calculation method used by Pianka; simply X/N, where X is the number of restaurant types common to two towns and N is the total number of sub-populations occurring in either; thus community similarity equals 1 when two towns are identical, and 0 when they share no restaurant types. The second new process was the development of an *Advertising Efficiency Index* to create adjusted *net* survival outcomes. That is, rather than only working with the *gross* survival outcomes produced by the life tables, a means of adjusting survival outcomes to account for differential advertising inputs was developed. Expressed as $S \times (1\text{-}DF^a)$, where S is the rate of survival generated from SPSS Survival Analysis, and DF^a is the *degree* and *frequency* of advertising observed. Also, simple correlations were used to gauge the nature of coactions occurring between restaurant types within and across towns and paired sample t-tests were used to compare resource availability between towns.

Methodological Soundness

In summary, the chosen method provided the researcher with access to various levels of ontological and ecological reality through which *new knowledge* about the assumed mechanism's tendencies are possible. Such new knowledge is possible through the combining of other discrete bodies of knowledge, for example, ecology, zoology and sociology in ways that introduce and/or generate *new approaches* and *methods*. Importantly, the process of retroduction provides the means for the researcher's observations of the Hobart Pizza industry to be creatively combined in a model building process from which to: 1) postulate a plausible generative mechanism, and then 2) determine if this mechanism is real (or imaginary) via empirical scrutiny.

To judge validity and reliability of qualitative research within the realism paradigm, Healy and Perry (2000) draw on the ontological, epistemological and methodological elements of the paradigm to propose six criteria. These are: ontological appropriateness, contingent validity, triangulation, methodological trustworthiness, analytic generalization and construct validity. The criteria have been strongly supported in the literature as appropriate for the realism paradigm (see Golafshani, 2003; Alam, 2005).

Chapter 7 addresses such issues and other likely issues for future uses of FA in an organizational studies context.

RESEARCH FINDINGS

This section presents a summary of the previously published findings (see Jones, 2009) for the 17 postulates discussed previously. This abbreviated discussion remains focused on each individual postulate ensuring continuity in terms of their development, empirical scrutiny and eventual discussion relative to the underlying research proposition. A summary of the findings for each postulate is now presented. The first set of postulates (1, 2 and 3) relate to the presence of harmful and non-harmful relations within the cryptic firm complex.

Postulate 1: *The degree of competition experienced by independent firms in the Pizza industry will be explainable by accounting for the type of resource, time of consumption, and specific location vis-à-vis each firm.*

Observational data from the town of Ripon is representative of the manner in which many Pizza firms avoid direct competition in the North Yorkshire/East Riding area. In Ripon, Firm A operates as a Pizza restaurant (positioned to couples) not delivering to homes, and not open for lunches. Alternatively, Firm B, although situated within a five-minute walk, and also a Pizza restaurant (positioned to families), opens for lunches later in the week, and delivers to home. Despite their close proximity, Firm A and Firm B seek a different resource, or customer type, at different times and at different locations (due to the provision of home delivery).

Another example is the relationship between the area's first franchised entrant (Franchise 1) and the next franchised entrant (Franchise 2). Franchise 1 is located downtown, serving lunch and early dinners in an affordable restaurant setting, but not providing home delivery. By contrast, Franchise 2 is located in the suburbs, not offering lunchtime service (except weekends) or restaurant service, only delivering or accommodating pick-up. Clearly they also do not compete head to head.

These examples are typical of the way in which Pizza firms organize their operations. They cater to different types of customers (price conscious, family oriented, business oriented, delivery oriented, etc.), in different locations and at different times. Informal interviews with various operators confirmed a lack of competitor focus regarding the operations of other local Pizza firms. Importantly, the Pizza firms did not market their operations to any of the other 22 towns investigated. Therefore, across the total number of

Pizza firms investigated, the actual possibility of interaction between shops was very low, and mainly restricted to the largest towns. In summary, there was sufficient evidence obtained from observational data and interviews to determine that local independent Pizza firms operating in the North Yorkshire/East Riding region experience very low levels of direct inter-firm competition from other Pizza firms.

Postulate 2: *The degree of competition experienced by independent firms in the Pizza industry can be inferred from the demonstrated endeavour of individual firms to acquire customers.*

Informal interviews and examination of past and current archival records suggest that a key difference between towns is the degree of advertising by Pizza firms to attract and retain customers. Pizza firms in smaller towns (for example Ripon, Stamford Bridge, Filey, Selby, Knaresborough, Withernsea and Easingwold) *connected* to the larger towns (for example York, Harrogate, Scarborough and Bridlington) tended to advertise more so as to maintain their individual presence. Whereas Pizza firms in *isolated* towns, located further away from larger towns (for example Goole, Thorne, Howden, Malton, Hornsea, Pickering, Market Weighton, Pickering, Pocklington, Helmsley and Kirkbymoorside) appeared less inclined to advertise.

Prior to the entry of Franchise 1 in the mid 1980s, Pizza firms, mainly found in large towns, and clearly as a new food type, required sufficient advertising to gain market awareness and acceptance. After Franchise 1 entered, less advertising was placed in the large towns, whilst it began to increase in the connected towns and continued to do so after the arrival of Franchise 2 in 1992. Conversely, the level of advertising in isolated towns remained comparatively low throughout the same period. These observations demonstrate a clear difference in the advertising practices of Pizza shop owners in the region. For example, Pizza shop owners in connected towns (for example Ripon and Knaresborough) report having to advertise to keep local business in their towns rather than allowing locals to dine out elsewhere in a nearby larger town. Respondents noted a perceived need to attract and retain local patronage, ultimately seen as also contributing to localized advertising wars with an *every man for himself* attitude surrounding such behaviours.

Alternatively, in the isolated towns, it was difficult to find such sentiment. The spatial proximity to larger towns reduced the attractiveness of locals traveling to larger towns to dine out. Essentially these Pizza firms had captive audiences who were regularly exposed to the televised advertising of both Franchise 1 and Franchise 2. Clearly, at this intermediate level of analysis a difference between the nature of competitive interactions between local Pizza shops operating in connected and isolated towns is observable. In summary, there was clear evidence that supports the notion that the competitive position of local Pizza firms, vis-à-vis their local marketplace, can be inferred by accounting for the nature of their advertising expenditure.

Postulate 3: *A lack of competitive behaviours associated with attempting to achieve resource ownership may indicate the presence of facilitative interactions.*

With regard to the possibility that the nature of coaction within the cryptic firm complex may aid firm survival, the above reported findings (Postulates 1 and 2) suggest a difference in coactions occurring between Pizza firms located in connected and isolated towns. To determine if facilitative coactions are occurring we need to consider this issue at the level of the town, rather that at the level of the *type of town* (connected or isolated). Four towns (Malton and Market Weighton, Ripon and Knaresborough) provided access to sufficient data from which to compare and contrast the nature of coactions vis-à-vis advertising and survival for all cryptic firm complex members. Table 5.3 illustrates the percentage of Pizza, Indian and Chinese firms in each town advertising for the period up to 1999 (<2000) and after 1999 (>1999). The percentages reported relate to the degree of actual advertising divided by actual possible advertising.

Table 5.3 Rate of advertising in connected and isolated towns

	Malton		Mkt Weighton		Ripon		Knaresborough	
	<2000	>2000	<2000	>2000	<2000	>2000	<2000	>2000
Indian	0%	20%	0%	40%	4%	13%	0%	27%
Pizza	9%	5%	13%	0%	38%	63%	15%	42%
Chinese	0%	18%	75%	0%	0%	40%	8%	8%
Overall	**5%**	**12%**	**75%**	**8%**	**18%**	**34%**	**9%**	**21%**

Leaving aside the Fish & Chip shops (who by-and-large don't use comparable paid advertisements), we observe a decrease in pizza advertising in isolated towns (Malton and Market Weighton) after 1999. By contrast, a substantial increase in advertising in the connected towns (Ripon and Knaresborough) is typically observed across all three restaurant types. Therefore, we would expect more competitive coactions between Pizza, Indian and Chinese (or Asian) firms in the connected towns and an increased possibility of positive facilitative coactions in the isolated towns. This was confirmed to be the case. In Ripon and Knaresborough respectively, the frequency of negative and/or positive population growth correlations is of equal proportions between Pizza, Indian and Chinese firms. Alternatively, in Malton and Market Weighton respectively, there are only positive (and highly significant) correlations.

Postulate 4: *Identification of the operational and external environments relating to specific firms will inform the degree of harmful or non-harmful relations between independent firms in the Pizza industry.*

As was demonstrated in Chapter 3, there is sufficient evidence to conclude that the firms under investigation experience different operating conditions. Specific factors that are reconcilable to the local operating environment and more broadly the external environment in each of the 23 towns are identifiable. Analysis of several variables (Guild Change (or change within the cryptic firm complex), Resource Abundance, Resource Change) and related diversity indices (Dominance, Margalef and FisherALPHA) all support the notion that individual firms operating in individual towns experience unique operational environments through which harmful and/or non-harmful relations with other related restaurants are mediated. Further, these variables relate to sources of energy and/or constraint within each town, providing insights into the nature of harmful and/or non-harmful relations that may occur and persist (as considered in Postulates 1, 2 and 3).

Postulate 5: *The external environment experienced by one or more independent firms in the Pizza industry is an identifiable feature that can be reconciled to their existence.*

The use of Canonical Discriminant Analysis has revealed significant inter-town differences related to spatial heterogeneity that has existed throughout the study period (see Chapter 3). To further explore (and confirm) the extent of such difference, Pianka's (1973) Community Similarity Index was also used to measure the extent to which the towns related to each cryptic firm complex differ, and to also compare any such difference across time. It was also observed that when the individual survival means for each of the 23 towns are compared for ten-year and 15-year time periods, a wide degree of variance between towns is demonstrated. Thus, it is confirmed that in addition to real and measurable differences between each town (and therefore differences in the local environments experienced), survival outcomes for all of the main restaurant types vary quite considerably across both time and space. As such, it can be concluded with a high degree of confidence that the external environment experienced by Pizza firms in the North Yorkshire/East Riding region is unique and reconcilable to their operations.

Postulate 6: *The operational environment experienced by one or more independent firms across time and space in the Pizza industry has an ecological dimension that is an identifiable feature that can be reconciled to their survival/demise.*

Clearly, as demonstrated in Postulate 4 and 5, there are significant inter-town differences related to spatial heterogeneity. The focus of Postulate 6 is upon the potential differential availability of resources to firms. This was measured through dividing the combined average spend per person on restaurant and take-away food in each town over time, by the number of firms operating in each town over time. Using a Paired Samples T-Test to compare the potential resource availability across both time and space, strong support for Postulate 6 is achieved given that 75 percent of all comparisons were significantly different (at .05 or better). Thus it can be concluded with confidence that the primary ecological dimension of each firm's operational environment does indeed vary in an identifiable and important way across both time and space. Such variance can be influenced by local economic growth/decline factors and other observable consumer trends.

Postulate 7: *The operational environment experienced by one or more independent firms across time and space in the Pizza industry has a selective dimension that is an identifiable feature that can be reconciled to their survival/demise.*

At the aggregated level, it would seem that independent Pizza firms held a survival advantage over all other restaurant types for five- and ten-year timeframes (81 percent and 72 percent compared to 60 percent and 44 percent respectively). However, the larger metropolitan areas (Harrogate and York) bias the sample due to their disproportionate size. Once the data are stratified into metropolitan, connected and isolated towns, a very different pattern emerges. Survival outcomes from Pizza firms in isolated towns are essentially 100 percent for both five- and ten-year timeframes. By contrast, in the connected towns, survival outcomes for Pizza firms are more like 60 percent (five years) and 50 percent (ten years). It is clear that the Pizza firms operating across the region experience a range of pressures from benign to difficult.

This observation is further supported when data related to actual Yellow Pages advertising spend are considered. Those Pizza firms located in isolated towns that have never used paid advertising in the Yellow Pages actually hold a survival advantage over those that have and/or those located in connected or large towns. Alternatively, in connected towns, Pizza firms that never placed paid advertisements in the Yellow Pages achieved worse survival outcomes than those that did frequently and/or occasionally. Further, Pizza firms in isolated towns, despite their low or non-existent Yellow Pages advertising spend hold a survival advantage over Fish & Chip shops, and Indian or Chinese restaurants. Conversely, in connected towns, Pizza firms, despite their larger Yellow Pages advertising spend do not hold a survival advantage over Fish & Chip shops or Chinese restaurants. In summary, it would seem that the differential survival of local Pizza firms within the 23 towns investigated is related to different types of environmental factors that act on Pizza firms on a town-by-town basis.

Postulate 8: *Whilst a group of independent firms in the Pizza industry may exist in a local area, each individual firm may experience/create different operational environments.*

There can be little doubt (as evidenced by the above discussion) that seemingly similar local Pizza firms may in fact actually experience fundamentally different operational environments. The evidence presented in relation to Postulates 1 through 7 confirm the presence of resource partitioning and most likely facilitation. These UK-based findings are consistent with those observed in Australia where the owners of Pizza firms located nearby to each other often spoke of the different operating conditions they encountered. In summary, local Pizza firms may operate in an external environment that is similar. However, the extent to which they share common operational environments is largely determined by the nature of coaction relations between themselves and other local Pizza firms, as determined, primarily, by their responses to their local conditions. Given that many are located in entirely different suburbs, provide entirely different services and/or face different coaction relations with other cryptic firm complex members, it should be expected that they would experience different operational environments.

Postulate 9: *The natural development of franchised Pizza firms in the Pizza industry will significantly alter the nature of the operational environments experienced by other associated firms.*

It was observed that the North Yorkshire/East Riding landscape was indeed altered by the presence of franchised Pizza firms. Both Franchise 1 and Franchise 2 represent advanced global franchise operations that have well-developed processes to ensure successful market development and market share capture. Further, as part of enormous UK operations, both relied heavily on television advertising to effectively and efficiently communicate their marketing messages to a specific region. Franchise 2 has developed targeted campaigns in conjunction with direct sponsorship of *The Simpsons* TV show that have lead to a phenomenon know as *The Simpsons Rush* (when a surge of delivery orders are received during the airing of the show). Just as a large oak tree growing alone in a field of daisies casts a large and ecologically significant shadow, so it would seem do the operations of the franchised Pizza firms. In comparison to all of the other main cryptic firm complex members, they have operational size and power that is not observed in the Indian, Chinese and/or Fish & Chip sectors.

Many similarities between the Australian and UK contexts were observed vis-à-vis the impact of franchised Pizza firms. In terms of stimulating demand for all Pizza firms, in the six-year period immediately after the entry of Franchise 1 into Harrogate, there are no recorded exits from the industry. Rather, the number of Pizza firms doubled by the onset of the 1989/1991 recession. This pattern is repeated across the other large towns. The arrival of Franchise 2 would seem to have impacted the market in several different ways. First, rather than positioning their operations similarly to those of Franchise 1, Franchise 2 positioned itself not as an affordable restaurant, but rather as a delivery/pick-up operation. As a result, whilst they increased primary demand for *take-out* pizza, they essentially competed against local delivery/pick-up pizzerias and not against Franchise 1.

Based on the 2001 census population figures, across the entire region only 23 percent of the population live within the operating range of a Franchise 2. Further, 57.3 percent of the local Pizza firms observed in this study operated outside the delivery/service zones of Franchise 2. About 66 percent of consumers in the region were exposed to the advertising of Franchise 1 and Franchise 2, despite not being serviced directly by the operations of either. Clearly, the advertising of the franchised firms favourably altered the operational environments of the independent Pizza firms.

Postulate 10: *Evidence of environmental modification in the Pizza industry should highlight which specific firms have (and have not) benefited due to change in their respective operational environments.*

It is a significant challenge to determine the degree to which Pizza firms operating in different locations and at different times survive better or worse in comparison to each other and/or other restaurant types. A specific challenge is to reconcile the positive or negative contribution made by franchise advertising to overall firm survival. SPSS Survival Analysis provides essentially a 'gross' survival outcome. Whilst data can be stratified into sub-sets that separate advertisers from non-advertisers, the challenge remains to determine 'net' survival outcomes that are adjusted for advertising. To address this challenge an *Advertising Efficiency Index* was devised to allow a net survival outcome to be considered. Expressed as $S \times (1-DF^a)$, where S is the rate of survival generated from SPSS Survival Analysis, and DF^a is the degree and frequency of advertising observed by independent Pizza firms.

Once the actual cost of advertising is applied to base survival outcomes generated from SPSS Survival Analysis, the differences between isolated and connected towns is clearly amplified, with firms operating in isolated towns gaining the most benefit. It would seem that the challenge of retaining custom from locals living in connected towns comes at a cost. One respondent stated that it was a case of *dammed if you do, dammed if you don't*. If firms in connected towns don't advertise they loose trade to the larger nearby towns. If they advertise, it creates a competitive rivalry within the cryptic firm complex that must be paid for by achieving even higher cash flow turnover.

Conversely, examination of local newspapers and business directories in isolated towns failed to find any level of consistent or meaningful advertising towards local consumers by the cryptic firm complex members. There was a sense that the locals provide a captive audience that does not require unnecessary communication to stimulate custom. Given that the isolated towns contain considerably smaller populations, individual cryptic firm complex members note word-of-mouth advertising as the best investment to be made.

In summary, it can be concluded that all pizzerias should gain some form of benefit from the advertising behaviours of Franchise 1 and Franchise 2 vis-à-vis increased primary demand for pizza. That said, clearly the *net* gain achieved is determined by the nature of resource partitioning (or isolation) across the landscape. *Quality* Pizza restaurants (especially in large towns) were very unlikely to compete directly with Franchise 1 and/or Franchise 2 and/or local take-away/delivery operators; therefore, they should gain regardless of location. *Local* Pizza firms would seem to gain no realizable advantage if they are located in connected towns, but stand to gain a considerable survival advantage if located in isolated towns. The key issue would seem to be the extent to which the franchised firms' advertising signal is: 1) received into a competitive or non-competitive local environment, and/or 2) is blocked by the clutter of other signalling that potentially reduced the clarity of the local 'pizza' signal.

Postulate 11: *Evidence of environmental modification in the Pizza industry may indicate the possibility that certain types of firms should inherit a survival advantage relative to other types of firms.*

The assumption that the advertising of franchised Pizza firms will alter the local environs of independent Pizza firms should be supported by evidence of new entrants inheriting a survival advantage relative to earlier entrants and any other members of the cryptic firm complex. Cross tabulations between the main restaurant types and survival/non-survival for three periods (Pre, before Franchise 1; Post-1, after Franchise 1; and Post-2, after Franchise 2) were used to consider this issue. At the regional level it was observed that Chinese food providers and Pizza firms had the highest level of new entrant survival for each period relative to Fish & Chip, Indian, and all other food providers.

However, once the data were stratified, clear differences were observed in connected and isolated towns. In connected towns, the probability of new Pizza entrants surviving across the study period is less than that occurring in isolated and large towns, and it is decreasing over time. Alternatively, in the isolated towns local pizzerias experience (relative to all other restaurant types) a higher probability of survival (relative to large and connected towns) at an increasing rate.

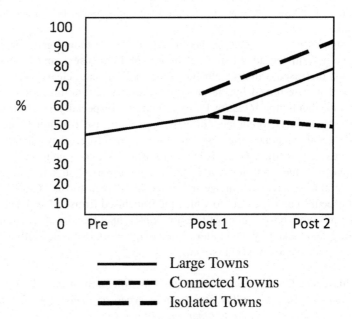

Figure 5.3   *New entrant Pizza survival by town type*

What can be inferred from this simple analysis, illustrated in Figure 5.3, is that new Pizza entrants in isolated towns appear to experience an operational environment with a strong ecological dimension that has: 1) been shaped by the constant advertising of the franchised Pizza firms, and 2) evolved towards positive/neutral coactions. Thus the potential negative impact of the selective dimension within their operational environment would seem to have been negated. Alternatively, new Pizza entrants in connected towns appear to struggle to survive (relative to the other restaurant types) due to: 1) the apparent lack of influence of the franchised Pizza firms' advertising, and 2) a higher level of negative/neutral coactions. Therefore, there are less available customers within their operational environment.

Postulate 12: *In Pizza markets featuring both franchised and independent firms, an invisible force capable of altering discrete operational environments is plausible, and its presence would be determined by the interaction of franchised and independent Pizza firms occurring across time and space.*

Discussions with restauranteurs, local consumers and service providers (for example, taxi drivers) confirmed the presence of an external stimulus (or an invisible force) that had the potential to increase the demand for pizza within and beyond the delivery zone of the franchised operators. Not only did Franchise 2 integrate their signal into one of the most popular sitcom satires, but they benefited from the relationship in such a significant manner that their brand recognition (Harris and Dennis, 2002) and profitability was increased whilst actual advertising spending was reduced (Makin, 2002), gains attributed to the emerging *Simpsons Rush.*

As previously noted, there is little doubt that the initial advertising of Franchise 1 and subsequent advertising of Franchise 2 has influenced the demand for pizza in a generalized way that has benefited other local Pizza firms. Consistent with the initial observations from the Australian context, the power of the franchised Pizza firms' advertising far exceeds that of other local Pizza firms and other restaurant types. It would seem logical that the close relationship between Franchise 2 and *The Simpsons* TV show has delivered benefits to both closely related target markets.

Postulate 13: *The presence of an invisible force will have identifiable transfactual conditions that relate to its tendencies to positively influence independent Pizza firm survival.*

The most insightful comments made by local consumers related to their actual consumption practices. Whereas those consumers located in connected towns acknowledged the likelihood that their potential spend (over any given period) on restaurant and take-way food would frequently occur, or *leak*, into food providers located in large towns, the same observation was not made for consumers located in isolated towns. This notion of possible leakage was discussed with several food providers, with confirmation that it was a serious concern for those food providers located in connected towns. Thus (as noted and discussed in Postulate 10), the variability in: 1) potential resource availability, and 2) *resource leakage* would seem to align to an escalation of advertising to retain custom from which negative coactions seemingly arise.

A logical conclusion to emerge from observations of each town, the individual levels of advertising and (previously) noted survival rates across each cryptic firm complex is that specific conditions can be ascribed to the presence of *Transferred Demand*. Firstly, the stability (or maintenance) of potential resource availability reduces the pressure on local food providers to advertise, especially where there is little resource leakage. In the absence of multiple competing local signals (attempting to *own* customers), the clarity of the signal emitted from the franchised Pizza firms is essentially amplified, thus stimulating demand for pizza and any other closely related substitutes (like Chinese or Indian).

Therefore, the observed survival advantage of Pizza firms in isolated towns would seem related to the efficiency of their advertising practices relative to those of other Pizza firms located in connected and large towns. Alternatively, there was no evidence found to support the notion that the signal emitted by the franchised Pizza firms was received by local consumers in connected towns with anything approaching the clarity of that occurring in the isolated towns. In summary, the proximity of each town to other towns is likely to reduce/increase the likelihood of leakage of potential consumer resources. Leakage of resources was observed to be associated with increased advertising that resulted in the accumulation of multiple signals that competed for receivers with the franchised Pizza firms' signals. In summary, there is support for Postulate 13.

Postulate 14: *The contingent conditions related to the tendencies of any such invisible force are explainable by an understanding of the variance occurring in the operational environments experienced by individual Pizza firms.*

As noted above, the potential for leakage of potential resources is related to a likely increase in negative coactions due to increased advertising. Given that there is no observed linear association between the level of advertising and firm survival in either large, connected, and isolated towns for any of the cryptic firm complex members, those local Pizza firms advertising in connected towns are likely to decrease their operating efficiency. However, they are also faced with a catch-22 situation where not advertising may not increase their survival prospects either.

Alternatively, the likely absence of a cluttered signalling environment in the isolated towns enables the signal from the franchised Pizza firms to *fertilize* the environment and stimulate local demand for pizza (and other close substitutes). In summary, the nature of selection occurring against local Pizza firms located in connected towns is a function of their town's proximity to larger towns which in turn is directly related to the prevailing selective environment experienced by food providers in connected towns. Likewise, the benign nature of the selection pressures in isolated towns (after the commencement of signalling by franchised Pizza firms) corresponds to the emergence of *fertilized* operational environments that complements the stability of local resources, again a function of the proximity of each town vis-à-vis the perceived preferences of local consumers. In summary, there is support for Postulate 14.

Postulate 15: *The degree to which an invisible force capable of influencing independent firm survival in the Pizza industry will be directly related to (or explainable by) an understanding of the operational environments experienced by individual firms.*

Of particular interest amongst the findings is the observation that firm survival observed at different levels differs dramatically (that is, at regional, individual town, and across types of towns). The above discussion has demonstrated both the varied survival outcomes across scale and location as well as the significant differences in environs experienced. There can be little doubt that the presence of an invisible force will logically form an active part of the operational environment of firms in isolated towns. In connected towns, the observations made by the various persons consulted leads one to conclude that it also forms an inactive (or suppressed) part of the operational environment of firms in connected towns. Likewise, differences in the nature of the operational environment experienced by local Pizza firms are traceable to the forms of coaction occurring between cryptic firm complex members; these coactions can be observed with accuracy only at the level of the town. In summary, there is support for Postulate 15.

Postulate 16: *Differential independent firm survival in the Pizza industry will therefore be related to differences observed in firm type and location.*

Observing the local Pizza firms at the level of the individual town exposes the researcher to significant variations in operating form (or structure), marketplace positioning, and exposure to a broad range of coactions. Once the breadth of such diversity is acknowledged, it is nigh on impossible to reassemble the Pizza firms into aggregated categories for any meaningful analysis. To do so would be to retreat from an *autecological* approach to understanding firm survival. For example, in the town of Malton, two Pizza firms operate on the high street. One is positioned as a restaurant, the other as an up-market take-away/delivery provider. In this general area, Chinese, Indian and Fish & Chip operators all provide restaurant level service. Less than 2 kilometres away, another two Pizza firms operate side by side with other food producers, all catering to price conscious consumers interested in take-away and delivery services. It is quite apparent the four Pizza firms essentially appeal to separate target markets, and/or are sufficiently distanced from each other, and/or provide a range of diverse services that differentiate each other to ensure survival.

In the larger town of Scarborough, local Pizza firms and Fish & Chip shops dominate cryptic firm complex composition. This is due to a lack of direct competition between franchised and local Pizza firms and the sustainability (or scalability) of the business model commonly employed by Fish & Chip shop owners. Conversely, in the connected town of Ripon, local preferences for Indian food and the retention of the traditional Fish & Chip shop have restricted traction by Pizza and Chinese firms within the local cryptic firm complex. In, summary, it was observed that any one type of Pizza firm (take-away, take-away/delivery, restaurant or restaurant/delivery) might hold a survival advantage not based upon the broad evolution of organizational form, but on the fit between that specific firm and its operational environment.

Put simply, the observed levels of spatial heterogeneity are not reconcilable at higher levels of scale and therefore explanations of firm survival are made and based upon local processes occurring independently in individual towns. In summary, the researcher's observations provide compelling evidence that explanations of differential Pizza firm survival in the study region are not reducible to a specific independent variable and must be explained by accounting for local variability on a firm-by-firm basis in relation to the local environment provided by separate towns. As a result, there is support for Postulate 16.

Postulate 17: *Collapsing firms into specialists and generalists will not give rise to a satisfactory explanation of the differential survival outcomes of similar types of firms operating in the restaurant and fast food cryptic firm complex in the North Yorkshire/East Riding region, as compared to that developed to explain the assumed presence of Transferred Demand.*

The resource partitioning theory of Carroll (1985) predicts that as markets mature and become more concentrated, specialists gain a survival advantage by out-competing or acquiring other generalists who also seek the market's middle ground. As this process occurs small niches open up that smaller specialists exploit. This scenario was not observed to occur in the Australian context, nor the UK context. As previously noted, the extreme limitations developed within Carroll's notion of resource partitioning render the concept ineffective within the context of this autecological investigation. There are several reasons that such an approach cannot be applied to investigating the survival of Pizza firms in this study.

First, there are no large generalists in the study to observe. The larger organizations (e.g. Franchises 1, 2 and 3) all scale the environment on a town-by-town basis (despite access to considerable group resources) as specialists, not generalists. Unlike the predictions (see Aldrich, 1999) that not all would survive, they do, servicing a distinct (narrow, yet sufficiently large) set of price conscious consumers without much evidence of overlap observed across major franchisors and independent firms.

Second, whilst more specialist Pizza firms are observed in the larger towns to serve a narrow customer type, it is by and large generalist Pizza firms that service a broader range of customer types in the small connected and isolated towns. The earlier predictions of Kangas and Risser (1979) that within smaller towns' firm survival would be explained by a proclivity towards operating as a generalist are confirmed. They felt that if the resource base was fluctuating (i.e. consumer preferences are changeable) then operating in a small town as a specialist would be too risky.

Third, classification of specialists and generalists across the life course of a particular firm and/or industry is challenging. For example, firms observed to be operating as specialists are also observed to have previously advertised in a manner that suggests a generalist style of operation, and vice-versa. As the environment has changed (for example, the advent of home delivery or the increased patronage of dine-in establishments) across the period of the study, many firms have adapted to those trends in a variety of ways. Given the inherent variability of organizational forms (with a potential to fluctuate), attempting to organize firms arbitrarily into specialist and generalist categories is deemed unwise. Such diversity of form across different environments is easily explainable by reference to the *original* theory of resource partitioning (Schoener, 1974) without having to try and satisfy the precise requirements of Carroll's (1985) later interpretation of this ecological process. In summary, the components of the proposed model of *Transferred Demand* would appear to offer more explanatory power than any attempt to define firms in the sample as specialists or generalists, firms who should conform to the predictive assumptions of the resource partitioning model developed within the context of the current organizational studies literature.

Overview of the Findings

Throughout this section, evidence from multiple sources, both quantitative and qualitative has been presented to: 1) describe the region and industry investigated, and 2) confirm/disconfirm the postulates developed earlier in the chapter. Across all 17 postulates, sufficient support has been found to confirm the logical presence of each postulate in the proposed model of *Transferred Demand*. Therefore, evidence has been presented that lends specific support to the underlying research proposition: *Transferred Demand is a force capable of positively altering the operational environments of firms, thereby enhancing survival, and its influence is determined by the interaction between franchised and independent firms and elements of the environment they share across time and space.*

THE PROCESS OF *TRANSFERRED DEMAND*

This section aims to explain the workings of the proposed model, uniting the components of the model of *Transferred Demand* that have been the focus of the postulate development. In doing so, additional insights from the broader ecological literature will be used to explain how the proposed model is claimed to have operated within the study areas during the life of this study. As such, this section contributes a novel explanation of firm survival to the organizational studies literature. Of particular interest is the contingent conditions argued to relate to the suppression and/or operation of *Transferred Demand*, conditions that have been modified by the environmental modification activities of firms operating in the study's geographical area of focus. Second, this section seeks to explain in detail the contribution this study makes to theory, method and practice within the context of organizational studies. Before articulating a complex theoretical explanation of firm survival, a simplified account of firm survival is presented to assist the reader's eventual comprehension as to how the components of the model of *Transferred Demand* unite and are bound together by expanded autecological arguments.

A Simplified Explanation of Firm Survival

The survival of local Pizza firms can be explained by the presence of *Transferred Demand* in the form of an advertising signal emanating from the everyday operations of franchised Pizza firms, across a heterogeneous environment. The influence and the non-influence of *Transferred Demand* can be explained as follows. In isolated towns, a lack of local advertising intensity results in the towns' boundaries effectively acting as a sounding board through which the external signalling (advertising) of franchised Pizza firms is amplified. The geographic location of the towns prevents the leakage of residential resources (their daily spend on food), which are essentially trapped within the towns' boundaries by the personal costs of travelling out of town to acquire a product/service that is available within the town. The result: demand for pizza increases as residents are exposed to a clear advertising message for a product/service that is available locally (though not from the advertiser). As a result of the impact of the external (franchising) signal, there is less need (for local firms) to signal internally, and indeed, we witness very low levels of local advertising. When we factor in the higher levels of Pizza firm survival in isolated towns (vis-à-vis connected and large towns) we can assume that the isolated Pizza firms have obtained an increased level of foraging efficiency (or the amount of internal energy used to acquire external energy) relative to other sub-populations.

Alternatively, in connected towns, the opposite process is evident. As a result of the proximity of the towns to larger more diverse populations, and the increased mobility of residents, historically it would seem that potential resources are lost from the towns as residents spend much of their potential daily spend on food outside their town of residence. The result is a competitive environment within which higher levels of advertising across all restaurant types is more common. The nature of these coactions transforms the towns' boundaries, appearing to make it less permeable to the incoming signal from franchised Pizza firms, so the sounding board effect is lost. Essentially, the degree of advertising locally dilutes the potential impact of the franchised signal. The outcome is the deflection of the signal. Demand for pizza is not increased, the need for local Pizza firms (and other restaurant types) to advertise to retain local custom (and achieve competitive positioning) increases, and the Pizza firms are locked into a competitive fight from which there typically are causalities. As the relative survival of Pizza firms in connected towns decreases, it can be assumed that they have achieved lower foraging efficiency relative to other sub-populations.

Therefore, the conditions (for isolated and connected towns) favourable to *Transferred Demand* relate to: 1) low levels of adversarial coactions, identifiable by low levels of advertising, and 2) the retention of residential resources within the local town. Under such conditions, the franchiser's signalling is clear and uninterrupted and can be captured and converted into revenues by the local firms. When both primary conditions are not met, the potential power of *Transferred Demand* is likely to be a lesser force relative to the presence of competitive interactions already occurring locally.

Deconstructing a Simplified Explanation of Firm Survival

This simplified explanation of firm survival was made possible because of the manner in which the components and boundaries of the research task emerged from the preliminary discussion earlier in the chapter. Five specific areas of focus were identified from which the construction of a model of *Transferred Demand* was possible. The five areas of focus are: non-harmful relations, environmental heterogeneity, the ability of firms to alter their environment, the presence of an invisible energy, and lastly, firm survival. These five areas again will serve as dimensions through which discussion of the process of *Transferred Demand* can proceed. The aim of this next section is to blend various concepts/theories and/or research methods (drafted in from the broader ecological literature) into a coherent explanation of firm survival. The requirements of this approach preclude the structuring of such discussion across each dimension individually (or sequentially). Rather, the collective relationship of the five dimensions (to and between each dimension) will be discussed in unison.

The Importance of Scale

In his seminal article on ecological scale, Wiens (1989: 385) asserted that to understand the nature of the *drama* occurring within the ecological theatre, we must view it from an appropriate scale. The explanation offered here for consideration has been crafted from an appreciation of how interpretation of the *drama* under investigation differs across different levels of scale. The following discussion will move from the level of the town, to the level of the region, and hover at the intermediate levels of the isolated and connected towns. Such movement ensures that this research opens itself to the opportunity of capturing a deeper level of understanding as to why Pizza firms are surviving in the North Yorkshire/East Riding Pizza industry. Thus, this research avoids committing what Babbie (2005: 102) labels an ecological fallacy, whereby assumptions are made 'that something learned about an ecological unit says something about the individuals making up that unit'. Furthermore, the challenge of accounting for processes that are contextually determined (Danermark, 2002) is essentially a scale dependent issue.

Returning to the simplified explanation of firm survival, the fundamental importance of scale reveals itself. At the regional (or aggregated) level, very little difference between the towns is observed across a range of demographic variables. Pizza firm survival is high relative to most other restaurant types but, consistent with the Australian context, differences are observable across towns based on their location. Clearly, there is evidence of differential survival outcomes that would logically seem related to environmental heterogeneity. Past studies (Carroll and Swaminathan, 1992) that operate at the level of populations typically invoke heterogeneity as a logical reason as to why specific (research) limitations must accompany their findings. However, the level of scale employed within the Pizza research presented above means that the obvious visibility of heterogeneity acts to motivate the researcher to uncover differences at a lower level, where any such heterogeneity is born.

At the level of the town, the researcher is immersed into a world of fluctuating variance where similarities are few and far between. The notion of using a Community Similarity Index (Pianka, 1973) to determine the similarity of the towns within the region seems never before to have been attempted. As noted earlier, an overall level of similarity (ranging from $\overline{X}$ = .39 in 1975 to $\overline{X}$ = .48 in 2004) demonstrates wide differences in community structure across the 23 towns investigated. Furthermore, the use of *Canonical Discriminant Analysis* confirmed: 1) the statistical significance of heterogeneity present, and 2) the various dimensions of its complex composition. Thus, while past studies often do not identify the presence of such factors that may contribute towards differential survival outcomes, this research explores and highlights them. Therefore, the explanation offered in this study is not from literature-based assumptions, but rather it has emerged from an (inquisitive) fascination of how and why the 23 towns differ significantly or marginally across a wide range of variables (for example, Guild change, Resource abundance, a range of Diversity indices, Resource change and Exit rates). This derives from the assumption that individual firms have a story of survival to tell. This has led to the identification of isolated and connected towns from which the explanation offered has been crafted.

Beyond Competition

Central to the explanation offered is a rejection that competition should automatically be assumed a widespread and pervasive feature of the environment, and/or a major influencer of community structures, as it is elsewhere (see Freeman and Hannan, 1983). In reality, this does not represent a bold move given the past rejection of such a dominant role for competition in the broader ecological literature (see Tokeshi, 1999; Walter, 1988). Consistent with accepted definitions of competition in the broader ecological literature (see Milne, 1961; Grime, 1979), it is through an understanding of how resources are captured by the Pizza firms that determinations of competition are stated. Therefore, room has been created for other (non-competition driven) explanations that could logically contribute to a more complete and *consistent* explanation of firm survival. Nevertheless, such denial can only be tolerated in light of supporting evidence. Qualitative evidence from interviews/conversations with restaurateurs/consumers and Yellow Pages data combined to confirm that the presence and/or intensity of competition that can be traced to variability across the same group of factors (related to environmental heterogeneity) that were identified using the process of *Canonical Discriminant Analysis*.

Several well-established (and fundamental) ecological concepts offer multiple pathways towards a more complete and consistent explanation of firm survival. However, in the absence of blindly assuming competition is acting uniformly as an efficient sorting process, this research is challenged with the task of attempting to explain how any other such explanations fit into an overall explanation of various coactions. The first alternative concept observed was that of facilitation. Consistent with Rathcke's (1983) notion of facilitation, understanding the extent to which cryptic firm complex members actually wanted to *own* consumer preferences, rather than *share* such preferences was central to allocating a role for facilitation in explaining survival outcomes. Further, there was no evidence found to suggest that in isolated towns any of the towns had moved towards a competitive phase identifiable by increased advertising and/or firm closures.

The next concept capable of contributing to the explanation offered was that of character displacement (Brown and Wilson, 1956). In this context, character displacement relates to occasions where differences among similar firms located close spatially are increased in regions where the firms co-occur but are reduced, minimized or lost where the firms' presence do not overlap. On two separate occasions character displacement was observable. First, despite Franchise 2 entering the industry with very similar positioning to Franchise 1 in the early 90s, over time the key positioning features of Franchises 1 and 2 diverged to the point where neither considers the other to be a direct (or significant) competitor. Second, and very noticeably, Chinese restaurants followed the trend of local Pizza shops delivering food. Thus, the process of convergent character displacement (as an explanation) fits nicely in contributing to the explanation of firm survival. That is, through repositioning and/or mimicking the traits of other members of the cryptic firm complex, firms avoided competing on a similar basis.

Once we are able to move away from Carroll's (1985) highly restrictive definition of resource partitioning to the more liberal (and original definition) of Schoener (1968; 1974), we can again explain an absence of competitive coactions in many towns. Rather than a futile focus on economies of scale and ambiguous attempts to classify firms as either specialists or generalists, we can focus on specific elements through which competition is enacted (for example, the nature of offering, the hours of operation, and the place of operation). As noted earlier, sufficient evidence was found to highlight the manner in which firms organized their operations to avoid direct competition. A fourth concept not directly observed (but likely to support aspects of the explanation offered), is that of functional redundancy (Lawton and Brown, 1993). Put simply, within a cryptic firm complex where multiple restaurant types provide the same (or very similar) function, there simply might not be a need for all *types* of firms to survive to ensure the complex retains its structure. Therefore, firms may suffer a form of environmental selection, rather than natural selection (Brandon, 1990). That is, it is the properties of the environment (the nature of consumer taste and availability of consumers) rather than the properties of the firms (their strategies and interacting elements) that may most explain their survival.

In summary, a range of alternative explanations that are well established in the broader ecological literature, better relate to the evidence provided and remove any need to assume the presence of competition as the underlying mechanism contributing to complex composition and/or evolution. Importantly, the explanation offered takes into account the actual (advertising) behaviour of the firms under investigation across time and space. Explicit in this acknowledgement of time and space is an ability to deconstruct the industry environment into discrete, localized environment neighbourhoods, and ultimately, unique operational environments that fit the requirements of individual firms.

Understanding Where the Heterogeneity Resides

To construct the explanation offered above, those factors that affect specific cryptic firm complex members in ways that influence survival outcomes had to be determined as being significant and measured/quantified (where this was possible). The idea of a firm's potential environment provided an excellent mechanistic conceptual basis to identify and isolate factors related to firms operating in individual towns. Overwhelming evidence was found that highly significant variance existed within and across all 23 towns during the entire period investigated. The beauty of discovering so much variance within and across the towns was that it reduced the temptation to assume that aggregating the data would simply produce intermediate points where sense could be made of the variance before it was lost at full aggregation. At full aggregation it is not possible to determine the extent of environmental heterogeneity as it relates to the operations of Pizza shops and/or all complex members. Put simply, the *unique relationships* between the firms and their local environs have traditionally been *averaged away* as Wiens (1989) has argued for ecological studies.

Therefore, the challenge is to start from the perspective of how the individual firms scale *their* environment. When we use the firms as measuring instruments (as Antonovics, Clay and Schmitt (1987) do with organisms) we are exposed to different degrees of heterogeneity that belong to a specific location. To put this issue into perspective, consider Ehrlich and Murphy's (1981: 615) warning against censuring (or aggregating) of populations that include more than one demographic unit (or selective neighbourhood). They state that 'attempting to study the dynamics of populations without defining demographic units is roughly analogous to studying the performance of 20 thermostatic heaters (each of which operates on a feedback principle to regulate temperature) in 20 different aquaria by pouring water samples from each aquarium into a common container and then measuring the temperature of the water in that container'. Clearly, within this study identifying, measuring and respecting the unique heterogeneity occurring within and across each of the 23 towns has avoided this problem.

Between the disaggregated and aggregated (levels of) data lay a potential explanation of firm survival. The challenge was to find factors (that despite the extreme nature of variance exhibited in each town) that enabled empirical scrutiny of the *assumed* model of *Transferred Demand*. The obvious factor was the propensity to advertise to attract resources. While it was not possible to split every town perfectly into isolated, connected or large categories, within a sufficient number of towns the nature of their advertising relative to their survival prospects and location was noticeable.

In summary, survival relative to advertising provided for a reasonably level playing field to compare Pizza firm survival in isolated and connected towns. A *reasonably* level playing field because it was obvious that the ecological process of succession (Connell and Slatyer, 1977) was occurring in each town as an isolated process with neither timing nor pacing in sync. Put simply, at the heart of explaining the heterogeneity observed across all 23 towns, was the challenge of not simply concluding that they are different, but rather, acknowledging that each town is out sync in its rate and/or stages of development. Nevertheless, the presence of *Transferred Demand* requires an acceptance that: 1) we can understand how firms can alter aspects of their operational environments, and 2) that we can understand how such change can contribute to above normal survival outcomes by local Pizza firms.

The Generation and Influence of Invisible Energy

Unlike past works that have acknowledged (but not explained) the likelihood that firms can change their environments (see Winter, 1964; Popper, 1972; Aldrich, 1979; Scott, 1987; Winter, 1990; March, 1994), the explanation offered here of *Transferred Demand* must account for the mechanism of, and conditions related to, how firms might alter their environments. In developing the environmental modification approach, using the works of Odling-Smee, Laland and Feldman (2003), a theoretically sound and well-developed framework was used to consider the issue of what *mechanism*, and what *conditions* could relate to firms altering their environment.

The central thesis of the model of *Transferred Demand* is that the natural development of franchised Pizza firms alters the environment in several fundamental ways. Consistent with Odling-Smee, Laland and Feldman (2003: 6), and from the perspective of our environment modification approach, the franchised Pizza firms not only modify their (operating) environment, but also the operational environment of other related restaurant types by directly affecting properties of the environment that they hold in common. Importantly, 'they not only contribute to energy and matter flow ... but in part also *control* them'. In doing so, franchised firms also make possible the ecological inheritance (by local firms) of an environment within which selection pressures have been lessened to the advantage of new entrants and existing firms.

Therefore, an entirely new explanation (within the context of organizational studies) emerges. Rather than focusing upon the inheritance from one firm to another (of routines associated with best practice) that provide a survival advantage, the explanation offered allows for firms to inherit different types of environments within which selection forces have been altered by the normal operations of more influential firms. That is, the franchised firms' powerful and effective advertising has modified the processes of selection experienced by some local Pizza firms. The argument contained within the explanation offered is that rather than assuming a survival advantage is explicitly gained from firms adapting to their environments, it is now demonstrated that for many firms the environment may well have been altered to better suit their normal (or pre-existing) operations.

DIFFERENT TYPES OF *TRANSFERRED DEMAND*

The challenge remains to explain more precisely what actual mechanism and related conditions explain the presence of *Transferred Demand*. In its most basic form, *Transferred Demand*[B] is argued to exist when a franchised Pizza firm operates in such a way as to stimulate consumer demand for all local providers of pizza. In both the Australian and UK contexts this was seen to occur immediately after the arrival of the first franchised Pizza firm. Relative to the advertising emanating from other restaurant types (including local Pizza firms), the franchise firm's advertising signal has an intensity and clarity that alters specific environmental factors (and increases consumer demand for pizza in general), and therefore reduces the potential impact of selection processes for all Pizza firms. So in its most basic form, *Transferred Demand*[B] is associated with an increase in the primary demand for pizza. Whilst the benefits gained by local firms would not be uniform, they would be expected to be essentially positive for essentially *all* local Pizza firms. In contrast, in its most complex form, *Transferred Demand*[C] is explainable with reference to several factors that in combination describe specific conditions under which only *some* local Pizza firms would gain benefits.

Within the particular context of this study, *Transferred Demand*[C] was observed to develop differently in Australia than in the UK due to differences in the operations of the franchised firms in both contexts. In Australia, Franchises 1, 2 and 3 were always direct competitors due to their pursuit of a common (price conscious) customer who sought delivery/pickup service. Alternatively, in the North Yorkshire/East Riding region the process of divergent character displacement resulted in two separate types of franchised Pizza operations emerging. One competed with local providers for home delivery/pickup in the late afternoon to late evening (Franchise 2) and another competed against local restaurant service style operators from lunchtime till early evening (Franchise 1). The extent to which local Pizza firms gained a benefit was largely dependent on the inheritance of a benevolent environment.

Where franchised firms were located in the same location as local Pizza firms (for example, large towns) the intensity of their signalling benefited locals in several ways and is explainable with reference to the process of resource partitioning. These firms differentiated with respect to such variables as the actual hours of operation, specific nature of offering, and location of each local firm dictate the *conditions* under which *Transferred Demand*[C] may assist survival prospects. Clearly those restaurant firms that are up market and licensed are positioned towards a different clientele than Franchise 1's family oriented (and more affordable) positioning. Likewise, those local Pizza firms that offer a broad range of food services (pizza, kebab, chicken and burgers, etc.) appeal to a far broader customer group than Franchise 2. Added to such positioning differences were influences from the actual location of each local Pizza shop and their specific hours of operation, as well as the conditions unique to each firm vis-à-vis the advertising signal presence generated by the franchised firms. However, in large towns, some local firms would not be expected to gain from *Transferred Demand*^{C}, specifically firms that are positioned too similarly to either Franchise 1's affordable restaurant style or Franchise 2's delivery/pickup service, especially in terms of hours of operation, specific offerings or location, will receive less (or no) benefit.

When local Pizza firms were located beyond the delivery boundaries of the franchised firms the benefits gained from their environmental modification behaviours were more obvious to discern. Rather than a specific focus on resource partitioning (and the avoidance of competitive coactions), now the focus is upon positive/negative coactions that are derived from the historical development of each town. In isolated towns, the primary conditions for *Transferred Demand*^{C} exist naturally, they being low levels of adversarial coactions and the retention of residential resources within the local town. Alternatively, in connected towns the reality of trying to attract the custom of more mobile residents naturally leads to more adversarial coactions. Therefore, the primary conditions noted within the explanation offered are met naturally within isolated towns, but not in connected towns.

In summary, while it is highly likely that clever operators in large towns have altered their operations to avoid direct competition, *Transferred Demand* is seen by and large to be a process related to specific properties of the environment (as determined on a firm by firm basis) that is unconsciously transferred to local firms. Its influence is governed by factors beyond the control of a single firm, but enhanced by the presence of non-adversarial behaviour. Under conditions of non-adversarial coactions and isolation, the advertising signal can be usefully thought of as a form of *emergy* (Odum, 1996). Odum defined *emergy* as available (or stored) energy of one kind previously required directly and indirectly to make a product or service that can be converted into useful energy by other entities within an ecosystem. There was little evidence in the UK context that local firms are aware of the benefit they gain from the invisible force that is *Transferred Demand*. Likewise, neither of the major franchised firms seemed aware of the (overall) positive influence their advertising had on the survival of local Pizza firms. Essentially, *Transferred Demand* can be categorized as a classic commensalism, where one firm benefits and the other remains unharmed, regardless of intention.

Visualizing the Generation and Influence of Invisible Energy

The apparent unawareness of the presence of *Transferred Demand* to many firms and the franchised operators raises a key question. How was the offered explanation developed, given the invisibility of *Transferred Demand*? Two factors combine to allow the model of *Transferred Demand* to be explainable in the context of this study. First, the ontological disposition of the researcher and second, his first-hand experience in franchised business contexts provide several foundational platforms to build from. Let us first consider the ontological dimension with reference to Table 5.4 below.

Table 5.4   Bhaskar's three overlapping domains of reality (a)

	Domain of Real	Domain of Actual	Domain of Empirical
Mechanisms	✔		
Events		✔	
Experiences			✔

Incorporating Bhaskar's (1975) stratified realities into the research process provides access to explanations that are built around a focus on generative mechanisms. Returning briefly to Bennett and George's (2003) notion that generative mechanisms are ultimately unobservable social processes that under specific conditions have the potential to transfer *energy* or information, and important point must be made. As noted earlier, while generative mechanisms may shape certain outcomes, they may also be shaped by other outcomes. Pre-existing competitive coactions provide for *other outcomes* that might act in a countervailing manner to deflect the potential influence of *Transferred Demand*.

With reference to Table 5.5, while the explanation developed thus far has occurred in the *domain of the empirical* (firm survival), it has done so mindful of the events that have occurred in the *domain of the actual* (increased consumer demand), events that are claimed to have been caused by the presence of advertising signals occurring under particular conditions in the *domain of the real*.

Table 5.5   Bhaskar's three overlapping domains of reality (b)

	Domain of Real	Domain of Actual	Domain of Empirical
Mechanisms	Franchise Advertising		
Events		Consumer Demand	
Experiences			Firm Survival

To achieve a fit between Bhaskar's (1975) stratified reality and the explanation offered required the use of the process of retroduction. Incorporating the researcher's current insights and wisdom from past business experience made possible the postulation of structures and mechanisms thought possible to cause the differential survival outcomes observed. So we hold possible the presence of a specific form of generative mechanism in the *domain of the real* with (potential) powers to cause events in the *domain of the actual*, that we could confirm or disconfirm in the *domain of the empirical*, by finding evidence for the postulates developed earlier in this chapter. The nature of the explanation offered has therefore been shaped by the researcher's past experience and current imagination and willingness to keep trying to fit consistent pieces to an ecological puzzle from outside the domain of organizational studies. In summary, support has been achieved for the initial research proposition, support that now facilitates a more precise definition of *Transferred Demand*.

Defining *Transferred Demand*

The working definition (and therefore research proposition) used thus far was that: *Transferred Demand is a force capable of positively altering the operational environments of firms, thereby enhancing survival, and its influence is determined by the interaction between franchised and independent firms and elements of the environment they share across time and space.* At this point we can now update this definition:

Transferred Demand is a form of emergy produced from franchisation that under certain conditions can alter the operational environments of firms in such a way that their survival may be enhanced.

Within this definition is the term *franchisation*, a termed coined and explained within this very discussion. Franchisation is the process through which an industry is transformed by the introduction of one or more franchised operators. The transformation is due to new ecological processes that alter the evolutionary outcomes (or trajectory) of the industry participants. Whilst it is common within the literature to assume negative impacts upon local business with the advent of franchising (see Stone, 1997), the findings of this study suggest that this assumption may fail to appreciate: 1) outcomes at localized levels, and 2) differences across industry types.

The definition provided is argued to accurately reflect the workings of *Transferred Demand* through the addition of emergy as an explanatory factor. In this case, emergy is previously used energy that remains stored in the environment capable of being converted to energy by other firms. The determinant of any such conversion is the particular conditions (previously detailed above) experienced by any particular firm. The remainder of this chapter discusses the contribution this study makes to the organizational studies and related literatures, but does also consider the limitations inherent within the study.

CONTRIBUTION EMERGING FROM THIS STUDY

This study represents a major departure from traditional approaches to the ecological investigation of firm survival in the organizational studies literature. By introducing new theories and methods, an entirely new set of insights have been developed. Thus, the decision to return to a range of foundational works, regardless of their domain of origin, would seem well justified. As a result, the theoretical concepts used throughout the study have accepted status in the broader domain of ecology and care has been continuously taken to ensure that at all times any such concepts have been applied within this study in a way *consistent* with their usage in the broader domain of ecology. The value in returning to original source documents, consulting ecologists of many types and clarifying the approach undertaken is evidenced in the following discussion.

Returning to the challenge of Sears (1935: 223), when the ecologist enters the study area, he or she 'sees not merely what is there, but what is happening there'. When the challenge of Sears is combined with Hodgson's (2001) *Principle of Consistency*, it is important to be armed with: 1), an appreciation of the foundations of ecological thought, and 2) an ability to apply such thought in a consistent manner. Conversations with a variety of ecologists have confirmed to the researcher that both prerequisites have been met within the requirements of this study. As discussed elsewhere (Jones, 2004; 2005;

2007; 2008; 2009), many intricate and ambivalent issues related to the usage of ecological/evolutionary theories have been encountered, and largely overcome throughout this study. Let us take the time to consider the nature of such issues.

What it Means to Use an Ecological/Evolutionary Approach

The fundamental task of any *ecological* approach is to 'delineate the general principles under which the natural community ... [under investigation] ... and ... its component parts operate' (Clarke, 1967: 18). This entails accounting for all *interacting* entities occurring within a *specific area* and understanding the coactions between each and the relations they experience with their environs. Such an approach is *evolutionary* to the extent that it also seeks to explain events occurring over time with reference to mechanisms of selection that act upon all manner of variations, some of which are retained during the entities struggle to survive. To accept the above description as describing the most basic requirements of adopting an ecological/evolutionary approach creates *consistency issues*. Therefore, this study does not seek to build directly upon work from within the organizational studies literature that claims to also use an ecological and/or evolutionary approach. Rather, it seeks to revisit the theoretical foundations of employing such an approach in the domain of organizational studies.

The first requirement is to be able to account for the nature of interacting entities within the particular community under investigation. At present, within the organizational studies literature no framework (consistent with the broader ecological literature) exists from which to examine the various types of relationships experienced between interacting entities. As previously discussed, it is common to adopt Aldrich's (1999) eight possible relations between organizational populations, assuming *commensalism* to be a descriptor for six of the eight relations. Despite assurances that such usage is appropriate from a sociological perspective (Aldrich, 2007); the field of organizational studies is not born from or solely dependent upon sociological perspectives. This study has resurrected Haskell's (1949) original coaction theory, establishing (for the first time) a consistent usage of the term *commensalism* between organizational studies and the broader ecological literature. Doing so introduces a well-established framework for categorizing coaction relations between any interacting entities. The next issue relates to the unit of analysis.

Perhaps the most obvious (yet most significant) contribution made to the domain of organizational studies is to reveal the actual complexity of the environments experienced by firms during the period of this study. Once we move to conceptions of the external, potential and operational environments directly linked to individual firms, we enhance our ability to more precisely capture the relationship between firms and their environments.

Within the current organizational studies literature explanations of firm survival are commonly shaped around assumed notions of ever-present competition. Often it is claimed that firms can out compete other firms by better adjusting their interacting elements to achieve better fit with their environment (Tushman and Romanelli, 1985; Levitt and March, 1988). Such claims are refuted (see Hannan and Freeman, 1989) by those who see the firms' essential, or core elements as relatively inert, and therefore difficult to change during times of environmental change. However, increasingly such extreme opinions are less about a dichotomy of opinion, and more about questions of how the processes of selection and adaptation interrelate (Levinthal, 1991). It is argued here, that regardless of which view is more dominant within the literature, any attempt to develop our understanding of why firms survive will be restricted by an inability to use appropriate ecological/evolutionary concepts and therefore ecological approaches. Let us consider a simple example.

The past work of Greve (2002: 847) provides a very interesting analysis of the importance of spatial heterogeneity to population evolution. Despite recognizing that 'organizations exist in a differentiated spatial ecology generated by past foundings and failures', the potential importance of the arguments presented are stymied by an apparent willingness to deal with this *new* issue, by using all the organizational ecology approaches developed (in the domain of organizational studies) since the seminal work of Hawley (1950). Thus a sociological paradigm of thought that excludes the most fundamental of ecological concepts is relied upon to make sense of spatial heterogeneity. Within the work of Greve, despite its availability, the simple concept of succession (so applicable to Greve's discussion) is not used. Neither is any consideration given to non-harmful coactions, nor is the issue of ecological scale employed. The point is, we as researchers of organizational phenomena have everything to gain from looking over the fence and shaking hands with the broader domain of ecology if we wish to claim we use such approaches wisely. During the past 30 years the field of organizational ecology has had hardly any influence outside 'the inner circle of its own parish' (van Witteloostuijn, 2000: 5).

Therefore, this study (metaphorically) has taken the opportunity to turn around to see where ecology has come from, before trying to extend its use moving forward. In summary, much new ground has been made by simply trying to be consistent. For example, by considering the environment to be firm dependent, we have an improved view of what exists for all (the external environment), but which may influence in different ways. We can consider how other firms might alter their operational environments, and how such environments can be formed from non-harmful interaction. We are able to conceive how some firms might have benefited from a process best labelled survival of the luckiest as their environment is altered in ways that immediately benefits them. We can also see that attempting to categorize firms as simply generalists or specialists is so problematic that it quite likely ignores that actual (alternating) function they perform within their location. We can also see that ignoring ecological scale is ignoring the very variance from which new and interesting explanations of firm survival might emerge. And finally we can see the potential danger of conducting any research that assumes the presence of competition without knowing: 1) what mechanisms act to produce negative coactions, and/or 2) don't account for patterns of attempted and/or actual resource capture.

Limitations of the Research

This study was conducted through the lens of transcendental realism. As such, the knowledge developed, while considered real is still held to be fallible. Realism holds that it may not be possible to observe every permutation relating to the generative mechanism. This study simply sought to confirm or disconfirm the model of *Transferred Demand* by finding support (or otherwise) for a series of postulates within the context of discovering a range of contingent conditions. It was not the aim of the study to *test* a theory, but rather to develop a model. This approach is in line with Moore and Upcraft's (1990) interpretation of how developing models leads to the eventual development of theories. A model of *Transferred Demand* is now developed and available to others for testing in future studies.

From an alternative perspective, the ontological approach employed imposes its own set of limitations; we would not expect another researcher who chose to investigate the same firms using a different approach, who gathered different data and analysed it differently, to draw the same conclusions. Of critical importance was the need to avoid committing an epistemic fallacy (Sayer, 2000) whereby scientific knowledge is derived only from what is directly given or observable (in the empirical domain). Therefore attention was given to what was possible, by using the process of retroduction within the context of a stratified reality. Perhaps the quote below best sums up the approach employed here and its limited need for generalization:

> An overall aim of science is to explain events and processes. To explain something implies (from the perspective of critical realism) first describing and conceptualizing the properties and the causal mechanism generating and enabling events, making things happen ... and then describing how different mechanisms

manifest themselves under specific conditions. This kind of investigation requires a methodological approach based on abduction and retroduction, and breaking with the so-called Popper-Hempel model of scientific explanations. (Danermark et al., 2002: 74)

Said another way, this study has the roots of its findings in the transfactual conditions it has explored. Danermark et al. (2002: 77) go on to say 'according to the realist concept of generality, scientific generalizations largely refer to transfactual conditions, to more or less universal preconditions for an object to be what it is'. Such comments build on Bhaskar's (1979: 227) view that 'scientifically significant generality does not lie on the face of the world, but in the hidden essence of things'. That said, whilst much of the variance in the landscape has been unearthed, it is more than quite likely that more remains to be discovered. Given the fact that many of the events under investigation had already occurred prior to the study's commencement, an outcomes-based explanation (see Mahoney, 2003) provided a logical approach to learning about the possible presence of a generative mechanism and its transfactual conditions. However, this may potentially reduce the acceptance of the findings by those that evaluate the validity and reliability of research in alternative ways. Therein lies a research limitation, but perhaps more accurately a research challenge, that of gaining legitimacy for the approach, findings and future research opportunities that arise from this study in the mainstream organizational studies literature. The remaining two chapters of this book focus upon these issues.

FINAL COMMENT: AN AUTECOLOGIST'S OPINION

Before this chapter concludes however, we should turn to the roots of the disciplines with which we are dealing, for any insights from such introspection. Both ecology and evolution (which were not initially differentiated from one another) and socioeconomics were developed during the Enlightenment, with the biological disciplines lagging. Few acknowledge the tension between ecology and socioeconomics, undoubtedly to the mutual detriment of the positive development of each. Ideology and idealization are thus still allowed to work their distorting influences, even on foundational statements. The reification of competitive selection, with density dependence the driving process, illustrates the extent to which such influences can affect interpretation and understanding. Perhaps the most damaging consequence, with respect to the topic of this book, is the accepted belief, in ecology as much as society, that the environment in which we live (along with all other organisms) is primarily competitive.

A further consequence, in OE and in demographic ecology, is the search for the general rules to which people, organizations and organisms are believed to respond. Such generalizations are, implicitly, natural laws or organising influences (Walter 2013). If organisms (including ourselves and our institutions) did respond to such influences, their nature and *modus operandi* would demand intimate understanding. Population and community ecology have delivered little in this regard. Besides, the theory associated with demographic ecology is clearly deficient, with the major problem being its exclusion from any consideration of the organisms themselves (Walter and Hengeveld 2014).

Alternative considerations should include, among their premises or foundational statements, the life and environment of the organisms themselves. Autecology does this explicitly (Walter and Hengeveld 2014). And that emphasis leads to perceptions of the ecology of organisms that are substantially different from those derived from demographic ecology. Perspectives of the environment, the organism–environment interaction, the relationships between organisms, and so on, all change fundamentally. And basic to the organism–environment interaction is an appreciation of the nature of environmental heterogeneity, mainly its structure and dynamics, and how it is affected by stochastic influences. All of this offers a tantalizing view of what is possible if we consider these aspects from the perspective of the individual organism (and its species-specific adaptations) or the individual firm (with its individualized sustenance activities). And so, too, we need to scrutinize the many derivative hypotheses that populate ecological writing, and have been applied to the life of firms. Those that relate to resource use and competition, in particular, need careful scrutiny as to their validity and utility. Naturally, the associated terminology also warrants scrutiny (Lambert and Hughes 1988).

The above suggestions all make sense for ecology (if one accepts the premises of autecology to start with). But how are we to apply such strictures to OE or FA? The obvious problem amplifies into several issues. Ecological theory has been transferred metaphorically to interpretation in the social sciences, in the form of OE (among other areas). Of itself, this is fine; our understanding, in general, depends on metaphor. But what if the principles of ecology (namely demographic ecology) were derived originally from socioeconomic perspectives in the first place? A compelling case has been made (see Young 1985; Todes, 1989). Clearly, Malthus and his followers saw the individual at the mercy of the competitive environment. And that is what defined their quality, and that settled their fate. The vast array of other environmental influences immediately became subservient to this dominating influence. These other influences are often mentioned, but their true relevance is downplayed along with the life of the organism. Autecology and firm autecology provide an opportunity to re-examine these basic tenets and to develop a more accurate and less idealized perception of our world. It asks of its proponents a willingness to understand the foundational premises around which research activity is organized and accomplished.

PART IV

Towards an Autecological Approach

6. Methodological issues

> Ecology has no aim, but ecologists have. The problems of ecologists are not fundamentally different from those of any other kind of naturalist. The superficial differences in aim are due to the different points of view, or methods of approach, rather than to any essential difference in the character of the problems. (Adams, 1913: 1)

The firms we seek to study autecologically are assumed to face problems, that while often similar in nature, occur at different times during their development, have potentially differing consequences, and may be solved through different means. The nature of such problem solving is of primary interest to us. Given the diversity of problems and opportunities firms deal with on a daily basis, we argue that it is logical that a great deal of variation will accumulate within various industry contexts over time. That variation, if not consistently and uniformly selected for and against, will result in diversity of firm structures, form and/or behaviour.

Such variation, complexity and diversity are present in all evolutionary systems (McShea and Brandon, 2010). Our specific interest however, is the firm's adaptive mechanisms/interacting elements and related environmental phenomena that interact to produce important ecological outcomes for individual firms. By studying the ecological significant activities of firms that produce adaptive or maladaptive outcomes, we can incorporate the spatio-temporal dynamics of higher-level evolutionary systems. Doing so enables us to transcend knowledge beliefs related to industries and build more precise knowledge about types of firms operating in specific industries.

This process of *knowing* preferences different ecological aims (Adams, 1913) and ecological data that others may categorize as annoying, or chaotic noise. This chapter seeks not to argue the merits of one approach versus another. Rather, we simply wish to provide clarity around the methodological and philosophical foundations of an autecological study of firms. Our suggestions are intended to signal our acceptance of methodological pluralism (Bell and Newby, 1977). We do not organize our data collection actions on the basis of assumed ecological laws that rely upon demographic ecology principles. Rather, we remain mindful of the idiosyncrasy of firms and the stochastic influences that would most certainly undermine the establishment of such convenient patterns, as expected in the OE approach. With this in mind, let us consider several methodological issues that must accompany the further development of our theory of the firm and its environment.

INFERENCE FROM PROXIES

Autecology is fundamentally concerned about individual-level behaviour. In the context of the study of firms, an autecological study is free to celebrate the opportunity to collect data that is largely free from inference. In other words, individual firms can represent themselves in datasets, rather than be inferred from information related to higher levels of aggregated data. Ecological inference (King, Rosen and Tanner, 2004: 1) 'is the process of extracting clues about individual behaviour from information reported at the group or aggregated level'. In OE studies, this issue has been identified as a cause for concern (Baum and Shipilov, 2006), given the OE preference towards generality over precision.

Our approach frees the researcher from making ecological assumptions about the process of competition and/or the presence of a carrying capacity and/or legitimacy as key factors through which to explain firm survival. In contrast to every other animal and plant that ecologists may choose to study, firms can be studied over long periods, in part because unique and accurate data related to their lifeline is available, and collected without the type of ecological inference typical in demographic studies.

Our firms have histories that have been recorded in various artefacts, they have voices through which to explain current and past behaviours, and their actions have typically been witnessed by many other firms and/or potential commentators. The autecological study of firms offers social researchers a unique opportunity to embrace the study of any firm's lifeline using many ecological theories and concepts, their application of which can be verified through conversations and other available records.

Such opportunities do warrant a warning, however. Hodgson's (2001: 90) *Principle of Consistency* specifies that, 'explanations in one domain have to be consistent with explanations in another, despite examination of different properties and deployment of different concepts'. This suggests that while autecological studies of the firm should enable the social researcher to get close to the problems and opportunities that firms confront, they must do so not having merely haphazardly borrowed concepts without fully understanding their consistency in usage. Two examples can quickly demonstrate this point.

The Challenge of Two Ecological Approaches

Throughout this book, we have championed an alternative ecological approach to the study of firms. We have drawn comparisons to the existing OE approach (see Table 1.1), identifying distinctly different principles upon which the two ecological approaches are developed. As argued previously (Hengeveld and Walter, 1999), these two approaches are mutually exclusive in that 'each of these paradigms dictates a different starting point for any ecological investigation and alternative investigation pathways' (Walter and Hengeveld, 2014: 10). As such, it is fairly obvious that each approach would most likely produce different interpretations and conclusions of similar phenomena. Understanding the assumptions that underpin each approach is a responsibility that falls upon each researcher.

Looking Outward

The second example is quite straightforward. In the early chapters of this book we have detailed the manner in which ideas have been imported from the natural sciences into the social sciences. We have highlighted the influence of sociology from the 1920s to present day in terms of how community and competition have been at the forefront of such development. We have also highlighted many translation errors, overlooked works and the isolation of such thinking from more general ecological thinking. An autecological approach to the study of the firm opens new avenues of interaction between practising ecologists and social scientists. Rather than learning our ecological craft from looking inwards, we can look outward and work with and learn from ecological experts whose knowledge is accepted across multiple domains.

GETTING CLOSER TO THE RESEARCH PROBLEM

In the previous chapter, the initial observations reported from the Australian context were inconsistent with assumptions of the regularly employed density dependence and competition models. Despite concerns (Petersen and Koput, 1991) that unobserved heterogeneity is not taken seriously, the *generality* of the density dependence approach within OE is preferred to the alternative aim of achieving greater 'precision of measurement and realism of context' (Singh, 1993: 471). As a result, many empirical findings (see Hannan and Freeman, 1989; Hannan and Carroll, 1992) regularly fail to find support in other studies of similar and/or the same phenomena (see Aldrich and Wiedenmayer, 1993). What is missing entirely is any real consideration of the individual firm and the unique problems and opportunities they confront. Instead, great faith is placed in the logical presence of a carrying capacity, despite the growing acceptance that calculating the carrying capacity of any population of firms is essentially impossible (as it is too, in ecology) given the influence of man's behaviour and use of technology to alter resource usage and availability (Cohen, 1995). As a result, all too often, ecological studies of firms remained too distanced from the subject matter they claim to investigate.

Ecologists have long known that size truly matters (Haldane, 1985), and the FA approach being proposed would enable such differences to be identified and understood. Following the logic of Grimm and Railsback (2005), the aim is not to replace the OE approach, but rather to offer an alternative approach through which new kinds of problems can be studied using new methods related to individual firms. As other mainstream ecologists have long advocated (see Price, Slobodchikoff and Gaud, 1984), ecology as a field must develop new approaches to better capture the life histories of that which it aims to study. Developments in ecology, and of course autecology, demonstrate ever-increasing sophistication in how we can imagine and study the many alternative adaptive solutions evolved by organisms to match the requirements of their ever-changing environment conditions.

Our approach returns a focus to Daubenmire's (1947) original concern for the *welfare* of that which is studied. By concerning ourselves with how firms change and/or retain their form, structures, functions and activities vis-à-vis the environmental circumstances they confront, we stay cognisant of all likely research problems, from the perspective of the firm. In this sense, the nature of the research problems that interest us relate directly to the adaptive mechanisms of these firms we can observe directly. Unlike the OE approach, we are not guided by law-like generalizations nor are we primarily dependent upon received data.

NATURE LOVES TO HIDE

It has been said that *nature loves to hide* (Morton, 2013), and in line with this view, Møller and Jennions (2002) highlight six factors that would also be expected to prevent organizational ecologists from being able to envisage, capture and explain all the variation present in their studies. First, the contexts we choose to study are not perfect, for there are lags between events and selection, and between selection pressures and responses that precede eventual selection (for or against). Second, there is inherent randomness in the contexts we study; no two towns, cities or regions are the same. Third, there are so many possible responses that firms can attempt to deal with perceived environmental change, yet typically only a few are focused upon. This leaves space for confounding variables to create sufficient noise to blur the assumed relationship between other variables. Fourth, many firms' actions vary considerably across time and space and are therefore difficult to measure. Fifth, it is difficult to capture the evolutionary past of all firms being studied. Thus, the capacity of each firm to respond differently is also difficult to explain. Last, the actions of one firm can alter (negatively or positively) the outcomes of other firms and their operational environments, a difficult dynamic to observe, let alone model.

We choose to accept the validity of these concerns. Our observations of firms and the environments they experience intuitively speak to all six concerns. We also recognize the 'particular way of doing science' (Cuddington and Beisner, 2005: 420) that is accepted in the demographic or OE approach. Rather than waste energy trying to propose new ways of doing science within an existing and established paradigm, we instead embrace these issues within an alternative paradigm. For the reasons outlined previously, the incommensurability (Kuhn, 1962: 150) that exists between OE and our FA approach is critically important to understand. First, as highlighted in Table 1.1, both approaches clearly focus on different problems and use different assumptions. Second, there is a high degree of meaning variance across the vocabularies of the two approaches. Third, both approaches essentially 'practice their trade in different worlds' making different ontological choices along the way.

These fundamental choices can be reduced to a preference of the dominance of the community over the individual or of the individual and its species-specific adaptations interacting with its local environment. This debate, as we noted earlier, has strong roots in the works of Park and Burgess (1921), on one side, and MacIver (1917) on the other. Bews (1935: 37) argued strongly that for human ecology (now OE) to advance, the interplay between these two competing positions would 'best be brought to light by the autecological method ... [where] ... instead of beginning with the community as a whole, the life of the individual is studied'. He felt that only through understanding the life-history of man's persistence through time could the process of adaptation to the environment be understood. In proposing our concern for each firm's lifeline to be understood we are aligned to the views of Bews. In doing so, we need to be ever mindful of several methodological issues.

IN EMERGENCE WE TRUST

Several years ago, Barney Glaser (2005) commented, in direct relation to the early stages of the study of Pizza shops presented in Chapter 5, that *all is data, keeping trying, it will emerge*. This book is the product of two inquiring minds that feel free to move between discipline boundaries and question the conventional wisdom often protected by the social and natural sciences. What we have come to recognize is the value of a common methodological approach to both *seeing* and *understanding* (Sears, 1935) the variance of ecological processes we investigate. Our past research approaches (Jones, 2009; Walter, 2013) clearly evidence a willingness to trust the data we engage with to reveal patterns and suggest what underlying processes or mechanisms generated those patterns. Further, we trust ourselves to step back and sort between these patterns to discern between those that are merely by-products of other patterns, and those that actually require direct consideration.

This data-driven approach is evident in both of our past approaches. For example, Jones (2009) moved from observations of firm survival in one context, to identifying the dimensions of a postulated explanation, to subjecting that proposed explanation to empirical scrutiny in another empirical context. Similarly, Walter and Hengeveld (2014) outline a three-step process to conducting autecological research. First, with reference to the adaptive mechanisms of organisms, identify related processes deemed central to the adaptive process. Second, inductively estimate the variables that determine the process under investigation. Third, develop testable analytical models that are mechanistic in nature. In both approaches, further data collection enables testing and refinement of the proposed models.

The issue here is that neither approach employs deterministic assumptions to guide the first-hand observations made with regard to *seeing* and *understanding* (Sears, 1935) the variance of the ecological processes we investigate. While ecology has been aligned with the 'unremitting search for causes' (Clements, 1935: 342) in both the natural and social sciences, our approaches in both domains truly embrace this notion in its original sense.

Accommodating the Observer's Experience and Reasoning

When we focus on the presence, operation and influence of mechanisms we must be mindful of the structures and conditions that surround assumed mechanisms (Fleetwood and Ackroyd, 2004). The study of mechanisms is by no means straightforward. Mechanisms have causal powers dependent upon the nature of the structures and conditions that surround them. We must be prepared to rely upon qualitative explanations of the presence and operation of mechanisms to visualize their operation (Sayer, 1992). In doing so we rely upon the experience and knowledge of the researcher to interpret and understand what they observe. Again, the importance of *seeing* and *understanding* (Sears, 1935) is critically important. There is a need to recognize the training and experience of the researcher doing the observations. In any given situation there will most likely be multiple mechanisms capable of potential interaction. Under certain conditions, one mechanism may temporarily hold sway over the potential influence of another, and vice versa. The ability to understand the actors and performances occurring in any ecological theatre is paramount to investigating mechanisms.

In this context, it is less important that researchers remain value *free* and/or value *laden* (Healy and Perry, 2000), but rather, remain value *aware*. The process of investigating the spatiotemporal dynamics of firms will always be influenced by the values of the researcher to some extent. Being attuned to the special ecological conditions that support the operation of ecological mechanisms through which firm survival can be explained is an acquired skill. It requires of the researcher an awareness and acceptance of the idiosyncrasy of firms and the stochastic influences that limit the formation of predictable patterns, or laws, that are expected when operating within the OE paradigm.

The ideas of Ragin (1994) help to explain the process that subconsciously occurs frequently when researchers enter the field. Ragin argues that the researcher relies upon particular analytic frames to draw upon certain theories to deductively see the world they wish to investigate. They also develop certain images of the world they investigate inductively to acquire evidence, or data. Ragin argues that most researchers combine these inductive and deductive processes through a process of retroduction. This is an important point, though one that can fall prey to confusion. There are many interpretations of the terms abduction and retroduction (see Hanson, 1958; Ragin, 1994; Danermark et al., 2002; Fleetwood and Ackroyd, 2004; Buchanan and Bryman, 2011), some of which are similar to one another, some that are not. We prefer to stay with the original works of Charles Peirce who coined the term 'retroduction'.

It has been argued that retroduction 'represents an attempt to overcome the pitfalls of purely inductive or deductive research processes' (Sæther, 1998: 246). Moreover, Peirce (1908: 104) argues that it is a form of reasoning through which 'spontaneous conjecture of instinctive reason' provides the intellectual foundations for new ideas to eventually be deductively explicated and/or inductively evaluated. Retroduction is an *initial* thought process through which the provisional plausibility of something is held to be possible. Peirce wonderfully captures the essence of the process when he says:

> The whole series of mental performances between the notice of the wonderful phenomenon and the acceptance of the hypothesis, during which the usually docile understanding seems to hold the bit between its teeth and to have us at its mercy–the search for pertinent circumstances and the laying hold of them, sometimes without our cognisance, the scrutiny of them, the dark labouring, the bursting out of the startling conjecture, the remarking of its smooth fitting to the anomaly, as it is turned back and forth like a key in a lock, and the final estimation of its plausibility, I reckon as composing the first stage of inquiry. (Ibid: 100)

For Peirce, such journeys via retroduction are essential for the development of new ideas from which deductions can be drawn and compared against future observations. Danermark et al. (2002: 96) argue that 'retroduction is about advancing from one thing ... and arriving at something different'. The notion of the fitting of an ever-altering conjecture to an anomaly perfectly describes the process of developing a model to explain the persistence of firms persisting across and within different operating conditions. At no point will the researcher be afforded any degree of security from the retroduction process, merely the confidence to 'enter ... [a] ... skiff of musement ... [and to] ... push off into the lake of thought' (ibid: 95), a journey where *all is data* (Glaser, 2001).

It is within this context that we highlight the need for the researcher to ensure familiarity with the history and present state of ecological thought before embarking on an autecological journey. It would make no sense to speculate upon the working of a firm's adaptive mechanisms whilst trapped in a cage built from a handful of thoroughly deterministic ecological laws. Thus, the methodological issues that arise in this discussion are quite challenging. In this sense, we accept the ideas of Ragin (1994), but with one important qualification.

Rather than seeing retroduction as a process of unifying deductive and inductive reasoning, we can view it as a scientific form of reasoning through *perceptive judgements* born from the researcher's life, and acted upon using combinations of inductive and deductive processes. That our actual representations of the social world are indeed linked to our values, and that we must remain *aware* of these values in terms of the choices we make and the limitations they may add to our endeavours. It is through such perceptive judgements that we can confidently rely upon the process of heuristic generalizations (Walter, 2013) to guide our autecological investigations. We can investigate the adaptive mechanisms and related sustenance activities of firms confident that through understanding their spatiotemporal dynamics we will develop ecological explanations of their persistence. Further, such observations can be modelled and combinations of inductive and deductive processes can be used to test the veracity of our initial and eventual reasoning.

DOING AUTECOLOGICAL RESEARCH

Given that firms are presently researched by social scientists using the OE approach, it is important that we clearly outline the difference methodologically between the OE approach and our proposed FA approach. With reference to the work of Walter and Hengeveld (2014) we can highlight a key difference. Importantly, OE assumes the existence of external laws (for example, population regulation and competitive exclusion) that are presumed to regulate population and community structures. In contrast, FA assumes no such external laws, so the responsibility is on the researcher to develop models of firm persistence vis-à-vis observed adaptive mechanisms. Thus, it is the properties of the individual firm, their organization and alteration within the firm, and their expression through the firm's interacting elements that we concentrate fully upon. Conversely, the OE approach is organized upon assumptions related to age, size and density issues that are expected to moderate the influence of competition and legitimacy within populations. From recognition of these fundamental differences, we can organize the process of autecological investigation.

The research presented in Chapter 5 was performed using a critical realist (Bhaskar, 1975) approach. This type of approach ensures a focus on mechanisms and the structures and the conditions related to their operation. In contrast to alternative empiricist or constructionist case study approaches, the emphasis upon structural processes and an openness to retroductive reasoning remains (Edwards, O'Mahoney and Vincent, 2014). This approach also enables the research process to combine elements of both intensive and extensive research designs (Harré, 1979), thus enabling multiple questions about mechanisms to be addressed simultaneously (Buchanan and Bryman, 2011). As such, this type of approach increases the likelihood of penetrating 'below the surface to identify underlying social mechanisms or generative mechanisms' (ibid: 534). This is done by employing two related forms of discovery logic. First, knowledge is developed about the presence of generative mechanisms. Second, knowledge is developed about the conditions that surround the operation (and non-operation) of such mechanisms.

Case studies provide the most likely research design vehicle to study in detail the activities and behaviours related to mechanisms in firms. These mechanisms are quite likely embedded in social processes, and are therefore difficult to identify, observe and understand from more typical survey data collection methods (Rouse and Daellenbach, 1999), and all the more so when the heterogeneity of the surrounding environments are also taken into account.

However, as is increasingly common today, a mixed method approach (Creswell, 2003) is advocated to enable the collection of data from historical archives, properties of the firm, semi-structured interviews, informal conversations, researcher observations and other collection methods. Such an approach increases the opportunity to achieve triangulated support for the developed postulates when developing and subsequently submitting models to empirical scrutiny. The use of mixed methods means that the weaknesses inherent in intensive or extensive case study approaches can be further negated. As has been demonstrated many times in the history of organization studies, such in-depth approaches have highlighted that firms are quite often 'of sufficient complexity that they are not fully known to the participants in them' (Buchanan and Bryman, 2011: 535). Under such circumstances, it is the ecological reasoning of the researcher that can advance an autecological investigation of the firm and its environment. No theory can be so precise as to explain in advance the operation of mechanisms (in unpredictable environments) that are influenced by chance, folly and perception. No theory of the firm can know in advance what actions and outcomes will eventuate from a combination of human agency, perceived problems or opportunities and unpredictable environments. This is the capricious micro-landscape of the autecologist who seeks to understand the sustenance activities of firms.

THE CRYPTIC FIRM COMPLEX

This chapter has outlined the methodological issues that would accompany an alternative ecological study of individual firms (or types of firms) and mechanisms through which they maintain their sustenance activities. There is a reason why the idea of an *individual* firm, or *type* of firm is stressed. The development of a FA approach must pay special attention to eliminate, as in biology (Paterson, 1993), the potential for cryptic species to be conflated inappropriately. As illustrated in Chapter 2, six sub-types of Pizza firms were recognized as belonging to a cryptic *firm* complex. Each type is a *true* firm, with a unique and identifiable ecology, but which is associated with morphological and physiological differences. That is, observable differences are evident in the form and structures used to develop, operate and modify the firm's functions and activities.

We argue that in the social sciences these concerns matter as much, if not more, than it does in mainstream ecological research, given the obvious implications for research design. Viewing firms from an autecological perspective increases the likelihood of the cryptic firm problem as being as big a concern in the social sciences as it is in the natural sciences. As noted earlier, in the natural world the information required to enable the replication of any form of life is stored with high accuracy and transmitted with equally high accuracy. Alternatively, the average firm does not maintain highly accurate stores of information from which to ensure its replication. When such replication is attempted, the fallible processes of learning and imitation are relied upon to transmit information from one firm context to another. We would therefore expect to observe a tendency towards increasing diversity during this evolutionary process (McShea and Brandon, 2010).

In addition, we have made the argument that spatiotemporal dynamics will also play a part in ensuring this tendency towards diversity, as individual firms in local environments evolve over time as they solve different problems related to their operating environment. Consequently, in any given industry, over time, we expect to see multiple forms of *firm-types* emerge. While many franchised firms do store and replicate information with higher degrees of accuracy, such firms are not numerically dominant across most industries. Thus, the likelihood of such a problem remains ever-present.

In mainstream ecology this problem has long been recognized, with Mayr (1957) connecting the issue of the species problem with the increase in autecological studies, where observing and understanding behaviour at the individual level was of primary importance to the researcher. Given that, by and large, we are not dealing with *interbreeding* situations between firms, in any biological sense, we need to develop our own processes of identification to manage this issue within a social context. Figure 6.1 represents the first step in our thinking in this regard.

Firm A	Firm B	Similarity
Functions	Functions	as a %
Activities	Activities	as a %
Form	Form	as a %
Structures	Structures	as a %

Degree
of Firm
Similarity

Figure 6.1   Firm similarity index

As discussed earlier, all firms demonstrate specific forms and structures across their lifelines. Likewise, all firms develop, use and modify specific functions and activities to enact their sustenance activities. Figure 6.1 directs the researcher's mind to the degrees of similarity between any two firms across these four areas of focus. In Chapter 5, Pianka's (1973) Community Similarity Index was used to assist in the process of making an ecological decision about the merits of aggregating data from various separate towns. Figure 6.1 extends the logic of such thinking, forcing the researcher to make comparisons between firms (across their functions, activities, form and structures) vis-à-vis the direct comparability and/or joint inclusion in a cryptic firm complex. While we acknowledge the substantial work required to complete this index, we also note our confidence in: 1) the need for such an index, and 2) the logic of our starting point.

While we are concerned that firms can be seen to differ across their form, structures, functions and activities, ultimately, we are more interested in how such differences have been created and maintained. How has an individual firm's interaction with its environment influenced its form, structures, functions and activities during and across its lifeline? What different types of sensory behaviour and/or interacting elements support persistence and how are they related to differences and/or similarities in form, structures, functions and activities? The autecologist must look beyond classifications in trade and telephone directories to ascertain that the firms we wish to study are identifiable by specific forms of organization, behaviour and environmental relations. McKelvey's (1982) thinking on homologous characters provides an outline of the taxonomic challenges of trying to sort firms into related and different types. Like McKelvey, we also see challenges in accounting for a potential larger number of homologous characters in the social sciences than in the natural sciences (due to previously discussed differences in information acquisition, use and transfer).

Therefore, in acknowledging the increased likelihood of the cryptic firm problem, we are also required to incorporate this concern into our research designs. Doing so will provide access to industry-based data concerning differences between firms concerning resource acquisition and usage, sensory behaviour, and lifeline development. We are confidently able to predict that the firms we wish to study are reducible to forms, structures, functions and activities, which is where our challenge begins. This sameness, or homology (Dawkins, 2009) is not easily traceable through ancient lines of decent. The indirect transmission of information and imperfect copying common to our contexts, means that our work will be best achieved embracing the tendency towards diversity we expect to see in cryptic firm complexes.

SUMMARY

Autecology represents a brave and exciting approach to the study of firms. It does so because of the manner in which it chooses to investigate the adaptive mechanisms of firms. As a result, different assumptions and research methods are required to account for the different individual behaviours expected to constitute a firm's lifeline. We have outlined the nature of the research design issues and challenges that are required to fully investigate and understand, in ecological terms, the presence of a firm over time and the related spatiotemporal dynamics that also determine the firm's lifeline. This is unashamedly a firm-centred approach that preferences the importance of ecological scale (Wiens, 1989) over generalized ecological laws that are assumed to most influence the survival of firms in communities and populations.

In doing so, we are free to act on Baum and Shipilov's (2006) call for greater consideration of spatial components, geographical barriers and/or localized resource environments in the ecological study of firms. We have explained the importance of *all being data* (Glaser, 2005) and the opportunities to use mixed method approaches to combine various forms of primary and secondary data with the spoken and written histories of individual firms and their environs. Our ecological aims (Adams, 1913) have been explained in good faith, not to compete with those of the more established OE approach, but to illustrate the unique nature and the strength of the proposed FA approach.

We recognize the challenge of adhering to Hodgson's (2001) principle of consistency. That has been a motivating factor in the collaborative nature of this work. We see great opportunities for social scientists to look outward and collaborate with practising ecologists in the natural sciences prior to planning and engaging in ecological studies of firms. This, we believe represents a great opportunity for researchers to learn how to get closer to the ecological phenomena they are naturally curious about. We will discuss further, in the following chapter, the types of research opportunities we believe this approach will enable us to address, and the insights this will bring to the socioeconomic understanding of firms and their operations.

An important point we have sought to communicate, is that our approach and motivations are well supported by past work that highlights the challenges of understanding the interplay between individual and community perspectives (MacIver, 1917), and proposing ideas that challenge the status quo (Kuhn, 1962). We have been quite candid about the willingness of the researcher to suspend judgement and trust that *understanding* will emerge from observation if given the chance. The key we believe is to remain aware of our values as we strive to become aware of the nuanced firm-level behaviours we observe. It is now time to consider the nature of research opportunities that can be addressed using an autecological approach.

7.   Opportunities and future directions

One difference is the level of aggregation the theory of the firm ought to address: is it one firm or a population of competing firms? Although the theory's label speaks of 'the firm' as if the theory deals with a single organization, the theory actually says little about the activities within a single organization. (Starbuck, Salgado and Mezias, 2006: 470)

In the Introduction to this work, we observed there is more than one theory of the firm, and that each one serves a particular purpose within different sub-domains of organizational research (Alvarez, 2003). What is missing in the theory of the firm is any true consideration of the individual firm, and its operating environment. Even in the resource-based theory of the firm, we need to reference other firms to enable judgments of competitive advantage to be made. In this book we have developed the outline of an autecological theory of the firm and its environment. Through this approach, the persistence through time of a single firm or multiple firms is explicable with reference to the adaptive mechanisms of the firm (or, the methods through which a particular firm engages with its operational environment). Through this approach we can enfold all the complexity of the firm's environment to achieve clarity, through the concept of the operational environment. In doing so, we believe we have advanced a truly alternative ecological approach through which to better understand the complex interplay between firm and environment. We note, too, the operational environment of any particular firm does potentially include other firms, each of which may influence that environment.

The object of science is to carry the light of understanding, to show us truth. If a piece of research aids us understand better, more fully, some aspect of this so complex universe of man and nature, then it is worthwhile. If it does not, then no parade of figures will make it anything more than labor lost. (MacIver, 1931)

In the spirit of MacIver (1968), we wish to be *honest witnesses* of the struggles and triumphs of the firm in its daily battle to reign supreme over the environmental conditions with which it interacts. When we speak of the firm, we refer to all firms, the large or small, physical or virtual, private or public, knowledge or asset intensive, and/or those deemed to be entrepreneurial or non-entrepreneurial. From our perspective, there are no firms in existence that are not worthy of our attention. In line with the reasoning of Haukioja (1982), when we observe a firm operating, we are observing a firm that to some degree is succeeding relative to the opportunities and problems that exist in its operational environment (although any assessment of future performance of such a firm would be based on speculation). As such, we see enormous opportunities to develop much more extensively our autecological theory of the firm and its environment. We believe that this outline of a new theory of the firm (and its environment) provides many opportunities for firms of all shapes and sizes to be investigated using a common approach. The remainder of this chapter will consider the nature and scope of these opportunities and act as an invitation to others to become further intrigued by such possibilities.

DRAWING TOGETHER QUESTIONS

An autecological theory of the firm and its environment is, perhaps surprisingly, holistic in approach, drawing upon many potential processes to explain ecological outcomes. Our attention is naturally drawn to the foundations of the firm, its learning abilities (Cyert and March, 1963), and the routines (Nelson and Winter, 1982) developed to facilitate standard operating procedures. We are intrigued by the ability of firms to search (Gavetti and Levinthal, 2000) for clues about stability and change in their operational environment, and the methods they use in this quest. More specifically, we are interested in knowing the type of knowledge the firm has of all factors in their operational environment, and the degree of comprehension regarding their interrelationships (Endsley and Jones, 2012).

We are also interesting in knowing about the degree and nature of attention (Ocasio and Joseph, 2005) paid to the reorganization of internal activities and interaction elements, and the interplay between top-down and bottom-up related pressures (Ocasio, 2011). As such, we scrutinize the nature of the network ties that facilitate both internal and external knowledge development, and subsequent knowledge sharing, that may support decision-making related to adaptive behaviours (Axelrod and Cohen, 1999). Therefore, the inherent tension related to the firm's exploration and exploitation efforts (March, 1991) are also of interest to us.

We are also curious about the extent to which Barnett and Sørensen's (2002) red queen effect is really present in industries, and how firms might actually alter the operational environment of other firms in the ways postulated by this approach. Indeed, we are not only interested in environment-to-firm influences, but also firm-to-environment influences and the ecological inheritance that may therefore result. While others explore new and exciting opportunities related to institutional environments (Gavetti et al., 2012), we, while sensing our connection to such work, remain committed to exploring the operational environment of the firm. This does not preclude a concern for the broader institutional, or external environment, but our focus is authentically firm-centred. We retain this focus because it is within the operational environment of each firm that we believe the truth about the relationship with the environment will be located.

A Fascination with All Performance

By declaring our interest in all firms, we therefore are interested in all measures of performance. We do not expect to see firms competing to out-perform other firms in the normal course of events, because the range of everyday processes to consider in operating a firm is vast. We are hoping to understand the ecology of all firms, transcending restrictive firm-level issues like size, age or education attainment. We do not doubt there is a place for strategizing for superior performance (McGahan, 2004), but see an advantage to remaining focused on the persistence of the majority, rather than on the survival of the fittest. As stated earlier, 'adaptive improvement is relative to the adaptive problem' (Sahlins and Service, 1960: 15). We can even imagine a scenario whereby firms decrease the nature of their complexity so as to meet the requirements of their local environment. For example, in line with industry trends, a firm adopts certain technologies that influence the nature of interaction between the firm and key stakeholders. Over time, the firm may determine that such potential advancement actually creates a mismatch between the firm and the requirements of its local environment. Despite what is happening elsewhere in the industry, this firm may achieve a better environmental match through simplifying the nature of its interacting elements.

Such an example of *specific* evolution (Sahlins and Service, 1960) represents the movement of ecological curiosity from outside the firm (Hannan and Freeman, 1977), to inside the firm. Adaptation and the learning and decision-making that would typically accompany such processes are of ecological interest to the autecologist. Instead of contrasting firms from most adapted to least adapted, in the sense of Sahlins and Service's general evolution, we choose to focus elsewhere. Our thinking in this regard brings to life past concerns for the individual behaviour of firms.

> The fact that we expect all organizations to seek the same state – self-control – does not mean that we expect all of them to attain it in the same way, with identical design, structures, or behaviour. It is essential that we find universals, but equally essential to find patterns in variations. (Thompson, 1967: 161)

We argue that society is filled with many potentially interesting ecological patterns (see Alderson, 1957) that relate directly and indirectly to firm persistence. However, past attempts to investigate firms ecologically have been ambushed by preference being given to one particular process, competition, simply because it has been assumed to be the driving force behind the initiation and success of firms. Other patterns tended to be pushed aside. We aim to breathe life back into the pioneering works of Thompson (1967), Lawrence and Lorsch (1967), Meyer and Rowan (1977) and Pfeffer and Salancik (1978) by adding one major difference to their thinking. The idea of an operational environment does not preclude the potential presence of a common external environment to which all firms in an industry are subject; we just think it unlikely. By first isolating each firm within its local environment we can understand the ramifications of grouping such firms at higher levels. This is the major benefit gained from releasing each firm from automatic association within a population (that is typically specified without identified reference points by an outside observer).

Having entitled each firm to exist within an operational environment, and to influence it, we immediately sidestep longstanding criticisms related to the study of firms. Concerns have been expressed with regard to a lack of control over the types of firms that have been aggregated into a population (Filley and Aldag, 1978) and that not all firms will inevitably share equal growth aspirations (Penrose, 1959). An inadequate appreciation that such growth aspirations not only may differ, but also may be inconsequential vis-à-vis other properties directly related to persistence (Whetten, 1988).

If we were to revisit Pfeffer and Salancik's (1978) resource dependence theory and redefine the firm's environment to be more consistent with our own thinking, it could be easily viewed as being autecological. Rather than assuming the environment is largely a constraining force determined by industry factors, we could step beyond this proposed enacting of environment, to deal more directly with the ways in which firms actually match the requirements of the environment, as well as modify it.

The same could be said of Child's (1975) strategic theory where the environment is defined so broadly that it is difficult to comprehend what the firm is considered to be responding to and shaping. Nevertheless, the original ideas of Child fit nicely with our sense of autonomy that an individual firm could demonstrate. Likewise, we find the idea of resource heterogeneity in the resource-based view of the firm (Barney, 1991) is intuitively obvious, but are left disappointed by an unwillingness to extend such independence to the actual environment in which firms operate. Once the researcher is emancipated from broad, complex and almost impossible to visualize conceptions of the environment, he or she is free to look closely at the nature and specifics of the firm–environment interaction.

We argue that once sufficient clarity is brought to bear upon the nature of such interactions, the notion of comparative firm performance becomes less interesting than the very persistence of any firm in a given environment. We feel it is significant that the lessons learned are will inevitably be substantially different, and much more revealing of the life of firms. For example, it is easy to compare the inefficiency of government-run firms versus private-run firms (van der Mandele and van Witteloostuijn, 2013), but that misses the point. The real issue relates to whether government-run firms match the requirements of their specific operational environment, what deficiencies may be present and, perhaps, whether their environment differs from that of private firms. They may, indeed, be as efficient as a private firm vis-à-vis their interactions with their own operational environment. By conflating the two operations into one environment it is easy, but incorrect, to make comparative judgments about efficiency. Using our approach, we can quickly recognize the more elastic ecological dimension within the government-run firm's operational environment. That dimension is highly unlikely to exist in an environment of the private-run firm, and this compromises all simplistic comparisons. Whether the provision of a substantial flow of funds to some government-run firms is good for society is not really an appropriate question for an autecologist, he or she merely needs to understand persistence in the context of such potential resource flows. Once the logic of such thinking is contemplated, we are free to also consider why some say that firm mortality declines with age, despite also finding that firm performance does not improve with age (Meyer and Zucker, 1989). Might it be related to how we define performance and what we put up for comparisons of mortality? This sounds like a research opportunity ripe for identifying cryptic firm complexes and how these should be treated and investigated.

Autecological Patience

A good working knowledge of organization theory provides a large toolkit of mechanisms—sometimes-true theories—for explaining the evolution of economic institutions, and there is sense in remaining agnostic ex ante rather than being wedded to, say, birth and death, or diffusion, or adaptation, as the true-or-false explanation. (Davis and Marquis, 2005: 340)

A virtue of the autecologist is patience. Walter (2013) notes that the autecological approach to understanding the responses of organisms emphasizes the species-specificity of interaction between the organism and its environment across its lifeline. The same emphasis applies to our FA approach. We must fully appreciate the nature of the firm's sustenance activities and the activity systems from which they are produced and supported in the first instance. Then we can concentrate on the nature of the interactions that take place between firm and environment. Developing such familiarity happens through remaining agnostic ex ante and being guided by heuristic generalizations. Doing so enables the researcher to deliberately observe the potential uniqueness of individual firms and find patterns associated with the spatiotemporal dynamics aligned to the lifeline of the firm/s in question.

By remaining open to the importance of spatiotemporal dynamics and the nature of the problems and opportunities encountered by any given firm, the autecologist remains free to draw upon many different ecological tools to explain the patterns that are perceived. Indeed, exposure to the 'cogs and wheels' (Hernes, 1998: 74), their forward, reverse and static motions, may enable the researcher to understand the invisible interaction between human agency, firm activities and internal and external environmental processes, only then can the selective environment even begin to be contemplated. The challenge we sense: to allow our observations to be also combined with our awareness of 'bits of sometimes-true theories' (Davis and Marquis, 2005: 340). Such a process can open a door to a new area of discussion in organization studies, that being the nature of selection.

EXPLORING SELECTION

With the exception of a few works (see Amburgey, Dacin and Kelly, 1994; Jones, 2007), the process of selection has remained quite simple in its description in the organizational studies literature. Firms are located in populations and these populations of firms experience selection for and against certain types of firms. The fundamental belief is that competition among the firms that make up the population is the driver for selecting *winners*. This is the essence of Darwinian selection (Brady, 1982; Paterson, 2005). Viewing firms at such an aggregated level thus enables us to assume that only a 'single pattern of selection' (Amburgey, Dacin and Kelly, 1994: 253) is acting upon the population we study. We see winners and losers and make sense of these outcomes based on our interpretation of a single process of selection. Actually, we can and should always have several processes of selection in mind when contemplating external selection acting on firms.

Selection, whichever process is responsible, may be disruptive, directional or stabilizing.

What is critically important is ensuring that we understand the level at which such processes of selection can be seen to act upon. While OE may infer that a single process of selection of acts upon a population of firms, this does little to help us understand the persistence (or not) of individual firms. We must observe selection at the level of what Hull (2001) terms the behavioural environment, what we call the operational environment. That is, selection is acting on individual firms, not upon a population of firms. To ignore this fact is to deprive the individual firm an opportunity to respond to perceived problems and/or opportunities in its operational environment. Herein lies the greatest opportunity for FA; to investigate and explain the process through which firms achieve environmental matching across their full lifeline, by responding to an array of potential selection processes.

The Firm–Environment–Selection Triangle

At present, no theory of the firm investigates the processes through which a firm deliberately (or non-deliberately) *alters* aspects of its local environment in ways that alter the match between the firm's interacting elements and the potential resources sought. Further, no theory of the firm currently investigates the *nature* of selection occurring upon firms, across their lifeline, and as mediated by their modification of factors within the firm's operational environment. Finally, no theory of the firm investigates the learning process through which firms make judgments about how to match the requirements of their environment through altering both the nature of their local environment and related selection processes.

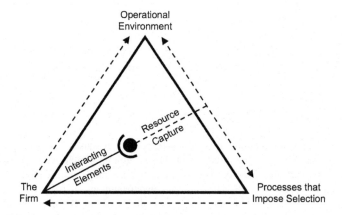

Figure 7.1 The firm–environment–selection triangle

Figure 7.1 illustrates the permanent relationship between a firm, its operational environment and the processes that impose selection upon the firm and its operations. No firm is immune from the realities that emerge from these permanent, yet malleable relations. Firms can receive feedback from their operational environment through the nature of selection they experience. They can also directly experience the nature of such selection via the degree of alignment between their interacting elements and the potential suite of resources available to capture. Illustrated in the centre of Figure 7.1, this relationship can be simply thought of as filling one's cup. As drawn in Figure 7.1, the firm is achieving a good fit between what resources are available and what they seek via their sustenance activities. However, the round ball could be drawn smaller or further away from the top of the cup, indicating the presence of too few resources or an inability to capture available resources.

As drawn, Figure 7.1 does not preclude the possibility that the firm has acquired the desired resources, but not yet fully exploited the resources efficiently. As noted earlier, ecological versatility (Mac Nally, 1995: 19) 'is a function of both resource exploitation and the relative availability of resources'. The nature of selection experienced by the firm provides the final say on the extent to which such ecological versatility has been achieved. Again, the nature of learning within a firm, its influence, positive or negative, on the decisions made to alter factors in the firm's operational environment to achieve this versatility is not investigated by any other theory of the firm.

Here is the opportunity for the full development of an autecological theory of the firm and its environment. What mechanisms facilitate this learning? How do such mechanisms influence the operation of other mechanisms through which environmental modification is possible? What countervailing mechanisms work against firms developing and/or maintaining ecological versatility? How do these mechanisms develop and mature across the lifeline of a firm to ensure persistence? To what extent is there diversity in the type and operation of mechanisms that can produce ecological versatility? These are just some of the unanswered questions awaiting the autecologist.

RESETTING ECOLOGICAL CURIOSITY

That a theoretical formulation is desirable because it makes it easier and more efficient to write more articles and books giving simple explanations for phenomena that are complex and diverse seems a strange justification for work that claims to be scientific. It confuses 'understanding' in the weak sense of making coherent and comprehensible statements about the real world with 'understanding' that means making correct statements about nature. It makes the investigation of material nature into an intellectual game, disarming us in our struggle to maintain science against mysticism. We would be much more likely to reach a correct theory of cultural change if the attempt to understand the history of human institutions on the cheap, by making analogies with organic evolution, were abandoned. What we need instead is the much more difficult effort to construct a theory of historical causation that flows directly from the phenomena to be explained. That the grand historical theorists of the past tried and failed to do this does not foreclose further efforts. After all, Darwin was preceded by eminent failures and even he did not get it all right. (Lewontin, 2005: n.p.)

Again, we are very mindful of the challenge of staying true to Hodgson's (2001) principle of consistency. We are confident that autecology offers social scientists a more appropriate ecological lens to study *actual* firms than the more demographically inspired OE approach, with its specific population/community focus, and thus its reliance on numbers (in the form of population density) to interpret the life, survival and demise of firms. The point Lewontin (2005) makes above is that we must combine curiosity with patience to allow the phenomena we study to guide our theory development. In this sense, the heuristic generalizing of Walter (2013) is a potential breath of fresh air to the ecological study of firms. OE and its various human ecology incarnations have all attempted to superimpose a rigid, biologically inspired, theoretical structure upon complex social phenomena, seeking confirmation along the way of already assumed outcomes. Conversely, FA seeks to draw *consistently* upon a raft of ecological concepts to explain observable complex phenomena that relate to firm persistence. It seeks to zero in on the mechanisms responsible for adaptive behaviour. It seeks to explain the spatiotemporal dynamics that relate to the firm's lifeline. It seeks to breathe new life into the mind of the ecologist-minded researcher of firms.

We believe the time is right to develop an alternative ecological approach to the study of the firm. Davis (2015) convincingly makes the case that of all the major paradigms in organizational theory (i.e. contingency theory, transaction cost economics, agency theory, resource dependence, population ecology and new institutional theory), only population ecology, or the OE approach of Hannan and Freeman (1977), has waned in recent times vis-à-vis the citations of these six approaches. Davis also notes that at a time in the world's history when more firms are succumbing to the challenges of their local environments, we need to prioritize what research questions must be directed at the firms of today if we wish to understand their origins, persistence and demise. We strongly believe that our autecological approach to the firm and its environment enables progress to be made about just how firms do maintain their persistence through time, during turbulent times, and the associated mechanisms developed, maintained, adapted and relied upon.

When we think we have *solved* a problem, well, by the very process of solving, new elements or forces come into the situation and you have a new problem on your hands to be solved. (Follett, 1937: 166)

Arguments based on structural inertia (Hannan and Carroll, 1992) largely ignore the fact that it is not the structures that are inflexible, but rather the habits of thought of man more generally that are inflexible (Veblen, 1922). But we can be much more optimistic about the ability of entrepreneurs and managers to solve problems on a day-to-day basis, because that in reality is why firms persist. Our approach reorients an ecological lens towards such awareness, learning and decision-making. We can not help but think that it is the inflexibility of past OE scholars rather than the managers of firms who have demonstrated the most inertia. Writing the foreword for Carroll's (1988) monograph, *Ecological Models of Organizations*, Amos Hawley made the most interesting of statements. With direct reference to, and acknowledging the logic of Fombron's (1988) contention that firms indeed do reshape their environments, Hawley (1988: xvi) noted 'this calls for a rethinking of the strategy of organization ecology. The proposal is unquestionably constructive. Perhaps, however, it is looking further down the road than organizational ecology should travel at this time'.

We agree. The OE approach is not designed to incorporate the proactive, environment shaping behaviours of managers and entrepreneurs, which is the role that FA now seeks to claim. Recently, the idea of an *ecological complex* (Jones, 2016) was suggested as a way of ensuring a tight focus remains upon the firm and its environment, so that the features of the firm and the factors of its operational environment are understood more precisely. Such clarity is required to ensure that firm-level behaviours, argued to relate to the modification aspects of the firm's operational environment, are understood in the context of the persistence of firms. Just as others have attempted before (see Astley and Fombrun, 1983), there are alternative ways to view firms ecologically, be that from a population or community perspective, or from the perspective of the individual firm and its distinctive ecology. Indeed, we truly believe FA is about connecting the threads of past thoughts and applying them to contemporary contexts.

New disciplines or fields of study do not spring to life fully formed, replete with arsenals of ideas, questions to be researched, theories to be tested, methods and tools to be used, or applications for their findings ready and waiting. Instead, they usually begin with glimmerings of new ideas or different perspectives, often developed as part of some seemingly unrelated discipline. These ideas or perspectives may lie dormant for some time, perhaps decades, while work in the mainstream field continues apace or evolves in different directions. At some point the ideas emerge again, prompted perhaps by thinking in other disciplines, new methods or technological advances, or simply someone reading the old papers in a fresh context and seeing things in a new light. The ideas and approaches begin to coalesce into something that has its own identity. The fusion of new or forgotten ideas and approaches is most likely to occur when different disciplines collide, drawing energy from the fringes that share a fascination with a common set of phenomena or problems. (Wiens et al., 2007: 1)

At present, this is our world, a space where lost ideas unite and everyday life is contemplated through the past thoughts and instincts of others long retired. We are excited to study the sensory abilities of firms and to develop a more concrete firm-level ecological approach to the study of firms. Like March (2010: 119), we too believe that 'adaptive improvement through deliberate problem solving is also an exquisite feature of human distinctiveness'. When it is also recognized that such behaviour, in changing one's environmental surrounds provides further *ecological* distinction (McKenzie, 1924), the true distinctiveness of FA is emphasized. Throughout this book we have championed a focus on the need to observe the adaptive mechanisms firms rely upon to maintain their persistence through time, so that we can understand how they operate and how they are (and can be) changed. We now invite you to contribute to the further development of this alternative paradigm. This work has offered many old and new ideas we believe can contribute to the development of an autecological approach to the study of the firm and its environment. Drawing upon the immortal words of Darwin (1859: 425) we believe, 'there is grandeur in this view of life'.

Glossary

A LEXICON FOR FIRM AUTECOLOGY

The ecological terms noted here are defined as for intended use in firm autecology (FA). Where usage differs from that already present in the organizational studies literature, an explanation is provided.

Adaptive Improvement The outcome of firms altering the feature–factor relationship between the firm and its operational environment to achieve a better match between a firm's interacting elements and the requirements and strictures of the local environment.

Adaptive Mechanisms See 'sustenance activities'.

Autecology As used here encourages researchers to contextualize ecological processes in terms of individual firms, their adaptive behaviours, the structure and dynamics of the environment, and their environmental interactions.

Autopoiesis In the context of this work relates to a firm's ability to build itself and maintain its persistence through time, with it both being and becoming to retain a match against changing environmental circumstances.

Coactions Are the nine qualitatively different systems relationships that can exist between two interacting entities. Adhering to Haskell's (1949) approach enables research to account for all of the negative, neutral and positive outcomes that are possible.

Common Environment A common environment is assumed to be present in organizational ecology, whereby firms designated to membership within a particular population experience homogeneous selection processes. In autecology, the environment is conceived at the level of the firm, not the population, and therefore far greater environmental variance is expected, and each is expected to interact with a unique subset of the environment as a whole.

Commensalism Refers to an interaction between two entities in which one benefits from the other, but the other is unaffected. First defined by van Beneden (1869) and its meaning in mainstream ecology has remained unaltered to present. Note, various definitions exist in the organizational studies literature (see Hawley, 1950; Aldrich, 1999); these tend to view commensalism as being directly related to competitive interactions.

Community In organizational ecology, is an observable number of interrelating populations. In autecology, the focus on individual firms relegates the concept to that of epiphenomenon.

Community Similarity Index In this context, is simply X/N, where X is the number of firm-types common to two towns and N is the total number of firm-types occurring in both; thus community similarity equals 1 when two towns are identical, and 0 when they share no firm-types.

Competition In this context, competition refers to the endeavour of two (or more) firms to gain the same particular thing, or to gain the measure each wants from the supply of a thing when that supply is not sufficient for both (or all), as consistent with Milne's (1961) definition for animals.

Corridor of Persistence Refers to the degrees of freedom afforded the firm's activities, products/services and identity by the operational environment. In essence, there is no identifiable equilibrium position possible in reality, but rather the relative degree of environmental stability determines the breadth of a buffer zone within which degrees of fitness are achieved.

Cryptic Firm Complex A group of firms that, despite being assumed similar, differ sufficiently across their form, structures, functions and/or activities, and environmental interactions that they cannot be seen as ecologically equal, vis-à-vis the adaptive mechanisms used to maintain their persistence.

Ecological Guild Consistent with Root's (1967) definition, we define a guild as a group of firms that seek to exploit the same types of resource in similar ways.

Ecological Inheritance The process through which entities inherit an environmental circumstance, either positive or negative, as a result of their influence on the environment, or that of other such entities.

Ecological Scale The observation and investigation of ecological processes at the scale at which firms respond to phenomena in their environment. It is expected that the ecological scale at which firms respond to their environment will vary in response to firm-level factors.

Ecological Versatility The degree to which firms can fully exploit the resources in their operational environment, with specific concern for gaining, processing and translating the resources to best match the requirements of their environment.

Emergy The energy independently (and generally) available that can be converted and used to the advantage of any given firm, for example, the positive (but incidental) influence from the advertising of another larger more powerful firm.

Environment See 'common environment', 'external environment', 'operational environment' and 'potential environment'.

Ephemeral Epiphenomena We see populations and/or communities as the transient by-product of individual-level behaviours, which means they are more conceptual than real.

Environmental Factors The sum total of all environmental phenomena that: are currently operationally related to a firm (its operational environment), were previously operationally related to a firm (its historical environment), may be operationally related to a firm in the near future (its potential environment), or are unrelated operationally to a firm, despite their spatiotemporal presence (its external environment).

Environmental Matching Firms persist in their operational environment through their ability to match the requirements of the environment, using their sensory abilities to ensure their environment does not exceed their individual tolerances.

Environmental Modification Occurs when a firm alters the feature–factor relationship that exists between the firm and its operational environment.

External Environment Broadly speaking, the external environment typically refers to the sum total of all factors external to the firm that may potentially influence its survival. More specifically, it is all factors external to the firm's operational environment, some of which may eventually become relevant to the firm through the firm's potential environment.

Facilitation Connotes positive interactions due to resource sharing within a guild, see Rathcke (1983).

Feature–Factor Relationship At any given moment in the lifeline of a firm, a constant relationship exists between the firm's features (form, structure, functions, activities) and the interacting elements they produce and all variable (or factors) present in the firm's operational environment.

Firm A firm is a non-autonomous entity, located in an operational environment, and is socially constructed, goal-directed, boundary maintaining and maintained through sustenance activities.

Firm Adaptation An outcome of multiple ecological processes acting upon firms that maintain their existence across time by matching the changing requirements of their operational environment.

Firm Features All firms, to varying degrees, are comprised of individual habits, firm routines, goals and boundaries. Together, these components produce interacting elements (humans, technology, products, services and the identity of the firm) that collectively are the features of the firm.

Foraging In this context, all firm-level behaviour aimed at acquiring, converting and utilising the resources needed to persist through time.

Generative Mechanisms Consistent with Bennett and George (2003), we view generative mechanisms as unobservable social, physical, and psychological processes that, under specific conditions, have the potential to transfer energy, information, or matter to other entities.

Heuristic Generalizations The process of elevating observable firm–environment interactions above popular single process explanations to frame which investigation questions are ecologically relevant.

Human Ecology See 'organizational ecology'.

Interacting Elements Three areas of interaction are: 1) human and technologically controlled activities, 2) the products and services produced, and 3) the actual identity of the firm.

Lifeline The life history of an individual firm, from which the different feature–factor relationships between firm and operational environment can be reconciled across time.

Organizational Ecology The study of firms (once aggregated into populations with unit character) in which assumptions are made about the tendency of firms to: operate as specialists or generalist, have limited adaptive abilities through structural inertia, and be subject to a common selection environment vis-à-vis the population to which they belong.

Operational Environment Refers to all observable environmental phenomena that are operationally related, directed, timed, ordered and spaced by and across the lifeline of a particular firm.

Operational Relations All observable environmental phenomena that are operationally related, directed, timed, ordered and spaced by and across the lifeline of a particular firm through which the interaction between firm and environment is knowable.

Persistence The ability of a firm to maintain operational relations with its local environment through time despite not always achieving optimal matching to its environment.

Population In organizational ecology is an observable number of firms deemed similar enough to belong to a population of firms. In autecology, the focus on individual firms relegates the concept to that of epiphenomenon.

Potential Environment The potential environment is simply a potential future state of the operational environment, including provision for new factors in the broader external environment to become relevant to the firm, and for the firm to modify the nature of its existing operational environment.

Principle of Consistency Defined by Hodgson (2001: 90): 'explanations in one domain have to be consistent with explanations in another, despite examination of different properties and deployment of different concepts'.

Resource Partitioning In organizational ecology, resource partitioning relates to increases in the failure rate of generalists and a lowering of the failure rate of specialists when market concentration increases. In firm autecology, is viewed as any difference in the resource utilization among related firms, specifically with reference to spatiotemporal and resource-type factor.

Retroduction A form of reasoning that occurs as an *initial* thought process through which the provisional plausibility of something is held to be possible.

Sensory Abilities The ability of firms to discern the nature of their environmental surrounds so as to increase the degree of situation awareness held within the firm.

Situation Awareness Defined as 'the perception of the elements in the environment within a volume of time and space, the comprehension of their meaning and the projection of their status in the near future' (Endsley, 1995: 36).

Sub-type A sub-type of firm describes a type of firm that comprises a cryptic firm complex, demonstrating different properties (e.g. form, structures, functions and/or activities) to closely related firms in a particular industry.

Survival See 'persistence'.

Sustenance Activities Can be considered regular, organized and enduring activities aimed at supporting firm survival (Gibbs and Walter, 1959). They are the mechanisms related to information gathering, sense-making and response, through which firms maintain their persistence.

Appendices

APPENDIX 1: LIST OF ALL 23 RESTAURANT TYPES

Pizza and:

- Asian
- Chicken
- Italian
- Seafood
- Indian
- Fish & Chip
- English
- General
- Steak
- Spanish
- French
- Kebab
- Sandwich
- Burgers
- Ice Cream
- Mexican
- Turkish
- Coffee & Teas
- American
- Japanese
- Pub Food
- Vegetarian

APPENDIX 2: NATURE OF DATA ANALYSED

The Retroduction-based Research Method

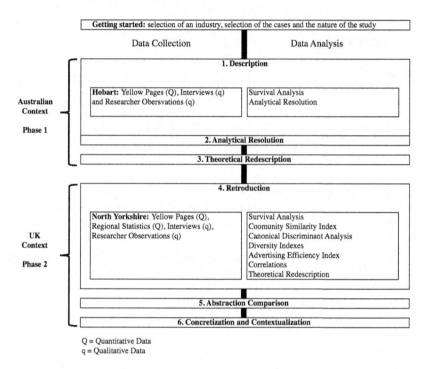

Q = Quantitative Data
q = Qualitative Data

The Retroduction Six-step Process

1. Description: Prepare a description of the phenomenon making use of the actors' accounts and a variety of sources.

2. Analytical Resolution: Distinguish various components, aspects or dimensions of the phenomenon and establish (tentative) boundaries to the components.

3. Theoretical Redescription: Interpret and redescribe the different components applying contrasting theoretical frameworks and interpretations in order to provide new insights (note: this activity sometimes referred to as 'abduction').

4. Retroduction: For each component, seek to identify basic, or 'transfactual' conditions, including structures, causal powers and mechanisms, that make the phenomenon possible.

5. Abstract Comparison: Elaborate and estimate the explanatory power of the structures, causal powers and mechanisms that have been identified during activities 3 and 4.

6. Abstract Comparison: Elaborate and estimate the explanatory power of the structures, causal powers and mechanisms that have been identified during activities 3 and 4.

References

Abatecola, Gianpaolo (2014), 'Research in organizational evolution, what comes next?', *European Management Journal*, **32** (3), 434–443.

Abernathy, William and K. Clark (1985), 'Innovation: Mapping the winds of creative destruction', *Research Policy*, **14** (1), 3–22.

Adams, Charles (1913), *Guide to the Study of Animal Ecology*, New York: The MacMillan Company.

Agarwal, Rajshree and D. Audretsch (2001), 'Does entry size matter? The impact of the life cycle and technology on firm survival', *Journal of Industrial Economics*, **49** (1), 21–43.

Alam, Ian (2005), 'Fieldwork and data collection in qualitative marketing research', *The Qualitative Report*, **8** (1), 97–112.

Alchian, Armen (1950), 'Uncertainty, evolution, and economic theory', *Journal of Political Economy*, **58** (3), 211–221.

Alcock, Alfred (1911), *Entomology for Medical Officers*, London: Gurney & Jackson.

Alderson, Wroe (1957), *Marketing Behavior and Executive Action: A Functionalist Approach to Marketing Theory*, Illinois: Richard D. Irwin.

Aldrich, Howard (1979), *Organizations and Environments*, Englewood Cliffs, NJ: Prentice-Hall.

Aldrich, Howard (1992), 'Incommensurable paradigms? Vital signs from three perspectives', in Michael Reed and Michael Hughes (eds), *Rethinking Organization: New Directions in Organization Theory and Analysis*, London: Sage Publications.

Aldrich, Howard (1999), *Organizations Evolving*, London: Sage Publications.

Aldrich, Howard (2007), *Personal communications*.

Aldrich, Howard and G. Wiedenmayer (1993), 'From traits to rates: An ecological perspective on organizational foundings', in Jerome Katz and Robert Brockhaus (eds), *Advances in Entrepreneurship, Firm Emergence, and Growth*, Greenwich, CT: JAI Press.

Allaby, Michael (2003), *A Dictionary of Zoology*, Oxford, UK: Oxford University Press.

Allee, Warder (1931), *Animal Aggregations: A Study in General Sociology*, Chicago: University of Chicago Press.

Alvarez, Sharon (2003), 'Resources and hierarchies: Intersections between entrepreneurship and business strategy', in Zoltan Acs and David Audretsch (eds), *Handbook of Entrepreneurship Research*, London: Kluwer.

Amburgey, Terry, D. Kelly and W. Barnett (1993), 'Resetting the clock: The dynamics of organizational change and failure', *Administrative Science Quarterly*, **38** (1), 51–73.

Amburgey, Terry, T. Dacin and D. Kelly (1994), 'Disruptive selection and population segmentation: Interpopulation competition as a segregating process', in Joel Baum and Jitendra Singh (eds), *Evolutionary Dynamics of Organizations*, New York: Oxford University Press.

Amburgey, Terry and J. Singh (2002), 'Organizational evolution', in Joel Baum (ed), *Blackwell Companion to Organizations*: Malden, MA: Blackwell Publishers.

Andrewartha, Herbert (1984), 'Ecology at the cross-roads', *Austral Ecology*, **9** (1), 1–3.

Andrewartha, Herbert and L. Birch (1954), *The Distribution and Abundance of Animals*, Chicago: University of Chicago Press.

Andrewartha, Herbert and L. Birch (1984), *The Ecological Web*, Chicago: University of Chicago Press.

Antonovics, Janis, K. Clay and J. Schmitt (1987), 'The measurement of small-scale environmental heterogeneity using clonal transplants of anthoxanthum ororatum and danthonia spicata', *Oceologia*, **71**, 601–607.

Astley, Graham (1985), 'The two ecologies: Population and community perspectives on organizational evolution', *Administrative Science Quarterly*, **30** (2), 224–241.

Astley, Graham and C. Fombrun (1983), 'Collective strategy: Social ecology of organizational environments', *Academy of Management Review*, **8** (4), 576–587.

Attiwill, Peter and B. Wilson (2003), *Ecology: An Australian Perspective*, Melbourne: Oxford University Press.

Audretsch, David (1995), 'Innovation, growth and survival', *International Journal of Industrial Organization*, **13** (4), 441–457.

Axelrod, Robert and M. Cohen (1999), *Harnessing Complexity: Organizational Implications of a Scientific Frontier*, New York: Free Press.

Babbie, Earl (2005), *The Basics of Social Research*, Sydney: Thomson Wadsworth.

Baldwin, James (1964), 'Stranger in the village', *The New Yorker*, available at http://www.newyorker.com/books/page-turner/black-body-re-reading-james-baldwins-stranger-village, accessed on 25/7/2016.

Barnett, William (1994), 'The liability of collective action: Growth and change among early American telephone companies', in Joel Baum and Jitendra Singh (eds), *Evolutionary Dynamics of Organizations*, New York: Oxford University Press.

Barnett, William and G. Carroll (1987), 'Competition and mutualism among early telephone companies', *Administrative Science Quarterly*, **32** (3), 400–421.

Barnett, William and T. Amburgey (1990), 'Do larger organizations generate stronger competition?', in Jitendra Singh (ed), *Organizational Evolution: New Directions*, Beverly Hills, CA: Sage.

Barnett, William and O. Sørensen (2002), 'The red queen in organizational creation and development', *Industrial and Corporate Change*, **11** (2), 289–325.

Barney, Jay (1991), 'Firm resources and sustained competitive advantage', *Journal of Management*, **17** (1), 99–120.

Bates, Timothy (1995), 'Analysis of survival rates among franchise and independent small business startups', *Journal of Small Business Management*, **33** (2), 26–36.

Baum, Joel (1996), 'Organizational ecology', in Stewart Clegg, Cynthia Hardy and Walter Nord (eds), *Handbook of Organizational Study*, London: Sage Publications.

Baum, Joel and S. Mezias (1992), 'Localized competition and organizational failure: The Manhattan hotel industry, 1898–1990', *Administrative Science Quarterly*, **37** (4), 580–604.

Baum, Joel and J. Singh (1994), 'Organizational hierarchies and evolutionary processes: some reflections on a theory of organizational evolution', in Joel Baum and Jitendra Singh (eds), *Evolutionary Dynamics of Organizations*, New York: Oxford University Press.

Baum, Joel and T. Amburgey (2002), 'Organizational ecology', in Joel Baum (ed), *Companion to Organizations*, Oxford, UK: Blackwell.

Baum, Joel and A. Shipilov (2006), 'Ecological approaches to organizations', in Stewart Clegg, Cynthia Hardy, Tom Lawrence and Walter Nord (eds), *Handbook of Organizational Study*, 2nd *Ed.*, London: Sage Publications.

Begon, Michael, J. Harper and C. Townsend (1996), *Ecology: Individuals, Populations and Communities*, Oxford, UK: Blackwell Science.

Bell, Colin and H. Newby (1977), *Doing Sociological Research*, London: Routledge.

Bender, Edward, T. Case and M. Gilpin (1984), 'Perturbation experiments in community ecology: Theory and practice', *Ecology*, **65** (1), 1–13.

Bennett, Alexander and A. George (2003), *Case Studies and Theory Development in the Social Sciences*, Cambridge, MA: MIT Press.

Berry, Brian and J. Kassarda (1977), *Contemporary Urban Ecology*, New York: Macmillan Publishing.

Bews, John (1935), *Human Ecology*, London: Oxford University Press.

Bhaskar, Roy (1975), *A Realist Theory of Science*, Leeds: Leeds Books.

Bhaskar, Roy (1979), *The Possibility of Naturalism: A Philosophical Critique of the Contemporary Human Sciences*, Atlantic Highlands, NJ: Humanities Press.

Blood, Douglas and V. Studdert (1988), *Baillière's Comprehensive Veterinary Dictionary*, London: Baillière Tindall.

Borradaile, Lancelot (1918), *A Manual of Elementary Zoology*, London: Oxford University Press.

Boucher, Douglas (1985), *The Biology of Mutualism*, London: Croom Helm.

Brady, Ronald (1982), 'Dogma and doubt', *Biological Journal of the Linnean Society*, **17** (1), 79–96.

Brandon, Robert (1990), *Adaptation and Environment*, Princeton, NJ: Princeton University Press.

Braun-Blanquet, Josias (1928), *Pflanzensoziologie*, Berlin: Springer.

Brelsin, Dermot (2014), 'Calm in the storm: Simulating the management of organizational co-evolution', *Futures*, **57**, 62–77.

Brown, William and E. Wilson (1956), 'Character displacement', *Systematic Zoology*, **5** (2), 49–65.

Bruderer, Erhard and J. Singh (1996), 'Organization evolution, learning, and selection: A genetic-algorithm-based model', *Academy of Management Journal*, **39** (5), 1322–1349.

Bruno, John, J. Stachowicz and M. Bertness (2003), 'Inclusion of facilitation into ecological theory', *Trends in Ecology and Evolution*, **18** (3), 119–125.

Bruyat, Christian and P. Julien (2001), 'Defining the field of research in entrepreneurship', *Journal of Business Venturing*, **16** (2), 165–180.

Buchanan, David and A. Bryman (2011), *The Sage Handbook of Organizational Research Methods*, London: Sage Publications.

Burkholder, Paul (1952), 'Cooperation and conflict among primitive organisms', *American Scientist*, **40** (4), 601–631.

Carolan, Michael (2005), 'Realism without reductionism: Toward an ecologically embedded sociology', *Human Ecology Review*, **12** (1), 1–20.

Carr, Edward (1965), *What is History?*, New York: Alfred A. Knopf.

Carroll, Glenn (1984), 'Organizational ecology', *Annual Review of Sociology*, **10**, 71–93.

Carroll, Glenn (1985), 'Concentration and specialization: Dynamics of niche width in populations of organizations', *American Journal of Sociology*, **90** (6), 1262–1283.

Carroll, Glenn (1988), *Ecological Models of Organizations*, Cambridge, MA: Ballinger Publishing Company.

Carroll, Glenn and A. Swaminathan (1992), 'The organizational ecology of strategic groups in the American brewing industry from 1875 to 1990', *Industrial and Corporate Change*, **1** (1), 65–97.

Carroll, Glenn and M. Hannan (2000), *The Demography of Corporations and Industries*, New Jersey: Princeton University Press.

Caves, Richard (1998), 'Industrial organization and new findings on the turnover and mobility of firms', *Journal of Economic Literature*, **36** (4), 1947–1982.

Chamberlin, Edward (1933), *The Theory of Monopolistic Competition*, Cambridge, MA: Harvard University Press.

Child, John (1969), *The Business Enterprise in Modern Industrial Society*, London: Collier-Macmillan.

Child, John (1972), 'Organizational structure, environment and performance: The role of strategic choice', *Sociology*, **6** (1), 1–22.

Child, John (1975), 'Managerial and organizational factors associated with company performance – Part 11. A contingency analysis', *Journal of Management Studies*, **12** (1–2), 12–27.

Child, John, K. Tse and S. Rodrigues (2013), *The Dynamics of Corporate Co-Evolution: A Case Study of Port Development in China*, Cheltenham, UK and Northampton, MA, USA: Edward Elgar Publishing.

Christensen, Clayton (2000), 'Meeting the challenge of disruption change', *Harvard Business Review*, **78** (2), 66–76.

Clarke, George (1967), *Elements of Ecology*, New York: John Wiley & Sons.

Clements, Frederic (1907), *Plant Physiology and Ecology*, London: Archibald Constable & Co.

Clements, Frederic (1916), *Plant Succession*, Washington: Year Book Carnegie Institute.

Clements, Frederic (1935), 'Experimental ecology in the public service', *Ecology*, **16** (3), 342–363.

Clements, Frederic and V. Shelford (1939), *Bio-Ecology*, New York: John Wiley & Sons.

Cohen, Joel (1995), *How Many People Can the Earth Support?*, New York: Norton.

Cohen, Wesley and D. Levinthal (1990), 'Absorptive capacity: A new perspective on learning and innovation', *Administrative Science Quarterly*, **35** (1), 128–152.

Connell, Joseph (1980), 'Diversity and coevolution of competitors, or the ghost of competition past', *Oikos*, **35** (2), 131–138.

Connell, Joseph and R. Slatyer (1977), 'Mechanisms of succession in natural communities and their role in community stability and organization', *American Naturalist*, **111**, 1119–1144.

Creswell, John (2003), *Research Design: Qualitative, Quantitative, and Mixed Methods Approaches, 2nd Ed.*, Thousand Oaks, CA: Sage.

Cuddington, Kim and B. Beisner (2005), *Ecological Paradigms Lost: Routes of Theory Change*, London: Elsevier Academic Press.

Cyert, Richard and J. March (1963), *A Behavioral Theory of the Firm*, New Jersey: Prentice-Hall.

Cyert, Richard and J. March (1992), *A Behavioral Theory of the Firm, 2nd Ed.*, Cambridge, MA: Blackwell Publishers.

Daily, Gretchen (1997), *Nature's Services: Societal Dependence on Natural Ecosystems*, Washington, DC: Island Press.

Dana, James (1872), *Corals and Coral Islands*, New York: Dodd & Mead.

Danermark, Berth (2002), 'Interdisciplinary research and critical realism: The example of disability research', *Journal of Critical Realism*, **5** (1), 56–64.

Danermark, Berth, M. Ekström, L. Jakobsen and J. Karlsson (2002), *Explaining Society: Critical Realism in the Social Sciences*, London: Routledge.

Darwin, Charles (1859), *On the Origin of Species by Means of Natural Selection, or, the Preservation of Favoured Races in the Struggle for Life*, London: John Murray.

Darwin, Charles (1881), *The Formation of Vegetable Mould, Through the Action of Worms, with Observations on Their Habits*, London: John Murray.

Daubenmire, Rexford (1947), *Plants and Environment: A Textbook of Plant Autecology*, New York: John Wiley & Sons.

Davidsson, Per and J. Wiklund (2001), 'Levels of analysis in entrepreneurship research: Current research practice and suggestions for the future', *Entrepreneurship Theory and Practice*, **25** (4), 81–99.

Davis, Gerald (2015), 'Celebrating organization theory: The after party', *Journal of Management Studies*, **52** (2), 309–319.

Davis, Gerald and C. Marquis (2005), 'Prospects for organization theory in the early twenty-first century: Institutional fields and mechanisms', *Organization Science*, **16** (4), 332–342.

Dawkins, Richard (2009), *The Greatest Show on Earth: The Evidence for Evolution*, London: Bantam Press.

DeTienne, Dawn, D. Shepherd and J. De Castro (2008), 'The fallacy of "only the strong survive": The effects of extrinsic motivation on the persistence decisions for under-performing firms', *Journal of Business Venturing*, **23** (5), 528–546.

Dew, Nick, B. Goldfarb and S. Sarasvathy (2006), 'Optimal inertia: When organizations should fail', in Joel Baum, Stanislav Dobrev and Arjen van Witteloostuijn (eds), *Ecology and Strategy*, London: Elsevier.

DiMaggio, Paul and W. Powell (1983), 'The iron cage revisited: Institutional isomorphism and collective rationality in organizational fields', *American Sociological Review*, **48** (2), 147–160.

Dingley, Fay and J. Maynard Smith (1969), 'Absence of a life-shortening effect of amino-acid analogues on adult *Drosophila*', *Experimental Gerontology*, **4**, 145–149.

Dobrev, Stanislav, A. van Witteloostuijn and J. Baum (2010), 'Introduction: Ecology versus strategy or strategy and ecology?', in Joel Baum, Stanislav Dobrev and Arjen van Witteloostuijn (eds), *Ecology and Strategy*, London: Elsevier.

Donaldson, Lex (1995), *American Anti-Management Theories of Organization: A Critique of Paradigm Proliferation*, New York: Cambridge University Press.

Durand, Rodolphe (2006), *Organizational Evolution and Strategic Management*, London: Sage Publications.

Dusenbery, David (1992), *Sensory Ecology: How Organisms Acquire and Respond to Information*, New York: W.H. Freeman.

Edwards, Paul, J. O'Mahoney and S. Vincent (2014), *Studying Organizations Using Critical Realism*, Oxford: Oxford University Press.

Ehrlich, Paul and D. Murphy (1981), 'The population biology of checkerspot butterflies (Euphydryas)', *Biologisches Zentralblatt*, **100**, 613–629.

Ellwood, Charles (1917), 'The present condition of the social sciences', *Science*, **46** (1194), 469–475.

Elster, Jon (1998), 'A plea for mechanisms', in Peter Hedstrom and Richard Swedberg (eds), *Social Mechanisms: An Analytical Approach to Social Theory*, Cambridge, UK: Cambridge University Press.

Elton, Charles (1927), *Animal Ecology*, London: Sidgwick & Jackson.

Emery, Fred and E. Trist (1965), 'The causal texture of organizational environments', *Human Relations*, **18** (1), 21–32.

Endsley, Mica (1995), 'Toward a theory of situation awareness in dynamic systems', *Human Factors Journal*, **37** (1), 32–64.

Endsley, Mica (2015), 'Situation awareness: operationally necessary and scientifically grounded', *Cognition Technology and Work*, **17** (2), 159–167.

Endsley, Mica and D. Garland (2000), *Situation Awareness Analysis and Measurement*, London: CRC Press.

Endsley, Mica and D. Jones (2012), *Designing For Situation Awareness: An Approach to Human-Centered Design*, 2nd *Ed.*, London: Taylor & Francis.

English, Wilke, J. Willems, B. Josiam and R. Upchurch (1996), 'Restaurant attrition: A longitudinal analysis of restaurant failure', *International Journal of Contemporary Hospitality Management*, **8** (2), 17–20.

Ericson, Richard and A. Pakes (1995), 'Markov-perfect industry dynamics: A framework for empirical work', *Review of Economic Studies*, **62** (1), 53–82.

Filley, Alan and R. Aldag (1978), 'Characteristics and measurement of an organizational typology', *Academy of Management Journal*, **21** (4), 578–591.

Flach, John (1995), 'Situation awareness: Proceed with caution', *Human Factors Journal*, **37** (1), 149–157.

Flattely, Frederic and C. Walton (1922), *The Biology of the Sea-Shore*, London: Sidgwick & Jackson.

Fleetwood, Steve and S. Ackroyd (2004), *Critical Realist Applications in Organization and Management Studies*, London: Routledge.

Follett, Mary (1937), 'The process of control', in Luther Gulick and Lyndall Urwick (eds), *Papers on the Science of Administration*, New York: Institute of Public Administration.

Freeman, John and M. Hannan (1983), 'Niche width and the dynamics of organizational populations', *American Journal of Sociology*, **88** (6), 1116–1145.

Fombron, Charles (1988), 'Crafting an institutionally informed ecology', in Glenn Carroll (ed), *Ecological Models of Organizations*, Cambridge, MA: Ballinger Publishing Company.

Fuller, George and H. Conrad (1932), *Plant Sociology*, New York: McGraw-Hill.

Gavetti, Giovanni and D. Levinthal (2000), 'Looking forward and looking backward: Cognitive and experiential search', *Administrative Science Quarterly*, **45** (1), 113–137.

Gavetti, Giovanni, H. Greve, D. Levinthal and W. Ocasio (2012), 'The behavioral theory of the firm: Assessment and prospects', *Academy of Management Annals*, **6** (1), 1–40.

Geels, Frank (2014), 'Reconceptualising the co-evolution of firms-in-industries and their environments: Developing an inter-disciplinary triple embeddedness framework', *Research Policy*, **43** (2), 261–277.

Gibbs, Jack and W. Martin (1959), 'Towards a theoretical system of human ecology', *Pacific Sociological Review*, **2**, 29–36.

Gibbs, Jack and W. Martin (1973), 'Towards a theoretical system of human ecology', in James Wittman (ed), *Selected Articles in Social Ecology*, New York: MSS Information Corporation.

Gibson, James (1979), *The Ecological Approach to Visual Perception*, Boston, MA: Houghton Mifflin.

Glaser, Barney (2001), *The Grounded Theory Perspective: Conceptualization Contrasted with Description*, Mill Valley: Sociology Press.

Glaser, Barney (2005), *Personal communications*.

Golafshani, Nahid (2003), 'Understanding reliability and validity in qualitative research', *The Qualitative Report*, **8** (4), 597–607.

Greve, Henrich (2002), 'An ecological theory of spatial evolution: local density dependence in Tokyo banking, 1894–1936', *Social Forces*, **80** (3), 847–879.

Grime, Philip (1979), *Plant Strategies and Vegetation Processes*, Brisbane: John Wiley & Sons.

Grimm, Volker and S. Railsback (2005), *Individual-based Modelling in Ecology*, Princeton: Princeton University Press.

Haldane, John (1985), *On Being the Right Size*, New York: Oxford University Press.

Hancock, Peter and D. Diaz (2002), 'Ergonomics as a foundation for a science of purpose', *Theoretical Issues in Ergonomics Science*, **3** (2), 115–123.

Hannan, Michael and J. Freeman (1977), 'The population ecology of organizations', *American Journal of Sociology*, **82** (5), 929–964.

Hannan, Michael and J. Freeman (1984), 'Structural inertia and organizational change', *American Sociological Review*, **49** (2), 149–164.

Hannan, Michael and J. Freeman (1986), 'Where do organizational forms come from?', *Sociological Forum*, **1** (1), 50–72.

Hannan, Michael and J. Freeman (1989), *Organizational Ecology*, Cambridge, MA: Harvard University Press.

Hannan, Michael and G. Carroll (1992), *Dynamics of Organizational Population: Density, Legitimation and Competition*, New York: Oxford University Press.

Hannan, Michael, L. Polos and G. Carroll (2007), *Logics of Organization Theory: Audiences, Codes and Ecologies*, Princeton: Princeton University Press.

Hanson, Norwood (1958), *Patterns of Discovery*, London: Scientific Book Guild.

Harré, Rom (1979), *Social Being: A Theory for Social Psychology*, Totowa, NJ: Rowman and Littlefield.

Harris, Lisa and C. Dennis (2002), *Marketing the e-Business*, London: Routledge.

Haskell, Edward (1949), 'A clarification of social science', *Main Currents in Modern Thought*, **7** (2), 45–51.

Haukioja, Erkki (1982), 'Are individuals really subordinated to genes? A theory of living entities', *Journal of Theoretical Biology*, **99**, 357–375.

Haveman, Heather (1992), 'Between a rock and a hard place: Organizational change and performance under conditions of fundamental environmental transformation', *Administrative Science Quarterly*, **37** (1), 48–75.

Hawley, Amos (1944), 'Ecology and human ecology', *Social Forces*, **22** (4), 398–405.

Hawley, Amos (1950), *Human Ecology*, New York: The Ronald Press Company.

Hawley, Amos (1968), *Human Ecology: A Theoretical Essay*, London: University of Chicago Press.

Hawley, Amos (1988), 'Foreword', in Glenn Carroll (ed), *Ecological Models of Organizations*, Cambridge, MA: Ballinger Publishing Company.

Hawley, Amos (1998), 'Human ecology, population and development', in Michael Micklin and Dudley Poston (eds), *Continuities in Sociological Human Ecology*, New York: Plenum Press.

Healy, Marilyn and C. Perry (2000), 'Comprehensive criteria to judge validity and reliability of qualitative research within the realism paradigm', *Qualitative Market Research: An International Journal*, **3** (3), 118–126.

Hegner, Robert (1924), 'Medical zoology and human welfare', *Science*, **60**, 551–558.

Hengeveld, Rob and G. Walter (1999), 'The two coexisting ecological paradigms', *Acta Biotheoretica*, **47** (2), 141–170.

Hernes, Gudmund (1998), 'Virtual reality', in Peter Hedstrom and Richard Swedberg (eds), *Social Mechanisms: An Analytical Approach to Social Theory*, Cambridge, UK: Cambridge University Press.

Hjalager, Anne-Mette (1999), 'The ecology of organizations in Danish tourism: A regional labor perspective', *Tourism Geographies*, **1** (2), 164–182.

Hodgson, Geoffrey (1993), *Economics and Evolution: Bringing Life Back into Economics*, Cambridge, UK: Polity Press.

Hodgson, Geoffrey (2001), 'Is social evolution Lamarckian or Darwinian?', in John Nightingale and John Laurent (eds), *Darwinism and Evolutionary Economics*, Cheltenham, UK and Northampton, MA, USA: Edward Elgar Publishing.

Hodgson, Geoffrey (2004), *The Evolution of Institutional Economics*, Cheltenham, UK and Northampton, MA, USA: Edward Elgar Publishing.

Holzapfel, Claus and B. Mahall (1999), 'Bidirectional facilitation and interference between shrubs and annuals in the Mojave Desert', *Ecology*, **80** (5), 1747–1761.

Hull, David (2001), *Science and Selection*, New York: Cambridge University Press.

Hunt, Selby (2000), *A General Theory of Competition: Resources, Competences, Productivity, Economic Growth*, London: Sage Publications.

Hutchinson, Evelyn (1957), 'Concluding remarks', *Cold Spring Harbor Symposia on Quantitative Biology*, **22** (2), 415–427.

Hutchinson, Evelyn (1965), *The Ecological Theater and the Evolutionary Play*, London: Yale University Press.

Jones, Colin (2004), 'An alternative view of small firm adaptation', *Journal of Small Business and Enterprise Development*, **11** (3), 362–370.

Jones, Colin (2005), 'Contemplating Knudsen's baseline: Where small is not so beautiful', *Journal of Small Business and Entrepreneurship*, **18** (3), 273–288.

Jones, Colin (2007), 'Using old concepts to gain new insights: Addressing the issue of consistency', *Management Decision*, **45** (1), 29–42.

Jones, Colin (2008), 'Imagining, developing and explaining the concept of Transferred Demand: Transcendental realism and entrepreneurship', *Proceedings of the 53rd ICSB Conference*, Halifax, Canada.

Jones, Colin (2009), 'Towards a consistent account of firm survival', Unpublished dissertation, University of Tasmania.

Jones, Colin (2013), *Teaching Entrepreneurship to Postgraduates*, Cheltenham, UK and Northampton, MA, USA: Edward Elgar Publishing.

Jones, Colin (2016), 'An autecological interpretation of the firm and its environment', *Journal of Management & Governance*, **20** (1), 69–87.

Jones, Clive, J. Lawton and M. Shachak (1994), 'Organisms as ecosystem engineers', *Oikos*, **69** (3), 373–386.

Jones, Geoffrey and D. Rocke (2002), 'Multivariate survival analysis with doubly-censored data: application to the assessment of Accutane treatment for brodysplasia ossi cans progressiva', *Statistics in Medicine*, **21**, 2547–2562.

Jovanovic, Boyan (1982), 'Selection and the evolution of industry', *Econometrica*, **50** (3), 649–670.

Kalnins, Arturs and K. Mayer (2004), 'Franchising, ownership, and experience: A study of pizza restaurant survival', *Management Science*, **50** (12), 1716–1728.

Kangas, Patrick and P. Risser (1979), 'Species packing in the fast-food restaurant guild', *Bulletin of the Ecological Society of American*, **60** (3), 143–148.

Kasarda, John and C. Bidwell (1984), 'A human ecological theory of organizational structuring', in Michael Micklin and Harvey Choldin (eds), *Sociological Human Ecology*, London: Westview Press.

Kimberly, John and R. Miles (1980), *The Organizational Life Cycle: Issues in the Creation, Transformation, and Decline of Organizations*, San Francisco: Jossey-Bass.

King, Andrew and C. Tucci (2002), 'Incumbent entry into new market niches: The role of experience and managerial choice in the creation of dynamic capabilities', *Management Science*, **48** (2), 171–186.

King, Gary, O. Rosen and M. Tanner (2004), *Ecological Inference: New Methodological Strategies*, New York: Cambridge University Press.

Klepper, Steven (1996), 'Entry, exit, growth, and innovation over the product life cycle', *American Economic Review*, **86** (3), 562–583.

Knudsen, Thorbjørn (2002), 'Economic selection theory', *Journal of Evolutionary Economics*, **12** (4), 443–470.

Krebs, John and N. Davies (1997), *Behavioural Ecology: An Evolutionary Approach*, Oxford: Blackwell Publishing.

Kropotkin, Peter (1902), *Mutual Aid: A Factor of Evolution*, New York: McClure Phillips & Co.

Kudo, Richard (1931), *Protozoology*, London: Bailliére, Tindall & Cox.

Kuhn, Thomas (1962), *The Structure of Scientific Revolutions*, London: University of Chicago Press.

Lambert, David and A. Hughes (1988), 'Keywords and concepts in structuralist and functionalist biology', *Journal of Theoretical Biology*, **133** (2), 133–145.

Langlois, Richard (1997), 'Cognition and capabilities: Opportunities seized and missed in the history of the computer industry', in Raghu Garud, Praveen Nayyar and Zur Shapira (eds), *Technological Innovation: Oversights and Foresights*, New York: Cambridge University Press.

Lawrence, Paul and J. Lorsch (1967), *Organization and Environment: Managing Differentiation and Integration*, Boston: Harvard University Press.

Lawton John and V. Brown (1993), 'Redundancy in ecosystems', in Ernst-Detlef Schulze and Harold Mooney (eds), *Biodiversity and Ecosystem Function*, Berlin: Springer-Verlag.

Levinthal, Daniel (1991), 'Organizational adaptation and environmental selection: Interrelated processes of change', *Organization Science*, **2** (1), 140–145.

Levin, Simon (1992), 'The problem of pattern and scale in ecology', *Ecology*, **73** (6), 1943–1967.

Levitt, Barbara and J. March (1988), 'Organizational learning', *Annual Review of Sociology*, **14**, 319–340.

Lewontin, Richard (1978), 'Adaptation', *Scientific American*, **239** (3), 157–169.

Lewontin, Richard (1983), 'Gene, organism, and environment', in Derek Bendall (ed), *Evolution From Molecules to Men*, Cambridge, UK: Cambridge University Press.

Lewontin, Richard (2005), 'The wars over evolution', *The New York Review of Books*, available at http://www.nybooks.com/articles/2005/10/20/the-wars-over-evolution/, accessed on 10/2/2016.

Luksha, Pavel (2008), 'Niche construction: The process of opportunity creation in the environment', *Strategic Entrepreneurship Journal*, **2** (4), 269–283.

Mac Nally, Ralph (1995), *Ecological Versatility and Community Ecology*, New York: Cambridge University Press.

MacIver, Robert (1917), *Community: A Sociological Study*, London: Macmillan and Co.

MacIver, Robert (1931), 'Is sociology a natural science?', *Papers and Proceedings of the American Sociological Society*, **25**, 33–35.

MacIver, Robert (1968), *As a Tale That is Told*, London: University of Chicago Press.

Mahoney, James (2003), 'Tentative answers to questions about causal mechanisms', *Proceedings of the American Political Science Association*, Philadelphia, PA.

Makin, C. (2002), 'Building a high street brand through a change in media strategy', *Institute of Practitioners in Advertising*, available at http://www.ipa.co.uk, accessed on 15/11/2016.

March, James (1991), 'Exploration and exploitation in organizational learning', *Organization Science*, **2** (1), 71–87.

March, James (1994), 'The evolution of evolution', in Joel Baum and Jitendra Singh (eds), *The Evolutionary Dynamics of Organizations*, New York: Oxford University Press.

March, James (2010), *The Ambiguities of Experience*, London: Cornell University Press.

Martin, Elizabeth (1983), *Macmillan Dictionary of Life Sciences*, London: Macmillan Press.

Martinez, Martha and H. Aldrich (2012), 'Evolutionary theory', in Daniel Hjorth (ed), *Handbook of Organisational Entrepreneurship*, Cheltenham, UK and Northampton, MA, USA: Edward Elgar Publishing.

Mason, Herbert and J. Langenheim (1957), 'Language analysis and the concept "environment"', *Ecology*, **38** (2), 325–340.

Mata, José and P. Portugal (1994), 'Life duration of new firms', *Journal of Industrial Organisation*, **7** (3), 227–245.

Maturana, Humbert and F. Varela (1980), *Autopoiesis and Cognition: The Realization of the Living*, London: Reidel Publishing Company.

Maynard Smith, John (1958), *The Theory of Evolution*, London: Penguin Books.

Mayr, Ernest (1957), 'The species problem', *A Symposium of American Association for the Advancement of Science*, Atlanta, December 1955.

Metcalf, Stanley (1998), *Evolutionary Economics and Creative Destruction*, London: Routledge.

Meyer, John and B. Rowan (1977), 'Institutionalized organizations: Formal structure as myth and ceremony', *American Journal of Sociology*, **83** (2), 340–363.

Meyer, John and W. Scott (1983), *Organizational Environments: Ritual and Rationality*, Beverly Hills, CA: Sage Publications.

Meyer, Marshall and L. Zucker (1989), *Permanently Failing Organizations*, London: Sage Publications.

Milne, A. (1961), 'Definition of competition among animals', in Fred Milthorpe (ed), *Mechanisms in Biological Competition*, New York: Academic Press.

McGahan, Anita (2004), *How Industries Evolve: Principles for Achieving and Sustaining Superior Performance*, Boston: Harvard Business School Press.

McKelvey, Bill (1982), *Organizational Systematics: Taxonomy, Evolution, Classification*, Los Angeles: University of California Press.

McKelvey, Bill (2002), 'Model-centered organization science epistemology', in Joel Baum (ed), *Companion to Organizations*, Thousand Oaks, CA: Sage.

McKenzie, Roderick (1924), 'The ecological approach to the study of the human community', *American Journal of Sociology*, **30** (3), 287–301.

McKenzie, Roderick (1934a), 'The field and problems of demography, human geography and human ecology', in Luther Bernard (ed), *The Field and Methods of Sociology*, New York: Ray Long & Richard R. Smith.

McKenzie, Roderick (1934b), *Readings in Human Ecology*, Michigan: George Wahr.

Mlinar, Zdravko and H. Teune (1978), *The Social Ecology of Change: From Equilibrium to Development*, London: Sage Publications.

Møller, Anders and M. Jennions (2002) 'How much variance can be explained by ecologists and evolutionary biologists?', *Oecoligia*, **134** (4), 492–500.

Moore, Leila and M. Upcraft (1990), 'Theory in student affairs: Evolving perspectives', in Leila Moore (ed), *Evolving Theoretical Perspectives on Students*, San Francisco: Jossey-Bass.

Morgan, George, N. Leech, G. Gloecker and K. Barrett (2004), *SPSS for Introductory Statistics*, London: Lawrence Erlbaum Associates.

Morris, Christopher (1992), *Academic Press Dictionary of Science and Technology*, New York: Academic Press.

Morton, Timothy (2013), *Realist Magic Objects, Ontology, Causality*, Michigan: Open Humanities Press.

Muller, Christopher (1997), 'Redefining value: The hamburger price war', *Cornell Hotel and Restaurant Administration Quarterly*, **38** (3), 62–73.

Muller, Christopher and C. Inman (1994), 'The geodemographics of restaurant development', *Cornell Hotel and Restaurant Administration Quarterly*, **35** (3), 88–95.

Muller, Christopher and R. Woods (1994), 'An expanded restaurant typology', *Cornell Hotel and Restaurant Administration Quarterly*, **35** (3), 27–37.

McShea, Daniel and R. Brandon (2010), *Biology's First Law*, London: University of Chicago Press.

Murmann, Peter (2003), *Knowledge and Competitive Advantage: The Coevolution of Firms, Technology and National Institutions*, Cambridge, UK: Cambridge University Press.

Nei, Masatoshi (2013), *Mutation-driven Evolution*, Croydon: Oxford University Press.

Nelson, Richard and S. Winter (1982), *An Evolutionary Theory of Economic Change*, Cambridge, MA: Harvard University Press.

Norgaard, Richard (2010), 'Ecosystem services: From eye-opening metaphor to complexity blinder', *Ecological Economics*, **61** (6), 1219–1227.

Ocasio, Willam (2011), 'Attention to attention', *Organization Science*, **22** (5), 1286–1296.

Ocasio, William and J. Joseph (2005), 'An attention-based theory of strategy formulation: Linking micro-and macroperspectives in strategy processes, *Advances in Strategic Management*, **22** (18), 39–61.

Odum, Eugene (1959[1971]), *Fundamentals of Ecology*, Philadelphia: W.B. Saunders.

Odum, Howard (1996), *Environmental Accounting*, New York: John Wiley & Sons.

Odling-Smee, John, K. Laland and M. Feldman (2003), *Niche Construction: The Neglected Process in Evolution*, Oxford: Princeton University Press.

O'Neil, Hugh and J. Duker (1986), 'Survival and failure in small business', *Journal of Small Business*, **24** (1), 30–37.

O'Reilly, Charles and M. Tushman (2004), 'The ambidextrous organization', *Harvard Business Review*, **82** (4), 74–81.

Park, Robert (1918), 'Community: A sociological study. Being an attempt to set out the nature and fundamental laws of social life. RM MacIver', *American Journal of Sociology*, **23** (4), 542–544.

Park, Robert (1936), 'Human ecology', *American Journal of Sociology*, **42**, (1), 1–15.

Park, Robert and E. Burgess (1921), *Introduction to the Science of Sociology*, Chicago: University of Chicago Press.

Park, Robert, E. Burgess and R. McKenzie (1925), *The City: Suggestions for Investigation of Human Behavior in the Urban Environment*, Chicago: University of Chicago Press.

Park, Thomas (1954), 'Experimental studies of interspecies competition', *Physiological Zoology*, **27** (3), 177–238.

Parsa, H.G., J. Self, D. Njite and T. King (2005), 'Why restaurants fail', *Cornell Hotel and Restaurant Administration Quarterly*, **46** (3), 304–322.

Paterson, Hugh (1993), *Evolution and the Recognition Concept of Species*, London: John Hopkins University Press.

Paterson, Hugh (2005), 'The competitive Darwin', *Paleobiology*, **31** (2), 56–76.

Pearse, Arthur (1926), 'The ecology of parasites', *Ecology*, **7** (2), 113–119.

Peirce, Charles (1908), 'A neglected argument for the reality of god', *Hibbert Journal*, **7** (1), 90–112.

Pennak, Robert (1964), *Collegiate Dictionary of Zoology*, New York: The Ronald Press Company.

Penrose, Edith (1959), *The Theory of the Growth of the Firm*, New York: John Wiley & Sons.

Perrow, Charles (1986), *Complex Organizations: A Critical Essay*, New York: Random House.

Petersen, Trond and K. Koput (1991), 'Density dependence in organizational mortality: Legitimacy or unobserved heterogeneity', *American Sociological Review*, **56** (3), 399–409.

Pfeffer, Jeffery and G. Salancik (1978), *The External Control of Organizations: A Resource Dependence Perspective*, New York: Harper & Row.

Pianka, Eric (1969), 'Sympatry of desert lizards (Ctenotus) in Western Australia', *Ecology*, **50** (6), 1012–1030.

Pianka, Eric (1973), 'The structure of lizard communities', *Annual Review of Ecology and Systematics*, **4**, 53–74.

Poole, Marshall and A. Van de Ven (2004), *Handbook of Organizational Change and Innovation*, New York: Oxford University Press.

Popper, Karl (1963), *Conjectures and Refutations*, London: Routledge & Kegan Paul.

Popper, Karl (1972), *Objective Knowledge: An Evolutionary Approach*, Oxford, UK: Clarendon Press.

Porter, Michael (1980), *Competitive Strategy*, Free Press: New York.

Porter, Michael (1985), *Competitive Advantage*, Free Press: New York.

Porter, Michael (1990), *The Competitive Advantage of Nations*, New York: Free Press.

Powell, Walter and P. DiMaggio (1991), *The New Institutionalism in Organizational Analysis*, Chicago: University of Chicago Press.

Price, Peter, C. Slobodchikoff and W. Gaud (1984), *A New Ecology: Novel Approaches to Interactive Systems*, New York: Wiley.

Ragin, Charles (1994), *Constructing Social Research*, London: Pine Forge Press.

Radosavljevic, Milan (2008), 'Autopoiesis vs. social autopoiesis: Critical evaluation and implications for understanding firms as autopoietic social systems', *International Journal of General Systems*, **37** (2), 215–230.

Rathcke, Beverly (1983), 'Competition and facilitation among plants and pollination', in Leslie Real (ed), *Pollination Biology*, London: Academic Press.

Rao, Haygreeva (2002), 'Interorganizational ecology', in Joel Baum (ed), *Companion to Organizations*, Oxford, UK: Blackwell.

Rees, William (1967), 'The Cnidaria and their evolution', *Proceedings of the Zoological Society of London*, March, 1965.

Reid, Leslie (1962), *The Sociology of Nature*, Baltimore: Penguin Books.

Reiners, William and J. Lockwood (2010), *Philosophical Foundations for the Practices of Ecology*, Cambridge, UK: Cambridge University Press.

Rittner, Don and T. McCabe (2004), *Encyclopaedia of Biology*, New York: Facts On File.

Rohde, Klaus (2005), *Nonequilibrium Ecology*, Melbourne: Cambridge University Press.

Rohde, Klaus (2013), *The Balance of Nature*, Melbourne: Cambridge University Press.

Root, Richard (1967), 'The niche exploitation pattern of the Blue-Gray gnatcatcher', *Ecological Monographs*, **37** (4), 317–350.

Rose, Steven (1997), *Lifelines: Biology Beyond Determination*, Melbourne: Oxford University Press.

Roughgarden, Joan (1979), *Theory of Population Genetics and Evolutionary Ecology: An Introduction*, New York: Macmillan.

Rouse, Michael and U. Daellenbach (1999), 'Rethinking research methods for the research-based perspective: Isolating sources of sustainable competitive advantage', *Strategic Management Journal*, **20** (5), 487–494.

Rumelt, Richard (1979), 'Evaluating competitive strategies', in Dan Schendel and Charles Hofer (eds), *Strategic Management: A New View of Business Policy and Planning*, Boston: Little, Brown and Co.

Sæther, Bjørnar (1998), 'Retroduction: An alternative research strategy?', *Business Strategy and the Environment*, **7** (4), 245–249.

Sahlins, Marshall and E. Service (1960[1973]), *Evolution and Culture*, Ann Arbor: University of Michigan Press.

Sayer, Andrew (1992), *Method in Social Science: A Realist Approach*, London: Routledge.

Sayer, Andrew (2000), *Realism and Social Science*, London: Sage Publications.

Schoener, Thomas (1968), 'The Anolis lizards of Bimini: Resource partitioning in a complex fauna', *Ecology*, **49** (4), 704–726.

Schoener, Thomas (1974), 'Resource partitioning in ecological communities', *Science*, **185** (4145), 27–39.

Schoener, Thomas (1982), 'The controversy over interspecific competition', *American Scientist*, **70** (6), 586–595.

Scott, Richard (1987), *Organizations: Rational, Natural, and Open Systems*, Englewood Cliffs, NJ: Prentice-Hall.

Sears, Paul (1935), *Deserts on the March*, Norman: University of Oklahoma Press.

Shriber, Michael, C. Muller and C. Inman (1995), 'Population change and restaurant success', *Cornell Hotel and Restaurant Administration Quarterly*, **36** (3), 43–49.

Singh, Jitendra (1993), 'Density dependence theory – current issues, future promises', *American Journal of Sociology*, **99** (2), 464–474.

Sober, Elliott (1984), *The Nature of Selection: Evolutionary Theory in Philosophical Focus*, Chicago: Chicago University Press.

Spencer, Herbert (1864), *Principles of Biology, Vol. 1*, London: Williams and Norgate.

Spomer, George (1973), 'The concept of "interaction" and "operational environment" in environmental analysis', *Ecology*, **54** (1), 200–204.

Stabell, Charles and Ø. Fjeldstad (1998), 'Configuring value for competitive advantage: on chains, shops, and networks', *Strategic Management Journal*, **19** (5), 413–437.

Stake, Robert (1995), *The Art of Case Study Research*, Thousand Oaks, CA: Sage Publications.

Starbuck, William, S. Salgado and J. Mezias (2006), 'The accuracy of manager's perceptions: A dimension missing from theories about firms', in William Starbuck (ed), *Organizational Realities: Studies of Strategizing and Organizing*, New York: Oxford University Press.

Stephens, David and J. Krebs (1987), *Foraging Theory*, Princeton: Princeton University Press.

Stevens, Martin (2013), *Sensory Ecology, Behaviour, & Evolution*, Oxford, UK: Oxford University Press.

Stone, K. (1997), 'Impact of the Wal-Mart phenomenon on rural communities', *Published Proceedings of Increasing Understanding of*

Public Problems and Policies, Farm Foundation, Available at: http://www.econ.iastate.edu/faculty/stone/10yrstudy.pdf, accessed on 17/10/2016.

Strong, Donald, D. Simberloff, L. Abele and A. Thistle (1984), *Ecological Communities: Conceptual Issues and the Evidence*, Princeton: Princeton University Press.

Stuart, Helen (1998), 'Exploring the corporate identity/corporate image interface: An empirical study of accountancy firms', *Journal of Communications Management*, **2** (4), 357–373.

Sumner, William (1902), *Earth Hunger and Other Essays*, New Haven: Yale University Press.

Teece, David (2016), 'Dynamic capabilities and entrepreneurial management in large organizations: Toward a theory of the (entrepreneurial) firm', *European Economic Review*, **86**, 202–216.

Teece, David, G. Pisano and A. Shuen (1997), 'Dynamic capabilities and strategic management', *Strategic Management Journal*, **18** (7), 509–533.

Thompson, James (1967), *Organizations in Action*, New York: McGraw-Hill.

Thomson, Arthur (1914), *The Wonder of Life*, London: Andrew Melrose.

Thomson, Arthur (1917), *The Study of Animal Life*, London: John Murray.

Tilman, David (1987), 'The importance of the mechanisms of interspecific competition', *American Naturalist*, **129** (5), 769–774.

Todes, Daniel (1989), *Darwin without Malthus: The Struggle for Existence in Russian Evolutionary Thought*, Oxford: Oxford University Press.

Tokeshi, Mutsunori (1999), *Species Coexistence: Ecological and Evolutionary Perspectives*, Oxford, UK: Blackwell Science.

Tosi, Henry (2009), *Theories of Organization*, London: Sage Publications.

Tsoukas, Haridimos (1989), 'The validity of idiographic research explanations', *Academy of Management Review*, **14** (4), 551–561.

Tsoukas, Haridimos and K. Dooley (2011), 'Towards the ecological style: Embracing complexity in organizational research', *Organization Studies*, **32** (6), 729–735.

Tushman, Michael and E. Romanelli (1985), 'Organizational evolution: A metamorphosis model of convergence and reorientation', in Barry Straw and Larry Cummings (eds), *Research in Organizational Behavior*, Greenwich, CT: JAI Press.

Utterback, James and W. Abernathy (1975), 'A dynamic model of product and process innovation', *Omega*, **3** (6), 639–656.

van Beneden, Pierre-Joseph (1869), 'Le commensalisma dans le regne animal', *Bulletins. Academie Royale de Belgique*, **2** (28), 621–648.

van Beneden, Pierre-Joseph (1876), *Animal Parasites and Messmates*, London: Henry S. King and Co.

Van de Ven, Andrew and S. Poole (2002), 'Field research methods', in Joel Baum (ed), *Companion to Organizations*, Malden, MA: Blackwell Publishing.

van der Mandele, Hugh and A. van Witteloostuijn (2013), *Free to Fail: Creative Destruction Revisited*, Cheltenham, UK and Northampton, MA, USA: Edward Elgar Publishing.

van Witteloostuijn, Arjen (2000), 'Organizational ecology has a bright future', *Organizational Studies*, **21** (2), 5–16.

Veblen, Thorstein (1922), *The Theory of the Leisure Class*, New York: Vanguard Press.

Vernon, Raymond (1966), 'International investment and international trade in the product cycle', *Quarterly Journal of Economics*, **80** (2), 190–207.

Wake, David, G. Roth and M. Wake (1983), 'On the problem of stasis in organismal evolution', *Journal of Theoretical Biology*, **101** (2), 211–224.

Wallace, Walton (1969), *Sociological Theory – An Introduction*, Chicago: Aldine.

Walter, Gimme (1988), 'Competitive exclusion, coexistence and community structure', *Acta Biotheoretica*, **37** (3), 281–313.

Walter, Gimme (2008), 'Individuals, populations and the balance of nature: The question of persistence in ecology', *Biology & Philosophy*, **23** (3), 417–438.

Walter, Gimme (2013), 'Autecology and the balance of nature – ecological laws and human-induced invasions', in Klaus Rohde (ed), *The Balance of Nature and Human Impact*, Melbourne: Cambridge University Press.

Walter, Gimme and R. Hengeveld (2014), *Autecology: Organisms, Interactions and Environmental Dynamics*, Florida: CRC Press.

Warming, Eugenius (1909), *Oecology of Plants: An Introduction to the Study of Plant Communities*, Oxford, UK: Clarendon Press.

Watt, Alex (1947), 'Pattern and process in the plant community', *Journal of Ecology*, **35** (2), 1–22.

Weick, Karl (1979), *The Social Psychology of Organizing*, Reading, MA: Addison-Wesley.

Wernerfelt, Birger (1984), 'A resource-based view of the firm', *Strategic Management Journal*, **5** (2), 171–180.

Whitehead, Alfred (1926), *Science and the Modern World*, Cambridge, UK: Cambridge University Press.

Wheeler, William (1910), *Ants: Their Structure, Development and Behavior*, New York: Columbia University Press.

Whetten, David (1988), 'Organizational growth and decline processes', in Kim Cameron, Robert Sutton and David Whetten (eds), *Readings in Organizational Decline: Frameworks, Research, and Prescriptions*, Cambridge, MA: Ballinger Publishing.

Wiens, John (1989), 'Spatial scaling in ecology', *Functional Ecology*, **3** (4), 385–397.

Wiens, John, M. Moss, M. Turner and D. Mladenoff (2007), *Foundation Papers in Landscape Ecology*, New York: Columbia University Press.

Williamson, Oliver (1975), *Markets and Hierarchies*, New York: Free Press.

Williamson, Oliver (1985), *The Economic Institutions of Capitalism*, New York: Free Press.

Wilson, David and J. Yoshimura (1994), 'On the coexistence of specialists and generalists', *American Naturalist*, **144** (4), 692–707.

Winter, Sidney (1964), 'Economic "natural selection" and the theory of the firm', *Yale Economic Essays*, **4** (1), 225–272.

Winter, Sidney (1990), 'Survival, selection, and inheritance in evolutionary theories of organization', in Jitendra Singh (ed), *Organizational Evolution*, London: Sage Publications.

Winter, Sidney (2003), 'Understanding dynamic capabilities', *Strategic Management Journal*, **24** (10), 991–995.

Wollin, Andrew (1995), 'A hierarchy-based punctuated-equilibrium model of the processes of emergence and change of new rural industries', Unpublished dissertation, Griffith University.

Young, Gerald (1974), 'Human ecology as an interdisciplinary concept: A critical inquiry', in Amyan MacFadyen (ed), *Advances in Ecological Research*, London: Academic Press.

Young, R.M. (1985), 'Darwinism is social', in David Kohn (ed), *The Darwinian Heritage*, New Jersey: Princeton University Press.

Young, Ruth (1988), 'Is population ecology a useful paradigm for the study of organizations?', *American Journal of Sociology*, **91** (1), 1–21.

Zahra, Shaker and G. George (2002), 'Absorptive capacity: A review, reconceptualization, and extension', *Academy of Management Review*, **27** (2), 185–203.

Zucker, Lynne (1989), 'Combining institutional theory and population ecology: No legitimacy, no history', *American Sociological Review*, **54** (4), 542–545.

Index

absorptive capacity 72
adaptive improvement 34, 63, 70, 171
    definition of 180
adaptive mechanisms *see* sustenance
    activities
Advertising Efficiency Index 119, 127
Alchian, A. 68
Aldrich, H. 4, 12, 24, 34, 60, 82, 98,
    101, 147
alternative ecological theory 3–19
    assumptions 5
Alvarez, S. 3
Amburgey, T. 99
Andrewartha, H. 3, 52
asymmetrical co-evolution 14
autecological patience 173–4
autecology
    definition of 180
    renaissance of 3
    theory 4
    see also firm autecology
autopoiesis 17, 24, 70–72
    definition of 180

Babbie, E. 136
Barnett, W. 99, 170
Bates, T. 112
Baum, J. 167
Bender, E. 101
Bennett, A. 110, 144
Bertness, M. 103
Bhaskar, R. 111, 115, 117, 144, 145,
    150
Birch, L. 3, 52
blanket benefit 94
Brandon, R. 50, 51, 107
Braun-Blanquet, J. 9
Brown, W. 103
Bruderer, E. 27
Bruno, J. 103

Bruyat, C. 33
Burgess, E. 8, 9, 159
Burkholder, P. 100, 101

canonical discriminant analysis 53,
    119, 123, 137–9
Carroll, G. 101, 102, 133, 138, 178
caveat 40
Child, J. 14, 17, 172
Clements, F. 9
coactions, definition of 180
coaction theory 100, 105, 106
commensalism 9, 10, 99–101, 147
    definition of 181
common environment 4, 5, 6, 23, 29,
    35, 43, 48
    definition of 180–81
community, definition of 181
community similarity index 52, 119,
    123, 137, 166
    definition of 181
competition 98, 99
    definition of 181
competitive relations 99–101
Conrad, H. 9
contingent conditions 115
corporate identity 27
corridor of persistence
    definition of 181
    environmental matching 69
critical realist approach 115
cryptic firm complex 31
    definition of 181
Cyert, R. 34

Danermark, B. 150, 162
Darwin, C. 14, 37, 179
Daubenmire, R. 3, 62, 158
Davis, G. 177
Dawkins, R. 76